"Dr. Chanequa Walker-Barnes is one of the most courageous and prophetic voices I know! For far too long, theology and narratives that shape reconciliation have been co-opted by whiteness and used from an individualistic lens. But there is hope! In *I Bring the Voices of My People*, Dr. Walker-Barnes gives us a new theological lens birthed from the margins that provides a more holistic approach to justice and racial healing. This is a must read for anyone serious about reconciliation. I highly recommend it!"

— BRENDA SALTER MCNEIL, author of *Roadmap to Reconciliation*

"Finally, someone is inviting us into reconciliation on black womxn's terms. And who better than Dr. Chanequa Walker-Barnes, who spectacularly shows us in *I Bring the Voices of My People* that a message that centers black womxn's experiences is a universally liberating message. I have experienced anti-black oppression in faith-based 'reconciliation' contexts, and Dr. Chanequa's words have invaluably supported my healing journey while also redirecting my steps toward justice practices that are not colonized by whiteness. 'Trust black womxn' is a phrase that often gets thrown around with little behavioral follow-up. Dr. Chanequa, a true sage, is telling us how to trust black womxn on the topic and practice of reconciliation. I'm following her lead and I hope you will too."

— CHRISTENA CLEVELAND, Director of the Center for Justice and Renewal

"Chanequa Walker-Barnes constructs a courageous womanist theology of racial reconciliation, drawing on a wide range of figures including womanist scholars, Alice Walker and her critical race theory, and Howard Thurman. What is so hopeful here, on a subject that has more often than not produced hopelessness and despair, is that Walker-Barnes puts forward a path that can lead to racial reconciliation, if not in my lifetime, then in the near, possible future. Walker-Barnes has offered us a challenge and an invitation; we should take them up by first reading *I Bring the Voices of My People*."

— PHILLIS ISABELLA SHEPPARD, Vanderbilt Divinity School

"Chanequa Walker-Barnes gives us new medicine, already tested through trials, and ready to address the sick ways Christians, especially evangelical Christians, think and talk about racial reconciliation. This beautifully written, sensitively personal, and analytically precise text may be the best book we have on racial reconciliation. Walker-Barnes, a womanist thinker of the highest order, has written herself into the required reading for every class that aims to consider race and reconciliation."

— WILLIE JAMES JENNINGS, Yale Divinity School

"A timely reminder of the role of context in determining not only when and where we enter but whose voices are missing from the work of repentance, a necessary component of reconciliation. In this Trumpian era, *I Bring the Voices of My People* is a must-read for anyone committed to naming, confronting, and dismantling White supremacy."

— ANGELA D. SIMS, President of Colgate Rochester Crozer Divinity School

"Chanequa Walker-Barnes offers an incredibly powerful analysis of racism and misogyny within the church and America. Her voice here and throughout her ministry is something all Christians need to hear in order to bring justice and reconciliation and to understand the work yet to be done. Her voice and her faith in God simultaneously provoke, humble, illuminate, and call us to action. Let us respond to her prophetic word."

— JIM WALLIS, author of *America's Original Sin*

"If the true work of a teacher is to help her students know what is at stake in the critical conversations of our time, then Chanequa Walker-Barnes can rightly be called a teacher of the church in twenty-first-century America. If you've seen enough to know that the legacy of white supremacy cripples Christians' capacity to build up communities of justice and reconciliation, *I Bring the Voices of My People* will help you avoid false hope, ask better questions, and find the partners you need on a faithful journey toward freedom."

— JONATHAN WILSON-HARTGROVE, author of *Reconstructing the Gospel: Finding Freedom from Slaveholder Religion*

"Some people are wise because they're near to God. Others are wise because of their social location and lived experience. And yet others are wise because they have studied the Word of God and the world we live in. Chanequa Walker-Barnes is all of the above. But there are people who are wise but are not very kind. And there are people who are kind but not very wise. Dr. Chanequa shines bright because she is both wise and kind, and our world needs both right now. She makes you want to hear more, dream more, be more. As a womanist of faith, she invites us to believe in something seemingly impossible, trusting that we have a God who specializes in the impossible. This book is a gift to the world, and so is Dr. Chanequa Walker-Barnes."

— SHANE CLAIBORNE, author, activist, and founder of Red Letter Christians

"In this superbly written book, readers will be exposed to a comprehensive and tightly argued work on historical racism, reconciliation movements, and the need for a robust and nuanced approach to understanding the experience of systemic oppression, engaging in truth-telling around white supremacy, and hearing and centering the voices of women of color. In some subjects, there exists the one book everyone needs to read. This is one of those books."

— KEN WYTSMA, author of *The Myth of Equality*

"Dr. Walker-Barnes takes readers through content that is typically not discussed within the paradigm of racial reconciliation. This voice in that conversation is a must read."

— REGGIE L. WILLIAMS, McCormick Theological Seminary

"Drawing on womanist theology, Chanequa Walker-Barnes rewrites all that we thought we knew about racism and reconciliation. After this book, no one will be able to talk about racial reconciliation in the same way again."

— J. KAMERON CARTER, Indiana University

PROPHETIC CHRISTIANITY

Series Editors

Bruce Ellis Benson
Malinda Elizabeth Berry
Peter Goodwin Heltzel

The PROPHETIC CHRISTIANITY series explores the complex relationship between Christian doctrine and contemporary life. Deeply rooted in the Christian tradition yet taking postmodern and postcolonial perspectives seriously, series authors navigate difference and dialogue constructively about divisive and urgent issues of the early twenty-first century. The books in the series are sensitive to historical contexts, marked by philosophical precision, and relevant to contemporary problems. Embracing shalom justice, series authors seek to bear witness to God's gracious activity of building beloved community.

PUBLISHED

Bruce Ellis Benson, Malinda Elizabeth Berry, and Peter Goodwin Heltzel, eds., *Prophetic Evangelicals: Envisioning a Just and Peaceable Kingdom* (2012)

Jennifer Harvey, *Dear White Christians: For Those Who Still Long for Racial Reconciliation* (2014)

Peter Goodwin Heltzel, *Resurrection City: A Theology of Improvisation* (2012)

Johnny Bernard Hill, *Prophetic Rage: A Postcolonial Theory of Liberation* (2013)

Liz Theoharis, *Always with Us? What Jesus Really Said about the Poor* (2017)

Chanequa Walker-Barnes, *I Bring the Voices of My People: A Womanist Vision for Racial Reconciliation* (2019)

Randy S. Woodley, *Shalom and the Community of Creation: An Indigenous Vision* (2012)

I Bring
the
Voices
of
My People

A Womanist Vision for Racial Reconciliation

Chanequa Walker-Barnes

WILLIAM B. EERDMANS PUBLISHING COMPANY
GRAND RAPIDS, MICHIGAN

Wm. B. Eerdmans Publishing Co.
4035 Park East Court SE, Grand Rapids, Michigan 49546
www.eerdmans.com

25 24 23 22 21 20 19   1 2 3 4 5 6 7

ISBN 978-0-8028-7720-8

Library of Congress Cataloging-in-Publication Data

Names: Walker-Barnes, Chanequa, author.
Title: I bring the voices of my people : a womanist vision for racial
     reconciliation / Chanequa Walker-Barnes.
Description: Grand Rapids : Eerdmans Publishing Co., 2019. | Series:
     Prophetic Christianity | Includes bibliographical references and index.
Identifiers: LCCN 2019017686 | ISBN 9780802877208 (pbk. : alk. paper)
Subjects: LCSH: Racism—Religious aspects—Christianity. | Race
     relations—Religious aspects—Christianity. | Reconciliation—Religious
     aspects—Christianity. | Womanist theology. | Racism—United States. |
     Race relations—United States.
Classification: LCC BT734.2 .W28 2019 | DDC 241/.675—dc23
LC record available at https://lccn.loc.gov/2019017686

For my students, who inspire me,
and for Micah, for whom I strive to create a more just world

Contents

Foreword

Twitter brings revelation. I realize we do not usually begin academic books with reflections on a Twitter thread, but I must start here.

The tech platform is where deep thoughts come together in 280-character bites, and threads and tags join together people who wouldn't usually find each other in conversations they don't usually have. As the divided church clashes in cyberspace, sickness is being revealed, and Twitter has become a prime space where information silos are disrupted. People with little exposure to conversations about race, gender, and equity have rare opportunities to consider ideas usually hidden from them by algorithms.

Recently, I wrote a #TwitterEssay on race, gender, and intersectionality within the evangelical church. I started, as usual, by defining the terms — racism, sexism, patriarchy, and intersectionality. If Chanequa's book had been published already, I would have quoted her and cited the reference. In her introduction she clarifies the relationships between all of these concepts: "The exclusion of women's racial experiences from dialogue on racial reconciliation is not simply a problem for women; it precludes any real understanding of the dynamics of race and racism." I agree and have come to understand that the points where these concepts intersect are the points of revelation, where the modus operandi of White patriarchy is clearest. Chanequa puts a point on it: "If we truly hope to work toward racial reconciliation, the perspectives of women of color must be moved from margin to center."

I continued the essay by responding to a prompt that asked me to describe my experience working at the intersections of race and gender in evangelical communities. Nowhere do the intersections of racism, sexism, and patriarchy overlap more so than within the top ranks of the flagship organizations of American evangelicalism. The White patriarchal DNA of evangelical America is on full display in the C-level executives within organizations such as *Christianity Today*, the Billy Graham Evangelistic Association, Cru, and The Gospel Coalition.

Chanequa's words reverberated through all of the organizations' website leadership pages. To get a clear diagnosis of the modus operandi of White patriarchy in these institutions, all one needs to look for are the women of color — especially Black women. We are not there. Black women are the greatest threat to White patriarchy in the US. InterVarsity Christian Fellowship/USA was the only one of these organizations with a Black woman in top leadership, but on their executive team of seven, where three White people — two of whom were women — and three Asian men communed in top leadership, there was only one Black woman. Perhaps as interesting, in InterVarsity's context, there were no Black men and no Latinx leaders at all.

Within hours of my posting the essay, several White men responded to the thread with angry objections. First, they insisted that I had defined racism incorrectly. Racism is prejudice. Power is not necessary to be racist. Second, they asserted that it is fine to have all-White leadership teams. It simply reflects who is most qualified for the job. And third, they claimed that I was guilty of putting words out in the world without taking responsibility for their repercussions.

My use of Twitter to craft an essay for the masses was, itself, an act of holy disruption that provoked the church to see and consider the intersections of racism and sexism in itself. This long gaze at the White male face of American evangelicalism did not, as some might argue, center whiteness. Rather, it revealed the yawning void in the center of evangelicalism. For we are not there. Black women are not there. Our stories are not there to inform the White male authorities' read of the Brown Virgin Mary's proclamation that the King of the Kingdom of God was on his way! Right now, she sang, we stand on the brink of an existential promise. We shall see it! Brown Jesus is coming, born of a Brown woman, in the context of Brown people struggling against colonization. We shall see the day, Brown Mary sang, when the low are brought high and the high are brought low!

And how could these White male leadership teams understand Mary's theological revelation? All of life has trained them not to see it — not to see her. White men who yearn to be reconciled with the people of color in the church across town were trained not to see the laws and structures that systematized the rape and exploitation of Brown people's great-grandmothers' bodies for White male profit. They were trained not to see the ways their theology did triple back-flips with a double twist to turn a story written by, for, and about Brown colonized women and men into one solely about individual spiritual salvation. As South African theologian René August says, "Who does that theology benefit?" White men benefit when Brown women and men forget the context of the gospel — the context of struggle against colonization. Thus, the gospel is gutted of good news for the majority of the world.

This picture that Dr. Walker-Barnes paints for us is far more than a Browner, more womanly take on racial reconciliation. This is a clarion call to renounce our colonized eyes — to allow ourselves to admit that we are blind and have not seen the Scripture — we have not seen Jesus — until we have seen him through a Brown woman's eyes. What she sees changes everything.

LISA SHARON HARPER
President, Freedom Road, LLC

Preface

One needs occasionally to stand aside from the hum and rush of human interests and passions to hear the voices of God. And it not unfrequently happens that the All-loving gives a great push to certain souls to thrust them out, as it were, from the distracting current for awhile to promote their discipline and growth, or to enrich them by communion and reflection. And similarly it may be woman's privilege from her peculiar coigne of vantage as a quiet observer, to whisper just the needed suggestion or the almost forgotten truth. The colored woman, then, should not be ignored because her bark is resting in the silent waters of the sheltered cove. She is watching the movements of the contestants none the less and is all the better qualified, perhaps, to weigh and judge and advise because not herself in the excitement of the race.

Anna Julia Cooper, *A Voice from the South*

I am a child of the South, a Georgia peach, born and bred in Atlanta. Not "Hotlanta," mind you, the sprawling, crowded, image-obsessed city that has almost completely squeezed out its poor and working-class citizens. I grew up in the Atlanta of the 1970s and 1980s: the city where tea was always served sweet; where Black pastors preached about racial politics; where the lifelong aim of poor and working-class children was to grow up to own a house in Cascade Heights, not a condo in Buckhead; where we looked to the annual June issue of *Ebony* magazine to see how many graduates of Frederick Douglass and Benjamin E. Mays high schools had made it onto their annual list of the nation's top Black high school seniors. I grew up in the Atlanta that was viewed as *the* big city by other southerners but that seemed slow and dull to my New York friends and relatives. I grew up in the Atlanta that gave Martin Luther King Jr. his dream and André Benjamin his drawl.

On both my maternal and paternal sides, I am the eldest of my generation, the first to be born and raised outside Jim Crow. Both of my parents had moved to Atlanta with their families when they were adolescents. My mother's family was the first African American family to move onto Fayetteville Street in southeast Atlanta; my father's was the second to move onto South Howard a few blocks away. In my families' five decades in those neighborhoods, we have seen them transform from working-class White to working-class Black to gentrifying hipster White communities that not even the most middle-class of us can afford.

Even as my families watched the For Sale signs go up, even as my great-uncle and his Vietnam vet buddies stood guard over my maternal grandfather's new home every night with high-powered rifles, moving to "The City Too Busy to Hate" must have felt like newfound freedom for my grandparents: for my paternal grandfather, a South Carolina–born Gullah bricklayer; for my maternal grandfather, who had to drop out of school to take care of his younger siblings while his parents and elder siblings worked their Mississippi sharecropper's farm; for my paternal grandmother, who on more than one occasion concealed my father underneath her long skirts as she walked past hooded Klansmen in Jacksonville; for my maternal grandmother, whose own uncle had been murdered and tossed onto his parents' porch in northern Mississippi because of his involvement in the civil rights movement.

But as they say, freedom is not free. As members of the first generation to benefit from the civil rights movement, my parents faced their own struggles. Being the first African American family to integrate the neighborhoods also meant that they were the first to integrate the schools. They met in eleventh grade when they were among the second class of African American students who integrated all-White Gordon High School (now McNair Middle School) in 1968. Integration never happened without resistance and without trauma. I have heard multiple stories about their traumatic experiences.

Growing up with this history, in this context, I found race was always part of my identity. In Atlanta, even serial killing was racialized. The Atlanta Child Murders began when I was seven years old. I vividly remember the day that the school bus turned into my apartment complex and all the mothers were outside. As we disembarked, a worried-looking mother stepped up to embrace each of us and rush us inside to give us the news: someone was killing Black children. Over the next year, each time another child's body was discovered, we would gather around the school playground at recess to share our families' conjectures: Is it the Klan? It must be the Klan. Who else would kill Black children? For southern Black third graders, knowledge about the Klan was commonplace. Racial knowledge was commonplace. It had to be if we were going to survive.

My own encounters with racism began in middle school, when I moved from the protective environment of predominantly Black schools to majority-White magnet schools. I was thirteen the first time that a store security guard stopped me on the way out and searched me. That was the same year that I participated in my first school protest over racism. In tenth grade I transferred to a school that was 80 percent Black but White-controlled. All of the administrators (except the head of the school's vocational program) were White, as were most of the teachers. The 20 percent White population and the three Korean American students (all brothers) were sequestered in advanced placement classes. White students always headed the student council. For at least a dozen years, the position of homecoming queen had followed a statistically improbable pattern of alternating between the races: Black one year, White the next. When I enrolled, information from my academic record was leaked to White classmates, who were told to "Watch out for that new Black girl. She's gonna steal your class rank." For most of them, that turned out to be true.

Ironically, at the time my mother, brother, and I were living in the family home of Hosea Williams, the civil rights legend who led the 1965 "Bloody Sunday" march across Edmund Pettus Bridge in Selma. His daughter, Elisabeth, and my mother have been best friends since shortly after my birth (they still are); they met after my mother started volunteering at the headquarters of the Southern Christian Leadership Conference. On more than one occasion, when we were down on our luck and needed a place to stay, the Williams family let us live with them. By my senior year, in fact, they constructed an apartment in the upper floor of their home for us. My earliest political conversations were with Mrs. Williams, discussing Jesse Jackson's presidential campaign and whether she planned to vote for him (she did, though she was terrified that he would be assassinated). It was on their bookshelves that I picked up *The Autobiography of Malcolm X* and *Bearing the Cross*, David Garrow's Pulitzer Prize–winning biography of King. By the time I reached my senior year, the fire for racial justice had long been lit in me. The racial incidents at school simply provided the accelerant.

The racism that I encountered in school also made me very antagonistic toward White people. Fortunately, in addition to my family's strong sense of racial identity, I had inherited a penchant for peace making from my grandmothers. Like my paternal grandmother in particular, I had—and still have—a sort of Pollyannaish tendency to see the best in people, to believe that people can and will choose to be their best selves. And like my maternal grandmother, I took seriously Jesus's commandment and example of loving our neighbors. It was my desire to combat my own racial hostility that led me to abandon my dream of going to Howard University and instead commit to attending a predominantly White institution (PWI) so that I could find the good in White people. To be honest, it didn't work. I did go to a PWI; I just didn't find the good. But it was the first step in my now thirty-year-plus commitment to racial justice and racial reconciliation.

That journey shifted into overdrive when, a few years after earning my PhD in clinical psychology, I more clearly heard the call to ministry and enrolled in the MDiv program at Duke Divinity School. The timing could not have been more fortuitous. I was at Duke at the same time as people like Jonathan Wilson-Hartgrove, Michael McBride, and Hannah Bonner. Brian Bantum was my preceptor in Willie Jennings's class, where he was laying out the ideas behind his soon-to-be award-winning book, *The Christian Imagination*. It was in Willie's class that I learned that Christian theology could help me address the problem of racism in ways that psychology could not. J. Kameron Carter and I parked in the same lot and often talked about his forthcoming book, *Race: A Theological Account*, and my burgeoning StrongBlackWoman project as we made the long walk down Chapel Drive to the Divinity School. I worked with Chris Rice and Emmanuel Katongole as they were launching the Center for Reconciliation, and I was a student in their first Journeys to Reconciliation course. It was at Chris's suggestion that I went to my first meeting of the Christian Community Development Association (CCDA), which eventually led to participating in their Emerging Leaders initiative and serving on the board. Also at Duke, I went on a pilgrimage to South Africa with Peter Storey, the former presiding bishop of the Methodist Church of Southern Africa and the architect behind the Truth and Reconciliation Commission. I participated in the Ubuntu program, a yearlong journey of racial reconciliation.

And all the while, that "yes, but" voice kept echoing in my head. The voice kept suggesting that something was missing in the conversation on racism and reconciliation that was happening in evangelical, mainline, and Black Protestant spaces. That "something missing," I finally figured out, was the voices of the women, especially those from my southern, working-class relatives, who carried centuries-old wisdom about how White folk behaved and how to survive them. It was through them that I had come to be a student of race, of racism, and of racial reconciliation. They were my earliest cultural studies professors, the type of women about whom Anna Julia Cooper wrote:

> Not by pointing to sun-bathed mountain tops do we prove that Phoebus warms the valleys. We must point to homes, average homes, homes of the rank and file of horny handed toiling men and women of the South (where the masses are) lighted and cheered by the good, the beautiful, and the true,—then and not till then will the whole plateau be lifted into the sunlight.

Only the Black Woman can say "when and where I enter,
in the quiet, undisputed dignity of my womanhood, without
violence and without suing or special patronage, then and
there the whole *Negro race enters with me.*"[1]

Here, then, I enter. Having been a quiet observer from my own vantage point as an African American Christian daughter of the South,
I add my voice to the cacophony of overwhelmingly white and male
voices on racial reconciliation. And I do not come alone, for I bring
the voices of my people with me.

1. Anna Julia Cooper, *A Voice from the South* (New York: Oxford University Press, 1988), 30–31.

Acknowledgments

A common question I get asked when people discover I am writing a book is, "How long have you been working on it?" I have been working on this book for at least a decade, beginning with my initial exposure to the Christian racial reconciliation movement through organizations such as the Duke Divinity School Center for Reconciliation, the Christian Community Development Association, and the Justice Conference. I am grateful for those who introduced me to this field and who have been my conversation partners (okay, sometimes dialogical combatants!), including Chris Rice, Emmanuel Katongole, Jonathan Wilson-Hartgrove, Shane Claiborne, Leroy Barber, and Soong-Chan Rah. I could not do this, of course, if it had not been for the sisters who have been treading this path longer than I have: Barbara Williams-Skinner, Brenda Salter McNeil, and Lisa Sharon Harper—I stand on your shoulders.

I could not have survived as an African American feminist in evangelical spaces without the support of friends who have supported and encouraged me (and let me vent!). I am especially grateful for Zakiya Jackson, Christena Cleveland, and Cathy Alexander. Z and C—y'all are priceless. And I must give a special shout-out to my "kick-ass-woke" sisters who provide laughter and consolation on a daily basis as we journey together through this space called white heterosexist patriarchy. Erna Hackett, Mayra Macedo-Nolan, Angie Hong, Audrey Velez, Nilwona Nowlin, and Sandra Van Opstal— may your lives be eternally free of man-babies and white woman tears.

A special thank you to Andrea Smith, who graciously allowed me to rework her three pillars of White supremacist heteropatriarchy for this text. I also express gratitude to Michael McGregor, the Collegeville Institute for Ecumenical and Cultural Research, and the participants of the 2016 "Apart, and Yet a Part" writing workshop, who provided feedback on this project in its earliest stage.

Over the past several years, I have taught multiple courses on racism, forgiveness, and reconciliation at the Mercer University McAfee School of Theology. Students in my 2016–2018 reconciliation courses have especially helped me to hone my ideas and have offered valuable commentary on the early drafts of these chapters. Thank you Linsey Addington, Kenya Anderson, Curtis Atkins, Jukabiea Barlow, Byron Bell, James Blay, Abigail Bradley, Tara Brooks, Darrick Brown, Timothy Careathers, Gina Catalano, Collier Cato, C. J. Chiles, Erica Cody, Sheknita Davis, Larry Debose, Colleen DeGraff, Charri Doyle, Quinta Ellis, Adam Gray, Lynne Green, Colin Holtz, Lindsey Huggins, Jose Jimenez-Abrams, Jeremiah Jones, Cora Kilgour, Cy Lynch, Sharolyn McDonald, Aaron McGinnis, Brittini Palmer, Adam Renner, Donail Sanders, Andrew Scott, Dominique Siler, Kristian Smith, Matthew Snyder, Timothy Sutton, Stacie Whalen, Laura Williams, and Deena Wingard (y'all thought I was playing when I said I would do this, didn't you?). And I cannot even say how grateful I am to Amanda Lewis and Jordan Sharp, who have been my research assistants on this project.

Thank you also to the faith communities that have accompanied me during this period, Eastside Church and the Nett Church, and to Decatur CoWorks for providing an awesome writing space and great coffee!

Of course, the Oscar for best supporting actors go to my immediate family: my husband, Delwin, my son, Micah, and my parents, Wali Sharif and Laquitta Walker. My parents were my earliest antiracist educators, and I continue to have conversations about race and racism with them (sometimes even before breakfast!). And Delwin and Micah continue to keep me grounded with their (okay, our) daily antics and laughter. We've been through a lot over the past few years, and I thank God for y'all every day.

Introduction

Keep moving. Keep breathing. Stop apologizing and keep
    on talking.
When you get scared, keep talking anyway. Tell the truth
    like Sojourner Truth.
Spill all the beans. Let all the cats out of all the bags.
If you are what you eat, you become what you speak.
If you free your tongue, your spirit will follow.
Just keep saying it, Girl, you'll get whole.
Say it again and again, Girl, you'll get free.

             Kate Rushin, "To Be Continued. . . . "

"Why am I here?" The question echoed in my head as it had on countless prior occasions. It seems that I cannot participate in a meeting or conference about Christian community development, social justice, or racial reconciliation without the question emerging at least once. As an African American woman, I am frequently reminded that these spaces are not my home. I am an outlier: I am neither White nor male, and I don't fit neatly into any of the typical Protestant boxes. I am too evangelical to be mainline, too mainline to be fully historical Black church, and too historical Black church to be evangelical. Sometimes I even feel too interfaith to be Christian. I am often alone in a room full of people—the only woman of color and even the only African American woman. The conversations in these spaces are often overtly patriarchal, dismissing women's experiences and expertise. These groups think diversity is achieved if they include men of color and White women, both of whom make pronouncements about race and gender that are assumed to capture everyone's experiences but that exclude those of women of color. I am often forced into the position of being the "Yes, but" voice. It is soul-wearying. And yet I—we—stay.

In the past two decades, racial reconciliation has emerged as an increasingly popular topic of academic discourse in the United States and South Africa. An inherently practical discipline, the field of reconciliation studies was birthed out of the experiences of evangelical Christian ministers and laypersons whose quotidian experiences crossed traditional boundaries of race and ethnicity within the church. In the United States, the racial reconciliation movement has strong roots in evangelical church and parachurch organizations. In 1997, for example, Promise Keepers—a predominantly White evangelical men's organization—launched a division on racial reconciliation and declared a lofty goal of eradicating racism in the church by 2000. The evangelical roots of the movement are beneficial in that the field has been first and foremost concerned with practical application. However, because of the emphasis upon male headship and female submission among evangelicals, men have dominated the movement and the literature.

In the United States, consequently, reconciliation has been largely framed as a movement aimed at obliterating racial barriers between African American and White men. The inaugural literature consisted primarily of autobiographical narratives of division, partnership, and friendship between Black and White men, including John Perkins and Wayne Gordon, Glenn Kehrein and Raleigh Washington, and Spencer Perkins and Chris Rice. As the field of reconciliation studies has developed into an academic discipline, the masculine preponderance has continued. The leading scholars in the field include J. Deotis Roberts, Curtiss Paul DeYoung, Allan Boesak, John Paul Lederach, Chris Rice, and Emmanuel Katongole. With few exceptions, women's voices and perspectives are largely absent. The result of this exclusively male gaze is a body of literature that examines race as a singular construct, ignoring the intersections between race, gender, and sexuality. *I Bring the Voices of My People* aims to disrupt this male gaze by centering the experiences and perspectives of women of color in its understanding of race, racism, and reconciliation. First, though, we must understand how we have arrived at this point.

Promise Keepers and the Birth of a Movement

In the United States, the surge of interest in racial reconciliation can be traced to movements in several evangelical organizations during the mid-1990s. To be clear, there were earlier events that set the stage, such as Tom Skinner's address, "The US Racial Crisis and World Evangelism," at InterVarsity's 1970 Urbana conference. The 1990s are distinctive in that several national and international evangelical organizations made racial reconciliation a prominent focus. In a 1997 article for *Christianity Today*, Andrés Tapia stated, "During the last several years, evangelicals have engaged in numerous initiatives in racial reconciliation, causing even the most jaded observers of race relations in the movement to take notice. The Southern Baptist Convention repented for its 'sin of racism.' The National Association of Evangelicals and the National Black Association of Evangelicals (NBEA) took significant steps toward healing their historic rift. Pentecostal denominational associations—one white, one black, which had originally split a hundred years ago—merged."[1] The most high-profile efforts, however, occurred within Promise Keepers.

In 1990, University of Colorado football coach Bill McCartney founded Promise Keepers (PK), which called upon men to commit themselves to seven promises: honoring Christ; developing friendships based upon trust and mutual accountability with "a few" men; practicing spiritual, moral, ethical, and sexual purity; building strong marriages and families through love, protection, and biblical values; supporting the mission of the local church through prayer, active

1. Andrés T. Tapia, "After the Hugs, What? The Next Step for Racial Reconciliation Will Be Harder," *Christianity Today*, February 3, 1997, 54.

involvement, and financial support; reaching beyond racial and denominational barriers; and influencing the world in obedience to the Great Commandment (Mark 12:30–31) and the Great Commission (Matt. 28:19–20). Based in Boulder, Colorado, PK quickly developed a national audience. By 1993, its Boulder conference attracted 52,000 men. In summer 1994, it held a series of six stadium rallies across the country, with hundreds of thousands of participants.[2] Two years later, it held twenty-two such rallies, which drew a combined total of 1,090,000 men.[3]

In 1996, PK made its sixth promise its primary focus: "A Promise Keeper is committed to reaching beyond any racial and denominational barriers to demonstrate the power of biblical unity."[4] PK's racial reconciliation emphasis was not simply a matter of rhetoric; the organization put substantial resources and support behind it. The commitment to diversity was born out in its hiring decisions. At its height, PK boasted a 437-member staff that was 30 percent people of color, including 16 percent African American, 13 percent Latino, and 1 percent Native American, making it arguably the most diversely staffed evangelical organization in the country.[5] In 1996, Raleigh Washington, African American pastor of Rock of Our Salvation Evangelical Free Church in Chicago, was appointed vice president of the organization. Washington headed a newly instituted reconciliation division, which was responsible for its racial and denominational unity efforts. The division was charged with developing educational curricula, including the "Eight Biblical Principles of Reconciliation," and dispersing $1.3 million that PK had raised for churches burned by arson. A national strategic manager was appointed for each major ethnic group.[6]

At its twenty-two stadium rallies in 1996, evangelical men—possibly for the first time—heard that racial reconciliation was not only

2. Howard A. Snyder, "Will Promise Keepers Keep Their Promises?" *Christianity Today*, November 14, 1994, 20.

3. Ted Olsen, "Racial Reconciliation Emphasis Intensified," *Christianity Today*, January 6, 1997, 67.

4. Promise Keepers, "7 Promises," https://promisekeepers.org/about/7-promises.

5. Olsen, "Racial Reconciliation," 67.

6. Olsen, "Racial Reconciliation," 67; Promise Keepers, "Eight Biblical Principles of Reconciliation," https://promisekeepers.org/about/faqs/faqs-controversy#eight.

valued, but also mandated, by the gospel.[7] Most of those men were White, but McCartney announced a goal of diversifying the rally audiences.[8] A clergy summit in Atlanta drew 39,000 clergy under the theme "Breaking Down the Walls." The audience, as with other PK events, was predominantly White but included significantly more African Americans, Asian Americans, Latino Americans, and Native Americans than previous rallies. The speakers were also diverse, with at least one person of color featured in each session.[9] On March 6 and 7, 1997, PK followed up with its first African American leaders' summit in Colorado. The meeting, which gathered more than one hundred clergy, was the first of a series designed to recruit more minority participation, building up to a national gathering for prayer and repentance to be held in Washington, DC, on October 4, 1997.[10] The event, "Stand in the Gap: A Sacred Assembly of Men," was part of PK's attempt to follow up on its vow to make racial reconciliation a central part of its work. More than half a million men gathered on the National Mall, where they heard founder McCartney declare the ambitious—and naive—goal of eradicating racism in the church by 2000.[11]

PK's attempt to disciple a million evangelical Christian men into the gospel of racial reconciliation was hardly a success. It met with considerable skepticism from Black and Latinx evangelicals. For example, after McCartney delivered a breakfast address at the 1995 gathering of the National Black Evangelical Association, one attendee demanded, "What is Promise Keepers going to say about the antiaffirmative action atmosphere in this country? . . . What are

---

7. Lisa Sharon Harper, *Evangelical Does Not Equal Republican . . . or Democrat* (New York: New Press, 2008), 93.

8. Olsen, "Racial Reconciliation," 67.

9. "Promise Keepers and Race," *The Christian Century* 113, no. 8 (1996): 254.

10. The PK gathering was held just two years after the Million Man March organized by Nation of Islam leader Louis Farrakhan. It drew many comparisons to the prior march. McCartney, however, was clear to draw a distinction between the two events, saying, "We are going to DC not to march, but to repent" (Olsen, "Racial Reconciliation," 67).

11. W. Terry Whalin, "Promise Keepers Gathers Black Leaders," *Christianity Today,* April 28, 1997, 84.

the men in the stadiums this summer going to hear about that? Will Promise Keepers stand up and be counted on this issue?"[12] In his *Christianity Today* article, Tapia asked,

> Does the white Promise Keeper wanting to hug me with reconciling fervor take into account that he may support immigration policies that make Latinos—whether US-born, legal immigrant, or undocumented—feel scrutinized every time they go to the doctor or take a child to school? that many Latinos could end up on the streets once welfare reform goes into full effect at the city and neighborhood level? that crackdowns on drugs are disproportionately applied to communities of color? that English-language-only initiatives create a climate where the desire to inculcate in my daughter my language and culture is seen as un-American? The next step for racial reconciliation needs to include rethinking the social and political issues that divide and exasperate our communities.[13]

The biggest challenge to PK's racial reconciliation focus, however, came from the White men who constituted its primary audience. In the year following the Washington, DC, gathering, attendance at PK events declined by more than 50 percent. In Emerson and Smith's pivotal book, *Divided by Faith,* McCartney attributed the decline directly to the racial reconciliation emphasis, stating: "To this day, the racial message remains a highly charged element of Promise Keepers' ministry. . . . [O]f the 1996 conference participants who had a complaint, nearly 40 percent reacted negatively to the reconciliation theme. I personally believe it was a major factor in the significant falloff in PK's 1997 attendance—it is simply a hard teaching for many."[14] Pretty soon thereafter, the movement that had once dominated media attention vanished from view for most Americans.

12. Kevin A. Miller, "McCartney Preaches Reconciliation," *Christianity Today,* June 19, 1995, 43.

13. Tapia, "After the Hugs," 54.

14. Michael O. Emerson and Christian Smith, *Divided by Faith: Evangelical Religion and the Problem of Race in America* (Oxford: Oxford University Press, 2000), 67.

Introduction

E-racing Gender: The Evangelical Paradigm

Despite its decreased prominence in the American religious landscape, PK's impact upon the evangelical approach to racial reconciliation endures for several reasons. First, while other national evangelical organizations, such as the Christian Community Development Association and InterVarsity Christian Fellowship, had an explicit—and justice-oriented—focus on reconciliation, the sheer size of PK's audience extended its potential influence much farther. Moreover, the target populations for CCDA and InterVarsity were highly selective; the former focused upon Christians who were living and serving in marginalized communities, while the latter was a college-based movement. Individuals in both of those organizations were likely more receptive to the language of racial reconciliation than the tens of thousands of evangelical men who packed stadiums at each of PK's rallies. Second, it is important to realize that these movements were not isolated from each other; there was considerable cross-pollination between them. For example, leaders within CCDA were frequent speakers at PK rallies, including CCDA's founder John Perkins and recent president Noel Castellanos. Raleigh Washington was a member of CCDA and pastored a congregation that had formed a strategic partnership with a community development ministry founded by CCDA board member Glen Kehrein. Perkins was a mentor for Brenda Salter McNeil, a former InterVarsity staff member who delivered a powerful sermon on racial reconciliation at its 2000 Urbana conference.

To some degree, then, the theology of racial reconciliation that emerged through the PK rallies shaped—and was shaped by—the dominant evangelical paradigm. Central to this paradigm was a belief that racism is a form of sin that results from division based on socially constructed categories of racial identity. Critical here is the idea that separateness—particularly that separateness evident among Christians during Sunday morning worship—is the "problem." The "solution," then, is togetherness. In *Dear White Christians*, Jennifer Harvey refers to this as "the reconciliation paradigm." She states:

> On the one hand, the reconciliation paradigm seems to claim
> that racial identities do not innately pertain to who we are as

7

human beings created in God's image. This version of reconciliation assumes that our separateness betrays a failure to understand our shared humanity as something that transcends our differences. The implications of this assumption seem to be that reconciliation would come if we honored the truth that at our core we are one and *the same*. On the other hand, these Christians argue that we must do better at learning about, understanding, and appreciating real differences among racial groups. This claim assumes that separateness comes from failing to value diversity enough. Reconciliation in this version becomes a matter of genuinely embracing *particularities*, or the ways in which *we are not the same*.[15]

Consistent with the evangelical emphasis on Christian identity being centrally expressed through the individual believer's personal relationship with God, the evangelical understanding of reconciliation focuses on: (1) transforming interpersonal relationships between Christians of different ethnic backgrounds; and (2) establishing racially diverse congregations. This was especially true for Promise Keepers. As Lisa Sharon Harper notes, "PK focused on individual responses to racism through personal relationship alone."[16] Thus it was that the sixth promise was limited to "reaching beyond . . . racial and denominational barriers," rather than dismantling structural barriers and working to ensure equity and equality. More recently, writings by progressive mainline Protestant clergy and academics have highlighted structural issues in racial reconciliation. Scholars like Allan Boesak, Curtiss Paul DeYoung, and Jennifer Harvey have each critiqued the interpersonal bias in the earlier literature and called for reparations as part of racial reconciliation.

Reducing racial reconciliation to interpersonal relationships presents a particular problem when participants are confronted with gender. In the evangelical worldview, women are seen primarily as wives, mothers, and daughters; that is, they are extensions of men

15. Jennifer Harvey, *Dear White Christians: For Those Still Longing for Racial Reconciliation* (Grand Rapids: Eerdmans, 2014), 28–29.

16. Quoted in Harvey, *Dear White Christians*, 104.

rather than human beings and leaders in their own right.[17] Male identity constitutes the basic human experience. Likewise, male racial identity constitutes the basic racial experience. Women are not seen as raced human beings; that is, they are not imagined as having experiences of race and racism that are distinct from their male counterparts. This is what enabled Bill McCartney to imagine that friendships between men of different races would singlehandedly eradicate the problem of racism, as he declared on the National Mall. In *Evangelical Does Not Equal Republican . . . or Democrat*, Lisa Sharon Harper describes her reaction upon realizing that PK's website made no mention of gender in its explanation of reconciliation:

> When I first logged on to the PK Web site, I wondered how they approached gender reconciliation and was struck by one thing. None of the seven promises address men's relationship to women. In the PK statement of faith, the sixth point reads: "All believers in the Lord Jesus Christ are members of His one international, multi-ethnic, and transcultural body called the universal church. Its unity is displayed when we reach beyond racial and denominational lines to demonstrate the Gospel's reconciling power." Gender reconciliation is not viewed as a way God displays his reconciling power, despite the reality that one of the first biblical relationships to shatter at the Fall in Genesis 3 was the relationship between men and women.[18]

During subsequent interviews with PK leaders, Harper pressed the issue of whether the organization was concerned about shaping how men related to women, particularly those who were not their romantic partners, such as women in their workplaces, their communities, and other settings. "The men were silent," Harper says.[19] PK, it seemed, was concerned with women only insofar as they were the wives or daughters of evangelical Christian men. Otherwise, women were invisible.

17. Harper, *Evangelical*, 114–15.
18. Harper, *Evangelical*, 108–9.
19. Harper, *Evangelical*, 110.

So too women—particularly women of color—have largely been invisible in the field of reconciliation. Reading lists on reconciliation usually include only male-authored texts, sometimes augmented by an autobiographical narrative by a female survivor of ethnic conflict outside the United States. For example, one mainline denomination's racial reconciliation curriculum includes a resource list of thirteen texts on racial reconciliation and the church; of these, only one has a female author, in this case, the final of four authors on a coauthored book. The results of this exclusively male gaze are a body of literature and an approach to reconciliation that are less about ending racism than they are about ensuring that White men and men of color have equal access to male privilege.

The exclusion of women's racial experiences from dialogue on racial reconciliation is not simply a problem for women; it precludes any real understanding of the dynamics of race and racism. Historically, women's bodies have been the sites upon which racial boundaries have been policed and racial wars have been fought. In the United States, for example, two of the primary ways by which White supremacist patriarchy has exercised its power have been by controlling what White women could do with their bodies and by demonstrating that Black women's bodies were violable. Thus, marginalizing the voices of women of color results in anemic understandings of racism that hinder our efforts toward reconciliation. If we truly hope to work toward racial reconciliation, the perspectives of women of color must be moved from margin to center.

Voices of Disruption

I Bring the Voice of My People aims to center the voices of women of color by using a womanist framework to construct a theology of racial reconciliation. I provide a full explanation of racial reconciliation later in this text, after first addressing the gaps in understandings of race, racism, privilege, and reconciliation that dominate popular Christian discourse and activism. A working definition that can guide readers in the first half of the book is this: *Racial reconciliation is part of God's ongoing and eschatological mission to restore wholeness and peace to a world broken by systemic injustice. Racial reconciliation focuses its efforts upon dismantling White supremacy, the systemic evil that denies and distorts the image of God inherent in all humans based upon the heretical belief that White aesthetics, values, and cultural norms bear the fullest representation of the imago Dei. White supremacy thus maintains that White people are superior to all other peoples, and it orders creation, identities, relationships, and social structures in ways that support this distortion and denial.*

I contend throughout this book that African American women, and women of color broadly, have a heightened stake in the dismantling of White supremacy, which intersects with other forms of systemic oppression to shape their realities. Thus, I use a womanist framework (in conversation with feminist theologies of other women of color). Taking its name from the word coined by Alice Walker,[20] womanist theology can be defined as

> . . . the systematic, faith-based exploration of the many facets of African American women's religiosity. Womanist theology is based on the complex realities of [B]lack women's lives. Womanist scholars recognize and name the imagination and

---

20. In the preface to *In Search of Our Mothers' Gardens: Womanist Prose* (San Diego: Harcourt Brace Jovanovich, 1983), Alice Walker provides the following definition of womanist: "**Womanist 1.** From *womanish.* (Opp. of 'girlish,' i.e., frivolous, irresponsible, not serious.) A black feminist or feminist of color. From the black folk expression of mothers to female children, 'You acting womanist,' i.e., like a woman. Usually referring to outrageous, audacious, courageous or *willful* behavior. Wanting to know more and in greater depth than is considered 'good' for one. Interested in grown-up doings. Acting grown up. Being grown up. Interchangeable with another black folk expression: 'You trying to be grown.' Responsible. In charge. *Serious.* **2.** *Also:* A woman who loves other women, sexually and/or nonsexually. Appreciates and prefers women's culture, women's emotional flexibility (values tears as natural counterbalance of laughter), and women's strength. Sometimes loves individual men, sexually and/or nonsexually. Committed to survival and wholeness of entire people, male *and* female. Not a separatist, except periodically, for health. Traditionally universalist, as in: 'Mama, why are we brown, pink, and yellow, and our cousins are white, beige, and black?' Ans.: 'Well, you know the colored race is just like a flower garden, with every color flower represented.' Traditionally capable, as in: 'Mama, I'm walking to Canada and I'm taking you and a bunch of other slaves with me.' Reply: 'It wouldn't be the first time'" **3.** Loves music. Loves dance. Loves the moon. *Loves* the Spirit. Loves love and food and roundness. Loves struggle. *Loves* the folk. Loves herself. *Regardless.* **4.**Womanist is to feminist as purple is to lavender" (xi–xii).

initiative that African American women have utilized in developing sophisticated religious responses to their lives.[21]

Womanist theology begins its analysis by understanding the lived experiences of African American women, including the ways in which they experience oppression and the ways in which they find hope and exercise agency in the midst of oppression. Emerging in the 1980s as a reaction to Black liberation theology and feminist theology, womanist theology privileges Black women's lives as "texts," sources of authority that can tell us something about the nature of God and about the nature of the human condition. It draws from the rich well of the beliefs, traditions, and practices that have enabled Black women to "make a way out of no way."

As Stephanie Mitchem notes, womanist theology asks the questions: "Where is God in the experiences of black women? By what name should this God be called? What does it mean to live a life of faith? How should black women respond to God's call?"[22] In the case of racial reconciliation, we might say that womanist theology asks the questions: "What do Black women's lives reveal about the natures of the 'powers and principalities'? How do Black women understand hope, forgiveness, and reconciliation in light of their experiences of oppression? What does healing look like for Black women? How should Black women respond to God's call to be ambassadors of reconciliation?" My preliminary answer to these questions, which I will work out in more detail in this book, is this: as a framework for thinking about and becoming the body of Christ, womanist theology offers two important gifts that advance our understanding of race, racism, and reconciliation. The first gift is intersectionality; the second is a wholistic view of healing and liberation.

Womanist theology, by definition, employs an intersectional framework as the lens through which to understand and interpret how systems of power and oppression interconnect to shape the lives of African American women. In other words, it recognizes that the

21. Stephanie Y. Mitchem, *Introducing Womanist Theology* (Maryknoll: Orbis Books, 2002), ix.
22. Mitchem, *Introducing*, 23.

experiences of African American women are not simply the sum of their experiences as women and their experiences as African American. Identity is not just additive; it is multiplicative. If I were writing it as an algebraic equation, I would write it like this:

$$RacialGenderIdentity = Race + Gender + (Race^*Gender)$$

In other words, African American women will share some experiences with African American men by virtue of their race, and they will share some experiences with all women by virtue of their femaleness. But their location at the intersection of race and gender predisposes them to experiences of gendered racism that are qualitatively and quantitatively different from those of African American men (and certainly from White men), White women, and sometimes even other women of color. The same, of course, is true for all men and women of color. For example, "driving while Black" is a form of gendered racial oppression in that it happens disproportionately to Black men. In chapter 2, I discuss some specific manifestations of gendered racism, including colorism, mammification, and hypersexualization, that are experienced frequently by women of color but that are largely ignored in our discussions of race and racism.

It is easy to think of this intersectional framework as an "alternative" or "add-on" perspective of race and racism. It is more important than that, though. Notice that in the equation above, race appears in two places: once on its own and again tied to gender. Most of our conversation about racial reconciliation, though, has focused on only one part of that equation: race alone. But the equation reveals that there is some knowledge to be gained about race that can be had only when we connect it to gender. I could say the same thing for class, sexuality, nationality, and many other categories of identity. In this book, I will focus mainly on race and gender.

In any society, the most marginalized people best understand the rules of the system, because they need to know the politics and dynamics in order to avoid being crushed by them. Women of color are often the marginalized among the marginalized. Our very survival depends upon knowing how the "isms" (or as I prefer to think of them, the "powers and principalities") work. We are constantly bending and genuflecting in order to fit into the small, contorted spaces that society has set for us. We are frequently hurting from the injuries we sustain when we dare to step out of place. And we are always aware that others—men of color as well as White women and men—do not have to bend and sidestep in the same ways or to the same degree. We thus have unique vantage points from which to view how the system works. Those who are serious about liberation and reconciliation would do well to sit at our feet and learn from us.

That brings us to the second gift: womanist theology is intrinsically wholistic. As Alice Walker noted in her original definition, womanists are "committed to the survival and wholeness of entire people, male *and* female."[23] This offers several significant implications for reconciliation. First, womanist theology uses the perspectives of African American women as a starting point from which to expand and encompass all of humanity. African American women have long been lauded as the caregivers of . . . well, the whole damn world. In my first book, *Too Heavy a Yoke: Black Women and the Burden of Strength,* I talk about why that is and what it means for the health and well-being of Black women. When it comes to justice and liberation, it means that African American women are concerned not just for our own healing and liberation; we want it for everyone. We know that ain't none of us free unless all of us are. And because we are experts at wearing the mask of the StrongBlackWoman to hide how we really feel, we know that external appearance is not a marker of internal health. Thus, womanists are concerned not just with the interpersonal but also with the intrapersonal, in other words, with the wounds that racism inflicts upon the self-image of people of color and the way in which it diminishes our capacity to see the image of God (*imago Dei*) stamped upon us.

At the same time, though, womanist theology will not allow us to limit reconciliation to the intrapersonal and interpersonal level. Feeling better about ourselves and getting along on the individual level do not racial reconciliation make. Indeed, womanists reject outright the notion that reconciliation can be reduced to interpersonal relationships because we are fully aware that *power* structures

23. Walker, *In Search of Our Mothers' Gardens,* xi.

relationships. We refute the notion that mere intercultural contact will reduce prejudice and increase harmony. We carry the cultural memories of mothers, grandmothers, and othermothers whose service as domestic workers for White men and women provided lots of intercultural proximity during slavery and Jim Crow. We share kitchen table talk with aunts and cousins who labor today as the new domestics: home care, nursing home, and hospice nursing assistants for elderly White people and nannies for the young. We know firsthand that such proximity does not protect us from the abuses of racism; it often renders us more susceptible. Womanists demand reconciliation that confronts inequalities in power, privilege, and access. Its telos is not simply the cessation of racial hostility; it is the establishment of justice and liberation for all women and men . . . regardless.

In essence, womanist theology takes all that you thought you knew about racism and reconciliation and tells you that you ain't nothing but a babe wandering in the wilderness. So come on over here, chile. Sit a spell and let the womenfolk teach you something about the ways of the world.

Chapter One

Racism Is Not about Feelings or Friendship

The word "racism" is too simplistic, too general, and too easy.
You can use the word and not say that much, unless the term is
explained or clarified. Once that happens, racism looks more
like a psychological problem (or pathological aberration) than
an issue of skin color.

> Doris Davenport, "The Pathology of Racism:
> A Conversation with Third World Wimmin"

An old adage says you should never talk religion or politics with
friends. It probably should say that you should never talk religion,
politics, or race. That, after all, has been the prevailing approach to
race in the United States since the decline of the Black power movement in the 1970s. Many Americans—namely, many White Americans—thought we had figured out the "race" problem with the passage of the Civil Rights Act of 1964 and the Voting Rights Act of 1965.
Talking about race from that point on was considered, well, racist.

Then came the 2008 presidential campaign of Barack Obama,
the man who would become the first African American US president.[1] Suddenly race was back at the forefront of US conversation.

---

1. My reference to Barack Obama as "Black" or "African American" is not meant
to obscure his biracial heritage but rather is intended to be consistent with how he has
self-identified and how he has been identified by the media and the public. During his

Every few days, news anchors and political pundits found some new way to inject Obama's blackness into the election. The coverage was distorted, confusing, and often contradictory. On the one hand, Obama was accused of playing identity politics if he raised issues of race or seemed to play into racial stereotypes. On the other, he was accused of racial inauthenticity if he did not. White political commentators continually raised the question of whether his blackness would dissuade White voters: *Was he too Black? Would he run a "race" campaign? Would White people actually vote for him, or would they say one thing in the polls and do another in the voting booth?* When it became apparent that he was generating White support, the questions shifted: *Was he Black enough? Would Black voters support him? Why wouldn't he run a race-based campaign?* When he secured the party nomination and then the presidency itself, the nation experienced a collective moment of self-congratulation. The tide had turned. We had finally moved beyond race. We were "postracial."

The postracial myth was one that few African Americans believed, especially those of us in the South. Southern African Americans knew all too well the tension of living in the "now and not yet." We knew that when it came to race, progress could be accompanied by regression and signs of hope could coexist with open hostility. For instance, we knew that Obama's election did not change the existence of "sundown" towns, cities where African Americans were not allowed after dark. Just two years prior to his election, I had attended a writing retreat in the north Georgia mountains. As my husband dropped me off at the retreat center on his way to visit family in Birmingham, I warned him to leave the area immediately. "*We* don't come up here." On the way out of town, he stopped at a gas station to fill up and to get a quick snack. As he wandered through the convenience store, the Black female store clerk—the only nonwhite person he had seen in the town—eyed him carefully. As he approached the counter, she said, "What are you doing here?" When he told her about the retreat and about my warning, she replied with concern, "Your wife was right. You hurry up and get back on down that road."

Senate term, for example, the Senate Historical Office designated him as the fifth—and at the time, only—African American serving in the US Senate.

Exploding the Postracial Myth

If anything, the eight years of Obama's presidency exploded the postracial myth. The racial progress marked by the election of the nation's first African American president met a swift backlash in the rise of the Tea Party. Two years after the Democrat Obama had carried a number of traditionally Republican states in the presidential election, the Republican Party was battling for its soul as Tea Party–backed ultraconservatives unseated more moderate incumbents in the House, in the Senate, and in gubernatorial elections across the country. While the central elements of the Tea Party platform—smaller government and lower taxes—resembled right-wing opposition to Democratic presidents, Tea Party rhetoric has been distinguished by one notable factor: the intense hostility aimed at Barack and Michelle Obama.[2] In a 2010 article for *Alternet*, Christopher Deis wrote:

> The deep ugliness and bigotry on display here is centered on a basic idea: Obama is not really one of "us." He, because of his race, his personhood, and his color can never be a "real American." For the Tea Party and right-wing populists, Obama is not fit to rule because as a person of color he is a perpetual outsider and racial Other. . . . Because Obama is not really eligible to be president, his office is not worthy of respect. Obama's presidency is itself illegitimate. By extension, the State is not worthy of respect or loyalty from its citizens.[3]

As Darrel Enck-Wanzer points out, President Obama has not been viewed as just an outsider; he has been depicted as a racial threat to White Americans.[4] From the ridiculousness of "birtherism" to the widely circulated racist depictions of the Obamas as gorillas, bar-

2. Darrel Enck-Wanzer, "Barack Obama, the Tea Party, and the Threat of Race: On Racial Neoliberalism and Born Again Racism" *Communication, Culture & Critique* 4, no. 1 (2011): 24.
3. Chris Deis, "The Tea Parties: Built on Fear, Violence and Race Resentment," *Alternet*, April 7, 2010, https://www.alternet.org/story/146190/the_tea_parties%3A _built_on_fear%2C_violence_and_race_resentment.
4. Enck-Wanzer, "Barak Obama," 26.

barians, and jihadi terrorists, the twenty-first-century Tea Party has whipped up a similar sort of frenzied racism as did D. W. Griffith's film, *The Birth of a Nation*, one hundred years earlier.[5] Released in 1915, it was the nation's first blockbuster and continues to be studied in film schools as a major turning point in cinematography, story-telling, and editing. Griffith's film portrayed African Americans as brutal savages prone to rape, simple-mindedness, and general de-bauchery. In contrast, it depicted the Ku Klux Klan as saviors who restored order to the post-Reconstruction South and saved the "help-less white minority." The film ushered in a renewed interest in the Klan, which had disbanded in 1869 but was reorganized following the film's release. Indeed, when *The Birth of a Nation* premiered in Atlanta, an advertisement for the Klan appeared alongside an ad for the film in the local newspaper.[6] Within six years, the organization had grown to nearly one hundred thousand members, and during the 1924 Democratic National Convention, forty thousand uniformed Klansmen paraded through Washington, DC.[7]

Like the growth of the Klan before it, the rise of the Tea Party seems to have ushered in a second Black nadir, a low point in US race relations characterized by high levels of antiblack racism and violence. The first nadir, which began just after the end of Recon-struction in 1877 and continued through the first two decades of the twentieth century, was marked by a record number of lynchings of Black men, women, and children. The second one is not altogether different, as the nation continually witnesses dozens of unarmed Black men, women, and children killed with impunity by mostly White police officers and civilians. It can be traced to July 13, 2013, when George Zimmerman was acquitted in the shooting death of Trayvon Martin, an African American teenager whom he had con-

5. The 1915 silent film, *The Birth of a Nation*, produced and directed by D. W. Grif-fith, is not to be confused with the 2016 film, *Birth of a Nation*, produced and directed by Nate Parker. Parker intentionally appropriated the name as a gesture of resistance toward the lingering influence that Griffith's movie has upon the film industry.

6. Southern Poverty Law Center, *Ku Klux Klan: A History of Racism and Violence*, 6th ed. (Montgomery, AL: Southern Poverty Law Center, 2011), 21, https://www.splcenter.org/sites/default/files/Ku-Klux-Klan-A-History-of-Racism.pdf.

7. Southern Poverty Law Center, *Ku Klux Klan*, 17, 22.

fronted in his neighborhood while Martin was walking home from a convenience store. Since Zimmerman's killing of Martin in February 2012, the death roster has been staggering: Kendrec McDade, March 2012; Rekia Boyd, March 2012; Shereese Francis, March 2012; Kimani Grey, March 2013; Jonathan Ferrell, September 2013; Miriam Carey, October 2013; Yvette Smith, February 2014; Eric Garner, July 2014; Michael Brown, August 2014; Kajieme Powell, August 2014; Ezell Ford, August 2014; John Crawford, August 2014; Akai Gurley, November 2014; Tamir Rice, November 2014; Anthony Hill, March 2015; Walter Scott, April 2015; Samuel DuBose, July 2015; Alton Sterling, July 2016; Philando Castile, July 2016; Tyre King, September 2016, Terrence Crutcher, September 2016; Keith Lamont Hill, September 2016; Jordan Edwards, April 2017; Charleena Lyles, June 2017; Stephon Clark, June 2018; Antwon Rose, June 2018; and many others.

Some of the victims were suspects in petty crimes; others had no criminal history. Some had histories of mental illness, as did Anthony Hill, a twenty-seven-year-old Air Force veteran who was killed after a neighbor called police asking for help for Hill, who was outside naked, crawling on the ground, banging on doors, and repeatedly jumping off his second-floor balcony. Many were simply minding their own business, as John Crawford was when he was killed from behind while talking on his cell phone in Walmart and holding an air rifle that he had picked up on the store shelves. Still others were actually looking to the police for help, such as Jonathan Ferrell, who was shot when he approached police for assistance after he had been involved in a car crash. Several others died in police custody, including Sandra Bland, who died in the Waller County, Texas, jail of mysterious circumstances after being arrested and jailed for failure to signal while turning; Joyce Curnell, who died of a stomach illness after being arrested at a South Carolina hospital when she refused to leave upon discharge; and Freddie Gray, who died after being taken on a "rough ride," a form of brutality in which police intentionally subject arrested persons to violent driving while the victims are handcuffed and unprotected by seatbelts.

The killings themselves were not new. African American communities have long complained about disparate treatment by police, but those complaints were routinely ignored or dismissed by White

Americans. The twenty-first century, however, brought two major technological shifts that changed public reaction: smartphones and social media. Suddenly, ordinary citizens had the capacity to record the arrests, and in some cases the killings, as they happened and then to broadcast them to the world. Incidents of police brutality that previously would have been unreported by major news media were now being reported constantly, even if only after several days of coverage in social media. For the first time, White Americans saw the disparities with their own eyes. They witnessed Eric Garner being choked to death by police on a Brooklyn corner. They saw Sandra Bland being thrown to the ground and arrested for a routine traffic violation. They saw a policeman leap out of his car firing at thirteen-year-old Tamir Rice. They witnessed Philando Castile bleeding to death in a car as his girlfriend and four-year-old daughter watched helplessly. Finally, scores of White "doubting Thomases" were able to put their fingers in the holes and to confirm the truth of the narratives being told by their Black and Brown sisters and brothers.

The killings gave rise to a twenty-first-century human rights movement: Black Lives Matter. Originally a hashtag created by three African American women—Patrice Cullors, Alicia Garza, and Opal Tometi—in response to the Zimmerman acquittal, "Black Lives Matter" became the rallying cry for mass action around the issue of antiblack police violence across the nation, in cities as diverse as Ferguson, Baltimore, Charlotte, Minneapolis, and Baton Rouge. The movement quickly became the focus of renewed right-wing ire, which fueled the 2016 presidential campaign of Donald Trump. The self-described "billionaire" businessman had a long history of making gestures toward a political career, stating an interest in running for the New York governor's office or the US presidency on multiple occasions. These gestures were usually seen as attention-grabbing media stunts. However, Trump began to garner attention from Tea Partiers in 2011 by becoming the first national figure to endorse their "birther" concerns, that is, the belief that President Obama had been born outside the United States and thus was not a citizen. In the year before Obama's reelection, Trump dominated media attention for six weeks by challenging the president's citizenship, at one point even stating that he would pay a private investigator to prove that Obama was born outside the country. When the White House finally settled the matter by releasing an image of Obama's birth certificate, Trump quieted about the issue. But his willingness to publicly question the legitimacy of the country's first African American president had harnessed a following.[8]

In his 2016 presidential campaign, Trump capitalized upon that following, building his brand as the candidate who was willing to trumpet the racial resentment of many far-right White conservatives. He made openly racist statements about Mexicans, African Americans, and Muslims, as well as heterosexist comments about women and LGBTQI persons. During the speech announcing his presidential bid, he broadly characterized the majority of Mexican immigrants as rapists, drug dealers, and criminals. "When Mexico sends its people, they're not sending their best. They're not sending you. They're not sending you. They're sending people that have lots of problems, and they're bringing those problems with us. They're bringing drugs. They're bringing crime. They're rapists. And some, I assume, are good people."[9] Trump's political rallies were often characterized by open violence toward and abuse of African American and Latinx attendees.[10] Just one week prior to the election, he received the enthusiastic endorsement of the Klan's newspaper. While he condemned the publication as "repulsive," he consistently refused to reject the Klan itself.[11] The morning following his election, a group of robed Klansmen stood on a highway overpass atop Interstate 40 in North Carolina, celebrating Trump's victory. Yet Trump reassured

8. Ashley Park and Steve Eder, "Inside the Six Weeks Donald Trump Was a Nonstop 'Birther,'" *New York Times*, July 2, 2016, http://www.nytimes.com/2016/07/03/us /politics/donald-trump-birther-obama.html?_r=0.

9. Washington Post Staff, "Full Text: Donald Trump Announces a Presidential Bid," *The Washington Post*, June 16, 2015, https://www.washingtonpost.com/news/post -politics/wp/2015/06/16/full-text-donald-trump-announces-a-presidential-bid/#ann otations:7472690.

10. Jose A. DelReal, "'Get 'em out!' Racial Tensions Explode at Donald Trump's Rallies," *The Washington Post*, March 12, 2016, https://www.washingtonpost.com /politics/get-him-out-racial-tensions-explode-at-donald-trumps-rallies/2016/03/11 /b9764884-e6ee-11e5-bc08-3e03a5b41910_story.html.

11. "Ku Klux Klan Supports Donald Trump for President," *Fortune*, November 2, 2016, http://fortune.com/2016/11/02/donald-trump-ku-klux-klan-newspaper/.

his largely White supporters that their resentment was not racist but rather a logical reaction to their marginalization by an increasingly privileged minority population.[12]

Despite the racism in Trump's campaign, many people in the United States believe that racism is largely nonexistent or, perhaps even worse, that it is caused by people of color talking about race. For example, in the weeks leading up to the 2008 South Carolina primary, one news station sent reporters to the state to ask whether race was an issue in the election. A middle-aged White woman unhesitatingly said, "Yes. We have a big problem with racism in this country." She went on to identify African Americans as the main racists. "They're always talking about it. Calling themselves African Americans. They're not African Americans. They're Americans and that's what they're supposed to be called." In the final year of Obama's presidency, an Alabama congressman labeled him the most "racially divisive, economically divisive president in the White House since we had presidents who supported slavery."[13]

Ultimately, the aftermath of Obama's election to the presidency revealed that racism remains America's "original sin" and that most Americans do not understand how to think or talk about race. Unfortunately, the latter is also the case for many people who embark upon the journey of racial reconciliation. As racial reconciliation has become more popular, people enter it with varying agendas and varying misperceptions of how race, racism, and reconciliation operate. Three such misperceptions seem to dominate the Christian racial reconciliation paradigm: (1) race is a social construct and therefore not real; (2) racism is the sin that results from division based upon the social construction of race; and (3) reconciliation occurs by increasing interpersonal contact between people of different races. In the remainder of this chapter, I draw upon critical race theory to challenge each of these assumptions.

12. Molly Ball, "The Resentment Powering Trump," *The Atlantic*, March 15, 2016, http://www.theatlantic.com/politics/archive/2016/03/the-resentment-powering -trump/473775/ .

13. Bradford Richardson, "Republican: Obama Most 'Racially Divisive' President Since Civil War," *The Hill*, January 15, 2016, http://thehill.com/blogs/blog-briefing -room/news/266075-republican-obama-most-racially-divisive-president-since-civil.

Constructing Race

Ironically, while race tends to be one of the most salient components of identity in the United States, it is an ambiguous term. In part, the ambiguity arises because the understanding of race has shifted considerably over time. The scientific perspective on race has evolved from understanding it as a biological reality to viewing it as a social construction.

Classical Racialism: Race as Biological Reality

Until recently, much of the thinking about race in the United States has been dominated by classical racialism, the belief that race is an ontological biological reality. That is, classical racialism held that "races are biologically distinct populations of human beings."[14] As a biological reality, race was believed to determine phenotype (observable characteristics such as skin color, facial features, hair texture) and to predict functioning across a wide range of areas, including intellectual ability, criminality, cultural aptitude, and morality.[15] These two elements—phenotype and functioning—are inseparable. From its very beginning, the project of classical racialism was synonymous with biological racism, the belief that White people are superior to all nonwhite groups and that this superiority is rooted in biology and genetics. A key interest of classical racism has been the production of racial taxonomies that categorized ethnic groups into races and rank-ordered them based upon characteristics such as skin color, hair type, and even skull size. In his 1735 text, *Systemae Naturae*, Swedish botanist Carolus Linnaeus identified four racial groups that corresponded to four continents: Americanus, Asiaticus, Africanus, and Europeanus. Others, such as Johann Blumenbach, Comte Joseph-Arthur de Gobineau, Herbert Spencer, and David Hume, followed

---

14. Jacoby Adeshei Carter, "Does 'Race' Have a Future or Should the Future Have 'Races'? Reconstruction or Eliminativism in a Pragmatist Philosophy of Race," *Transactions of the Charles S. Peirce Society* 50, no. 1 (2014): 34.

15. Carter, "Does 'Race' Have a Future," 35.

suit, in some cases elaborating upon Linnaeus's taxonomy. While they differed in the numbers of races that they identified, each agreed that Europeans were superior.[16]

The Rise of Scientific Racism. In the nineteenth century, the rise of the scientific age gave further credence to classical racialism. Scientists began using craniometry—the measurement of human skulls—to "prove" that there were distinct differences in brain size among the races. The methodology is laughable by today's standards. The researchers would often initially classify skulls in racial groups based upon the geographic location in which the skull was found and the skull's size and shape. Skulls with larger size and symmetry were usually classified as European, and those that did not fit the researcher's expectations were eliminated from analysis. Unsurprisingly, then, the analysis would find that Caucasians had larger skull sizes than did Native Americans or Africans. While the methodology may have been a joke, its results were not. Policymakers used arguments of genetic inferiority to justify the Indian Removal Act of 1830, which enabled the mass displacement and extermination of tens of thousands of Native Americans.[17] Classical racialism, then, has always been a political and theological theory as much as it was a scientific theory. It was developed, at least in part, to justify the extermination of the Indigenous peoples of the Americas and the enslavement and brutal treatment Africans in the Western world.

The Eugenics Movement. Notably, scientific racism did not end with the cessation of slavery. In the twentieth century, classical racialism paved the way for the eugenics movement, which purported that race was biologically linked not only to intelligence, but also to traits such as criminality, poverty, alcoholism, laziness, and morality.[18] For eugenicists, the future of civilization would require selective breeding to ensure the purity of the racially superior (conveniently, northern

16. Tanya Golash-Boza, *Race and Racisms: A Critical Approach* (New York: Oxford University Press, 2015), 24.
17. Golash-Boza, *Race and Racisms,* 25–27.
18. Golash-Boza, *Race and Racisms,* 40.

and western European groups) as well as forced sterilization of the racially unfit (a broad category that included Jews, Native Americans, and Africans). The writings of eugenics scholars were foundational in the philosophy, policy, and leadership of Adolf Hitler. His attempts to preserve the purity of the Aryan race begin with the passage of the Law for the Prevention of Hereditarily Diseased Offspring in 1933, which mandated sterilization, by force when necessary, of anyone diagnosed with conditions believed to be hereditary, including blindness, epilepsy, physical deformity, intellectual disability, and chronic alcoholism. This law resulted in the forced sterilization of four hundred thousand Germans.[19] When sterilizing "inferior" Aryan Whites proved to be an ineffective method of creating a racially pure society, Hitler turned to euthanasia and eventually to the gas chambers.

The horrors of the Holocaust did not bring an end to eugenics. Between 1929 and 1974, the state of North Carolina forcibly sterilized more than seventy-six hundred people, primarily poor women, men, and sometimes children who were identified by social workers based upon low academic performance or "unwholesome" home environments.[20] White backlash to the civil rights movement included a rise in sterilization of Black women in the South. Dorothy Roberts provides a detailed account of this history in *Killing the Black Body*:

> During the 1970s sterilization became the most rapidly growing form of birth control in the United States, rising from 200,000 cases in 1970 to over 700,000 in 1980. It was a common belief among Blacks in the South that Black women were routinely sterilized without their informed consent and for no valid medical reason. Teaching hospitals performed unnecessary hysterectomies on poor Black women as practice for their medical residents. This sort of abuse was so widespread in the

19. United States Holocaust Memorial Museum, "The Biological State: Nazi Racial Hygiene, 1933–1939," Washington, DC: United States Holocaust Memorial Museum, July 2, 2016, https://www.ushmm.org/wlc/en/article.php?Module Id=10007057.

20. Irin Carmon, "For Eugenic Sterilization Victims, Belated Justice," MSNBC, June 27, 2014, http://www.msnbc.com/all/eugenic-sterilization-victims-belated-justice.

South that these operations came to be known as "Mississippi appendectomies."[21]

By the 1970s, of course, eugenics legislation had been repealed. The continued sterilization of African American, and eventually Latina American, women was done under the auspices of providing health care.[22]

In 1994, psychologist Richard Hernstein and political scientist Charles Murray published *The Bell Curve*, in which they argued that racial and ethnic differences in intelligence (IQ) test scores are largely attributable (by 40 to 80 percent) to genetic makeup. They made policy recommendations to reduce immigration into the United States, which they believed to be responsible for decreasing IQ scores nationwide. They also made a case for ending affirmative action. The book received widespread cultural and academic criticism as an example of racist science and "anachronistic social Darwinism," with many noteworthy scholars pointing out serious problems with its theoretical assumptions and statistical methodologies.[23] Notably, the Pioneer Fund—a now-defunct organization criticized for its ties to eugenics and classified as a "hate group" by the Southern Poverty Law Center—funded much of the research in the book.

In 2015, Richard Lynn published the second edition of his book, *Race Differences in Intelligence*, in which he argued that there are innate and heritable differences in intelligence that are tied to climate. Lynn argued that the longer winters of the Northern Hemisphere produce populations with higher IQs. Thus, he found that Europeans and East Asians (specifically, Chinese, Japanese, and Koreans) are genetically predisposed to having higher IQs than are other

21. Dorothy Roberts, *Killing the Black Body: Race, Reproduction, and the Meaning of Liberty* (New York: Pantheon Books, 1997), 90.

22. Nicole L. Novak et al., "Disproportionate Sterilization of Latinos under California's Eugenic Sterilization Program, 1920–1945," *American Journal of Public Health* 108, no. 5 (May 2018): 611–13.

23. Stephen Jay Gould, "Curveball: A Review of Herrnstein and Murray's The Bell Curve," *New Yorker* 70, no. 39 (November 28, 1994): 139.

geographic populations, including southeast and southern Asians, Native Americans, Pacific Islanders, and Africans.[24]

Classical Racialism Debunked. Despite the continued publication of such texts, classical racialism has been thoroughly discredited by the overwhelming majority of scientists and anthropologists. Ironically, it was the insistence upon race as a biological reality that undermined the viewpoint. By its own logic, classical racialism meant that scientists should be able to use biological data to distinguish between distinct racial groups. As philosopher Jacoby Adeshei Carter explains, it "requires that the populations referred to by racial terms be clearly distinguishable from other populations by either ancestry or essence that corresponds directly with biosocial phenomena such as intelligence, cultural and moral aptitude. But there are no rigidly distinct populations like that."[25] That is, there are no distinct genetic or otherwise biological markers of racial differences. Moreover, the existence of mixed race groups further muddies the ontological waters. Social and natural scientists have successfully demonstrated that such clearly distinct populations do not exist and that the concept we know as "race" has no essential biological foundation. Advances in genomic science have solidified this view, which is now known as the "ontological consensus."[26]

24. Richard Lynn, *Race Differences in Intelligence: An Evolutionary Analysis*, 2nd ed. (Arlington, VA: Washington Summit Publishers, 2015).

25. Carter, "Does 'Race' Have a Future," 37.

26. Carter, "Does 'Race' Have a Future," 35. There are scholars who continue to argue for the scientific basis of race. In his 2012 book, *Preludes to Pragmatism: Toward a Reconstruction of Philosophy*, Philip Kitcher argues that race is both socially constructed and biologically real. Using evolutionary biology as an example, he asserts that the human species could be divided into subcategories with "distinctive and salient clusters of significant genotypic and phenotypic traits" that could be regarded as races (Carter, 29). The rationale of Kitcher's argument is based upon the evolutionary biological concept of "reduced interbreeding . . . [which] occurs whenever members of one population are geographically separated and mate with one another more frequently than they mate with members of other populations" (Carter, 31). Over time, this can produce populations that, while not unique species, have clusters of unique genetic, and even phenotypic, traits (Carter, 31). Among humans, this might correspond to putative racial differences. He conceptualizes races as "populations that have been re-

Social Constructionism: Race as Human Invention

But if race is not a biological entity, what is it? People who accept the ontological consensus still maintain widely varying perspectives on race. On one end of the spectrum is racial eliminativism, which holds that since, from a purely scientific perspective, "there is nothing in the world that corresponds to our use of the term 'race,'" the concept should be eliminated.[27] On the other end of the spectrum is social constructionism, which holds that race is "a socially real phenomenon with no causually determinative biological underpinnings."[28] In other words, social constructionism argues that race is not a real entity in the way that, for example, we might think of an orange as a real entity. An orange exists, regardless of whether we see it, notice it, or name it. It is not just an idea or concept; it is a *real thing*. No matter if we call it an orange, naranja, or chungwa, its existence and properties do not change. Race, on the other hand, is a human invention, and a relatively new one at that. Its invention coincides with Western expansionism, colonialism, and the transatlantic slave trade.

Western Expansion and the Invention of Race. The phenotypic characteristics that we attribute to racial differences are markers of historical geographical isolation. That is, even before the concept of race was invented, the fairest peoples on earth were clustered on the continent of Europe, the darkest peoples on the continent of Africa, and so on. Each population reproduced within itself because it was geographically isolated from the others. Over time, this meant that certain biological patterns became evident among them. For example, the peoples of Africa developed a genetic mutation that protected them from the malaria that was common to their geographic region, but that also predisposed them to a debilitating disease called

---

productively isolated for substantial periods of time that bear phenotypic features that people find important and noticeable" (Carter, 41). Carter ultimately rejects Kitcher's view, arguing that it "does not yet establish that the conception of race that we in fact retain ought to be a biological one, as opposed to a merely social and constructionist view of race" (Carter, 46–47).

27. Carter, "Does 'Race' Have a Future," 30.
28. Carter, "Does 'Race' Have a Future," 35.

sickle cell anemia. The fair-skinned peoples of Europe developed a susceptibility to a different disease, cystic fibrosis. As each group reproduced within itself, it reproduced those genetic risks, along with phenotypic traits like skin color and hair texture. There were distinctions within each group, of course. Indeed, genomic science has found that there is generally more genetic variability within racial groups than there are across them.[29] But throughout most of human history, race was a nonexistent concept; it was all about tribal or national identities that marked shared phenotype as well as shared histories, cultures, and geographies.

When transoceanic travel conquered geographic isolation and brought the peoples from different continents together, it laid the foundation for the concept we now know as race. When the light-skinned peoples of Europe encountered the dark-skinned peoples of Africa, phenotype was the most salient marker not just for geographic origin, but also for beliefs and customs about clothing, food, spirituality, family, housing, government, and so on. If the two groups had met on terms of equal power, the meaning ascribed to the differences in skin color might not have been very significant. Unfortunately, it was a rigged encounter from the beginning. While Europeans were not the first to make transoceanic voyages, their foray coincided with two scientific advances that proved fortuitous for them and disastrous for the peoples of Africa, the Americas, and maritime Asia, namely, advances in maritime technology and in weaponry. Thus, when the British, French, Dutch, Spanish, and Portuguese set sail for the shores of other continents in the late fifteenth century, they did so in the fastest, lightest ships that had ever been designed and they were armed with the most efficient killing machines. Not only could Europeans claim that they were superior to the darker-hued peoples of the world, they could enforce their dominance and power.

29. The Human Genome Project, for example, found that 99.9 percent of human DNA sequences are identical. Of the 0.1 percent of human variation, only 3 to 10 percent is accounted for by ancestral migration patterns. (Wendy D. Roth and Biorn Ivemark, "Genetic Options: The Impact of Genetic Ancestry Testing on Consumers' Racial and Ethnic Identities," *American Journal of Sociology* 124, no. 1 [July 2018]: 158.)

Still, the concept that we now know as race was not fully formed until the advent of the Atlantic slave trade. It was in the dungeons of the slave ports on the West African coast and in the bowels of the slave ships that the Fante, Igbo, Yoruba, Mandinka, and Wolof became simply "Black," a term that signaled not just skin color and geographic origin, but also enslaveability. Since then, the concept of race in the United States has been shaped by a forced-choice mentality, in which people ascribe, or are assigned, to a single category. This makes sense given the country's history. Since the arrival of Europeans on the shores of North America, race has been a high-stakes category that wholly constrains a person's opportunities. Racial categories in the United States were constructed to "flatten" a person's identity so that the person fit easily into one box. Being White meant that you were free; being Black meant that you were enslaveable; and being Indigenous meant that you were extinguishable. Throughout US history, the task of every immigrant group has been to prove themselves "not Black," that is, not enslaveable. For western European immigrants, this has meant becoming inscribed into the racial category of whiteness. For other ethnic groups, it has meant reinforcing one's non-blackness.

(Re)making Racial Designations. Once racial designations were established, each group maintained its racial boundaries through intragroup marriage and procreation. Until the 1967 Supreme Court decision in *Loving v. Virginia*, interracial marriage was illegal throughout the southern United States.[30] Thus, even as the country's population diversified, intimacy and reproduction largely occurred between people who have shared racial identities, which include not only phenotypic traits, but also shared cultural, political, social, and geographic histories. The genetic risks associated with those shared histories were also passed down along racial lines, further supporting

30. With the exception of ten states that never passed antimiscegenation laws, interracial marriage and intimacy was illegal in most of the country at some point. Several states repealed the laws in the late nineteenth century, and most other non-southern states followed suit in the post–World War II period. The southern states, however, never repealed their antimiscegenation legislation; those laws were invalidated with the *Loving* decision.

the illusion that race was a biological concept even as social constructionism was at work.

The racial category of whiteness demonstrates this more than any other. Our understanding of who counts as "White" has shifted, and continues to shift, dramatically throughout US history. Initially limited to people from northern and western European countries, the category of whiteness was expanded over time to include the Irish, Italians, and most recently, Jews. The determination of race was often a matter for the legal system, as it had significant implications for immigration and citizenship. In *Race and Racisms: A Critical Approach*, Tanya Golash-Boza states:

> For centuries, the citizenship and racial statuses of people living in the United States were questioned and challenged. Some immigrants, like Mexicans and Armenians, could be classified as white. Before arriving in the United States, Armenians, like Japanese and Italians, were not white. They had not yet been assigned a race. Eventually, each national-origin group in the United States was assigned a racial category. The assignment of whiteness to Armenians and Italians and non-whiteness to Japanese would have enduring effects on their social location in the United States. . . . The relationship between common knowledge and law is circular. When judges decided who was legally white, they were not able to separate themselves from the unconscious biases inherent in common knowledge. At the same time, their decisions reinforced common knowledge about who was not white. Similar processes occurred with identification of the Irish, Jews, and Italians, people who today are nearly universally accepted as white.[31]

Modern Racial Designations. Today, racial designations—that is, the racial category to which a person ascribes and/or is assigned—are based upon a combination of factors such as phenotype, continental ancestry, shared history, and self-identification. The US Census

31. Golash-Boza, *Race and Racisms,* 49.

recognizes five racial categories: White, Black or African American, American Indian or Alaskan Native, Asian, and Native Hawaiian or Other Pacific Islander. Hispanic or Latino is viewed as a separate ethnic—rather than racial—category because persons of Hispanic or Latino descent may be of any race. While the census recognizes that racial identities are not biologically based, it continues to rely on essentialist understandings of race to categorize people into distinct groups based upon phenotype and presumptions about genetic history. Despite all scientific evidence to the contrary, the US Census continues to treat race as a mathematical formula, wherein a person can be 50 percent White, 40 percent Black, and 10 percent Native American. There is no US parallel to the Latin American concept of *mestizaje*, which recognizes the blending of races or cultures. It was not until 2000 that individuals were able to select multiple racial identities on the Census. People who do so are still required to endorse the specific racial categories that make up their identity. Of course, even at the individual level, those categories can change. For example, there is an effort under way to add "Arab" as a new census designation for people from the Middle East and North Africa, who have traditionally been categorized as White. Far from being fixed, ontological realities, then, racial categories are highly malleable; they shift over time and space. They always have; they probably always will.

Social Construction and the New Racism

The heart of the social construction argument is the idea that racial categories are not based in biological differences but are instead constructed by societies. They have meaning only because society gives them meaning. Recently, this has become a key element in the Christian racial reconciliation movement. Race, many argue, is not something that God created or even sanctioned; it is a human construct that imposes distinctions that are not based in reality. Since race is an illusion that creates sinful divisions within humanity, reconciliation, then, must involve obliterating those divisions and the racial categories that cause them.

This is a flawed argument. Indeed, social constructivist arguments are generally unhelpful in ameliorating modern racism. It made more sense to rely upon them during the civil rights movement, when the main argument for Jim Crow segregation was that Blacks and other people of color were ontologically inferior to Whites. In that case, an ontological argument required a constructivist rebuttal. Social constructivism was the argument used to expose the wizard behind the curtain. It was designed to establish the normality and full humanity of people of African descent by offering scientific evidence that racial identities are grounded in social, cultural, and historical rather than biological realities. Today—hardcore supremacists notwithstanding—it is rare to find people making explicit arguments about inferiority based upon biology or genetics. Nowadays people tend to invoke color-blind racism.

The New Default: Color-Blind Racism

In *Racism without Racists*, Eduardo Bonilla-Silva argues that color blindness became the dominant US racial ideology following the civil rights movement.

> Compared to Jim Crow racism, the ideology of color blindness seems like "racism lite." Instead of relying on name calling (niggers, spics, chinks), color-blind racism otherizes softly ("these people are human, too"); instead of proclaiming that God placed minorities in the world in a servile position, it suggests they are behind because they do not work hard enough; instead of viewing interracial marriage as wrong on a straight racial basis, it regards it as "problematic" because of concerns over the children, location, or the extra burden it places on couples. Yet this new ideology has become a formidable political tool for the maintenance of the racial order. Much as Jim Crow racism served as the glue for defending a brutal and overt system of racial oppression in the pre-civil rights era, color-blind racism serves today as the ideological armor for a covert and institutionalized system in the post-civil rights era. And the beauty

of this new ideology is that it aids in the maintenance of white privilege without fanfare, without naming those who it subjects and those who it rewards. . . . Thus whites enunciate positions that safeguard their racial interests without sounding "racist." Shielded by color blindness, whites can express resentment toward minorities; criticize their morality, values, and work ethic; and even claim to be the victims of "reverse racism."[32]

The Four Frames of Color-Blind Racism. Bonilla-Silva identifies four central "frames" for color-blind racism: abstract liberalism, naturalization, cultural racism, and minimization of racism. The first frame, abstract liberalism, is the foundation of color-blind racial ideology. Liberalism, in this case, does not refer to a place on the political spectrum (i.e., conservative versus liberal, right versus left). Rather, it refers to liberal humanism, the core philosophy undergirding Western modernity that emphasizes individualism, universalism, egalitarianism, and meliorism ("the idea that people and institutions can be improved"). Abstract liberalism, then, dismisses the reality of racism or the need for corrective action to ameliorate racial inequality by using the language of equal opportunity, meritocracy (the idea that success is the result of individual merit), government non-intervention (the idea that social change should result from voluntary action and not from government legislation or action), and individual choice.[33]

The second frame, naturalization, justifies and dismisses racial disparities by claiming that they occur naturally rather than as the result of intentional practices and policies of exclusion. This frame is often employed by Whites to rationalize school and neighborhood segregation.[34] For example, employing the naturalization frame, a White Christian might claim that worshipping in an all-White con-

---

32. Eduardo Bonilla-Silva, *Racism without Racists: Color-Blind Racism and the Persistence of Racial Inequality in America*, 4th ed. (Lanham, MD: Rowman & Littlefield, 2014), 4.

33. Bonilla-Silva, *Racism without Racists,* 74, 80–84.

34. Bonilla-Silva, *Racism without Racists,* 76, 84.

gregation is acceptable because people "naturally" gravitate toward people who are like them.

The third frame, cultural racism, explains racial disparities as resulting from cultural differences between racial/ethnic groups. It is a form of "blaming the victim" in which racial disparities are acknowledged as real but are attributed to presumed cultural characteristics of racial/ethnic minorities themselves.[35] In some cases, historical circumstances of slavery and Jim Crow may be acknowledged as the "cause" of Black inferiority. However, these circumstances are posited to exert their effect through their impact upon cultural characteristics such as family structure, work ethic, lack of interest in education, and the "culture of poverty." The essence of this frame is this: *Racial disparities exist and are cause for concern, but they result from the behavior and attitudes of people of color, not from racist policies, practices, and experiences.* This frame is particularly pernicious in that it is one that ethnic minorities themselves can easily internalize.

Finally, the fourth frame, minimization of racism, simply posits that racial discrimination is a phenomenon of the past that no longer impacts the lives and the opportunities of ethnic minorities. Alternatively, people using this frame may acknowledge that discrimination continues to exist but that it is an aberrant occurrence.[36] This frame is often used in response to antiblack police violence. With each new incident that garners national attention, many White Americans resort to "bad apple" logic, refusing to believe that the repeated violence is a symptom of a systemic problem and instead attributing it to the isolated behavior of a few "bad" police officers. This frame is also evoked when people claim that racist attitudes, beliefs, and behavior belong only to "evil" White people.

Using interview data, Bonilla-Silva demonstrates how Whites invoke each of the four frames of color-blind racism. In particular, he notes that these frames are not mutually exclusive; Whites tend to use them in combination. Moreover, he notes that Whites use these frames regardless of their stated feelings about people of color, that

35. Bonilla-Silva, *Racism without Racists,* 76, 87–88.
36. Bonilla-Silva, *Racism without Racists,* 77.

is, whether they sympathize with the plight of people of color or whether they feel hostility toward them.[37]

Example: The Moynihan Report. The US Department of Labor's 1965 report, *The Negro Family: A Case for National Action*, is a good example of color-blind racism.[38] Commonly known as the Moynihan Report, it was written by Daniel Patrick Moynihan—a social scientist who was then assistant secretary of the US Department of Labor and who would eventually serve four terms in the Senate—to address the "new crisis in race relations" following the passage of the Civil Rights Act of 1964. Notably, Moynihan was a liberal Democrat considered to be sympathetic to African Americans. His report began by acknowledging that, despite the victory of the Civil Rights Act, the struggle for racial progress was ongoing. He posited that despite improvements in income, education, and standard of living for African Americans, their circumstances were deteriorating relative to White Americans, rather than improving.[39] Moynihan's report evoked at least two frames of color-blind racism: minimization of racism and cultural racism. He acknowledged that racism was a continuing social problem. However, he minimized its impact upon the material realities of African Americans and instead argued that the primary impediment to Black progress was a cultural characteristic resulting from the experience of slavery, namely, a deficiency in the structure of Black families:

> The fundamental problem, in which this is most clearly the case, is that of family structure. The evidence—not final, but powerfully persuasive—is that the Negro family in the urban ghettos is crumbling. A middle class group has managed to save itself, but for vast numbers of the unskilled, poorly educated city working class the fabric of conventional social relationships has all

37. Bonilla-Silva, *Racism without Racists,* 78.

38. Daniel Moynihan, *The Negro Family: The Case for National Action* (Washington, DC: US Government Printing Office, 1965), http://www.dol.gov/oasam/pro grams/history/webid-meynihan.html.

39. Moynihan, *The Negro Family,* introduction.

but disintegrated. There are indications that the situation may have been arrested in the past few years, but the general post war trend is unmistakable. So long as this situation persists, the cycle of poverty and disadvantage will continue to repeat itself.[40]

Largely ignoring historical and systemic forces such as slavery, political and social disenfranchisement, economic oppression, and lack of educational opportunity, Moynihan attributed racial disparities to the failure of African Americans to develop and maintain patriarchal family structures. And this, in turn, he blamed upon the unnatural strength of African American women.[41]

An Impregnable Fortress. Color-blind racism is especially difficult to dispel because the four frames "form an impregnable yet elastic wall that barricades Whites from the United States' racial reality."[42] The solidity of the wall "provide(s) whites a seemingly nonracial way of stating their racial views without appearing irrational or rabidly racist."[43] And the flexibility of the walls allows the discourse of racism to shift in response to discrepant information.

> Color-blind racism's frames are pliable because they do not rely on absolutes ("All Blacks are . . . " or "Discrimination ended in 1965"). Instead, color-blind racism gives some room for exceptions ("Not all Blacks are lazy, but most are") and allows for a variety of ways of holding on to the frames—from crude and straightforward to gentle and indirect. . . . The pliability of the color-blind wall is further enhanced by the style of color blindness. For instance, if whites find themselves in a rhetorical bind, such as having disclosed a personal taste for whiteness or a dislike for blackness, they can always utter a disclaimer such as, "I am not prejudiced," or "If I ever fall in love with a black person,

40. Moynihan, *The Negro Family*, introduction.
41. For a fuller description of Moynihan's use of the trope of the Black matriarch, see Chanequa Walker-Barnes, *Too Heavy a Yoke: Black Women and the Burden of Strength* (Eugene, OR: Cascade, 2014), 110–17.
42. Bonilla-Silva, *Racism without Racists,* 95.
43. Bonilla-Silva, *Racism without Racists,* 96.

the race thing will never be an obstacle for us getting together." They can tiptoe around the most dangerous racial minefields because the stylistic elements of color blindness provide them the necessary tools to get in and out of almost any discussion.[44]

The flexibility of color-blind racism means that reliance on social constructionist understandings of race is an insufficient method for combating racism and working toward reconciliation.

Socially Constructed Yet Real

Earlier, I stated that social constructivist arguments were necessary to expose the wizard behind the curtain of Jim Crow racism, which relied upon pseudoscientific claims that Blacks were inherently genetically inferior to Whites. Today, the primary challenge for racial justice is not exposing the wizard behind the curtain. It is revealing how the wizard exerts its power in visible and not-so-visible ways. It is exposing the powers and principalities of racism in a "postracial" age. Social constructionism takes us only so far in doing that. That is because the social constructionist argument is, first and foremost, an argument about the *scientific* utility of race as a variable for analysis; hence, the racial eliminativist assertion that race is not a biological reality and thus should not be treated as such in scientific research. This does not mean, however, that scientists believe that the concept of race has no social or cultural significance. In other words, the fact that race is socially constructed does not mean that it is not real.

Take another social construct, for example, breakfast. Breakfast is generally defined as the first meal of the day. Around the world, though, there are different standards—different social and cultural constructions—of what constitutes breakfast. As I write this, I am sitting in a lakefront retreat center in Minnesota, where I have just enjoyed a breakfast of yogurt, granola, and blueberries. That is breakfast here. For my Mississippi and South Carolina–born African American grandfathers, that would not be breakfast; it would hardly

44. Bonilla-Silva, *Racism without Racists,* 96.

be considered food. For my Indonesian stepmother, that might be the early morning snack eaten while cooking breakfast, which usually includes fried rice. What is considered breakfast in any particular place is socially constructed as a complex and dynamic interplay between the foods that are local to the area, cultural preferences in cooking methods, and work patterns, among other factors. But breakfast is also very real. At this moment, my belly is full of a social construction. A social construction is fueling my body.

Race is much like that. Race is a construction, and it is also real. It is real because it makes a tangible impact on people's material lives. In fact, race is not just a social construction; it is a legal, political, and perhaps even economic construction. Lauren Lucas, a legal scholar specializing in constitutional and criminal law, points out that while the construction of race has shifted over time, from a legal perspective, race remains an important category. Inasmuch as society imbues phenotype with particular meaning about a person's racial identity, physical appearance—that is, the degree to which a person appears to be "raced"—matters.[45] This is especially the case in the context of the equal protection doctrine, where race continues to be defined and shaped by those who wield power in the legal system.

> Because race is a social and legal construct, in the context of doctrine, it is malleable by those wielding power over the law. Therefore, under the current regime, the power to make legally significant decisions about how race is defined and who will be considered a member of what race is held primarily by the government—whether the executive, legislature, or judiciary. To the extent that the Supreme Court continues to allow the limited use of race-based classifications, at least some of the justices appear unlikely to accept more nuanced understandings of how members of a minority race should be defined; instead, they seem drawn to formulations based in ancestry, without regard for cultural affiliation or other factors.[46]

45. Lauren Sudeall Lucas, "Functionally Suspect: Reconceptualizing 'Race' as a Suspect Classification," *Michigan Journal of Race & Law* 20, no. 2 (Spring 2015): 262.
46. Lucas, "Functionally Suspect," 257.

Race, then, is an important and powerful legal construct. Because of the existence of historical and contemporary race-based discrimination, race is a protected category. Removing it from social, legal, and political discourse significantly hinders our ability to address current and historical discrimination.

Is Symmetrical Treatment the Answer?

At the same time, though, significant problems in how race is treated in the legal field (which includes doctrine and legislation at all levels of government) pose a barrier to justice. The US legal system employs a decontextualized approach in which it makes assignments to and judgments about a person's racial identity without consideration of historical and contemporary patterns of discrimination and powerlessness. In other words, while it acknowledges that race is a socially constructed category, it deliberately ignores the circumstances of inequality in which the categories were constructed. This is the foundation for color blindness, which treats all racial identities as the same and views any disparate treatment as discriminatory. Ironically, the doctrine of color blindness is rooted in the "separate but equal doctrine" established by the 1896 *Plessy v. Ferguson* case, which established that segregation between races was permissible as long as the law was color-blind in allowing each group equal treatment.[47] When the 1954 *Brown v. Board of Education* case nullified the *Plessy* ruling, "the rhetoric of color-blindness was reformulated to refer to the equal treatment of *individuals* by not discriminating among them. Under this new rhetoric of color-blindness, equality meant treating all individuals the same, regardless of differences they brought with them due to the effects of past discrimination or even discrimination in other venues."[48]

This modern reformulation of color blindness calls for "symmetrical treatment," which ignores markers of difference. Thus, the

---

47. Patricia Hill Collins, *Black Feminist Thought: Knowledge, Consciousness, and the Politics of Empowerment*, 2nd ed. (New York: Routledge, 2000), 277.
48. Collins, *Black Feminist Thought*, 279.

court holds that it is equally wrong to reject Blacks from employment opportunities due to race and to attempt to atone for prior discrimination by favoring race in college admissions decisions. This blanket approach to race ultimately lacks coherence. In its failure to recognize the political and social contexts that give differing significance to different racial identities, it rejects the notion that "one size does not fit all" when it comes to justice and that there may be some circumstances in which differential treatment across racial groups is necessary to correct for the pervasive impact that race has upon political and social life.[49]

While Lucas's argument is specific to the legal arena, it has significant implications for racial reconciliation in the body of Christ. Symmetrical treatment is the dominant Christian approach to racial reconciliation. The argument follows along these lines:

1. Race is socially constructed, that is, a human rather than divine creation.
2. Race obscures God's intentions for humanity; therefore, it is sinful.
3. All racial categories are equally sinful, that is, blackness is as problematic as whiteness.
4. The solution is for Black people to stop seeing themselves as Black, for White people to stop seeing themselves as White, and for all of us to see ourselves as Christians.

I have intentionally invoked a White-Black racial binary here, for reasons that I will explain shortly. For now, it underscores the point that the "problem" that confronts us within racial reconciliation is not the existence of race. After all, there are countless socially constructed categories of identity that we use without question. Whether we are Kenyan or Dominican, Democrat or Republican, Baptist or Episcopalian, evangelical or mainline, progressive or conservative—those are all social constructions; yet, to my knowledge, no large-scale conversations are being held about the sinfulness of those distinctions or the need to eradicate them. And while millions

49. Lucas, "Functionally Suspect," 257.

of lives have been claimed by wars between countries whose very identities are based upon boundaries imagined by humans, there is no push to abolish nationality as a category of identity. The discomfort with the idea of race, then, is not really about ontology or constructionism. It is about the discomfort with acknowledging the real problem: racism, or more specifically, White supremacy.

Racism Is about White Supremacy . . . Period

The focus on race as an illegitimate construct has strongly—and wrongly—shaped the understanding of racism within the Christian movement for racial reconciliation. People often view racism as social division based on race; that is, racism occurs when people align and separate themselves based on their affinity for people of the same race and their hostility toward people of other races. A popular way to put this has been to define racism as "prejudice plus power," that is, it is having the personal power to act on one's feelings about racial difference. This understanding reduces racism to the level of affect and interpersonal relationships: racism occurs because of how we as individuals feel about other ethnic groups; reconciliation occurs when we eliminate our negative feelings about other racial groups and establish relationships across race.

But racism is not about our feelings. Nor is it about the attitudes, intentions, or behavior of individuals. Racism is an interlocking system of oppression that is designed to promote and maintain White supremacy, the notion that White people—including their bodies, aesthetics, beliefs, values, customs, and culture—are inherently superior to all other races and therefore should wield dominion over the rest of creation, including other people groups, the animal kingdom, and the earth itself. White supremacy is a systematic way of ordering societal systems, ideologies, and relationships so that political, economic, cultural, and social dominance accrues to Whites. It exists independent of any individual person's feelings toward people of other races. Because the term "White supremacy" has become identified with terrorist and hate groups, people rarely use it in discussing racism and reconciliation, instead opting to use the less harsh term, "White privilege." But White privilege exists because of White supremacy. That is, White privilege consists of the advantages inherent in being categorized as White in a society that views whiteness as superior.

A Matter of Power

A critical concept implicit in this understanding of racism and White supremacy is that of *power*. Racism upholds White supremacy through its use of power. People often confuse power with economic indicators such as wealth, political position, or occupational status. Thus, power is believed to be an attribute of people who are very wealthy, who are politically connected, or who are high-level executives or professionals. Instead, as Collins and Bilge observe, "Power relations are about people's lives, how people relate to one another, and who is advantaged or disadvantaged within social interactions."[50] Power is not something that individuals possess; rather, it is "an intangible entity that circulates within a particular matrix of domination and to which individuals stand in varying relationships."[51] In other words, power exists beyond the individual but can be employed by individuals depending upon their relationship to it. In a White supremacist context, those identified as White have more ready access to power relative to people of color. In a White supremacist system, whiteness functions as a form of currency that grants access to rights, privileges, and protections that are not accessible—or that are less accessible—to others.

Collins notes that racism operates through a complex matrix of four types of power: structural, disciplinary, hegemonic, and interpersonal. Structural power involves the way in which societal systems and institutions are structured to create and reproduce patterns of racial injustice over time, including in educational, economic, government, criminal justice, housing, and health care systems. The

50. Patricia Hill Collins and Sirma Bilge, *Intersectionality: Key Concepts* (Cambridge: Polity Press, 2016), 7.
51. Collins, *Black Feminist Thought*, 274.

disciplinary domain includes the regulations and practices that sustain bureaucratic systems, as well as the "gatekeepers" who control who can access and benefit from these systems. The hegemonic domain consists of the ideologies, ideas, images, and symbols that shape how we think about the world, such as our ideals about femininity, masculinity, intelligence, professionalism, and leadership. It includes the stereotypes that form our basest assumptions about what racial identity represents: from the "hot-blooded Latina" to the doting mammy. Finally, the interpersonal domain includes the ways in which individuals and groups interact with one another.[52]

Example: The Housing System

The real-estate market provides a good example of the ways in which these domains collude to impact the material realities of people of color. A few years ago, my family became the first nonwhite family to purchase a house on our street in a historically White suburb on the northeast side of Atlanta. The prior occupants, like many of our neighbors, had lived in the home for nearly fifty years, raising their children there. It's a wonderful community full of kind people who actually brought baked goods over when we moved in (I thought that only happened in the movies). When a Cuban American family on the next street suffered a fire that destroyed their home and vehicles, our neighbors galvanized. By the end of the day, the family had received a donated SUV, clothes, shoes, and toiletries to tide them over as they looked for temporary housing. These are people whose kindness seems to know no racial bounds.

It bears repeating that racism is not about our feelings. The fact that our neighborhood remained White for so long is a result of racism within the structural domain. Most of our elderly neighbors purchased their homes in the sixties, when legalized housing segregation would have barred African Americans from the commu-

---

52. Collins, *Black Feminist Thought*, 276–88; Bonnie Thornton Dill and Ruth Enid Zambrana, *Emerging Intersections: Race, Class, and Gender in Theory, Policy, and Practice* (New Brunswick, NJ: Rutgers University Press, 2009), 7–11.

nity. Today, disparities in intergenerational wealth mean that even highly educated, middle-class African Americans cannot afford the high down payments required in the post-mortgage crisis economy. FHA loans are the primary path to home ownership for people of color in the United States. But FHA appraisers have been systematically devaluing the homes in our neighborhood for the past few years. Consequently, several realtors in the area advise sellers to work only with buyers who have non-FHA loans or cash-only offers. My family was a direct victim of the FHA practice of undermining sales by underappraising homes in established neighborhoods. In our case, the appraisers deemed the lower level family room in a split-level home to be a "basement" (despite the home having a separate basement). This meant that they appraised the home at a value that was considerably less than our offer (and also less than the local county property tax appraisal), which threatened to nullify the sale. Fortunately, we were working with a seller and two realtors who really wanted to make the deal work. Our realtor steered us to a mortgage broker who found another loan product with a similar down payment requirement. Following our home closing, the realtors and mortgage broker filed an official letter of complaint with FHA based upon our case.

This example points to another set of problems at the disciplinary level, where the gatekeepers to these systems can block access. This could include the FHA appraisers who systematically undervalue properties in established communities, a practice that steers people of color disproportionately toward newly constructed homes that are often further away from the city center and that are less likely to appreciate in value. Other gatekeepers include realtors who steer clients toward "the right kind" of neighborhoods, and the mortgage brokers who influence which clients get which interest rates. At the hegemonic level, those individuals' decisions are informed by societal ideals and stereotypes regarding what constitutes a "good" or "fitting" neighborhood, such as low density of people of color, or who is likely to be a worthwhile client (in my case, being a seminary professor at the nearby university helped). Finally, people of color experience racial microaggressions in this system on a day-to-day basis, such as the messages on our neighborhood listserv that warn of suspicious—and nearly always Black—strangers walking or driving through the community (the interpersonal domain).

This example demonstrates the inefficiency of focusing discussions of racism and reconciliation upon the interpersonal domain, that is, on how people feel about and behave toward each other. Collins's conceptualization recognizes the importance of interpersonal relationships but also highlights the ways in which relationships are embedded within and reflective of a larger system of oppression. While each domain serves a particular purpose, they are interrelated and cannot be separated. Collins notes: "The structural domain organizes oppression, whereas the disciplinary domain manages it. The hegemonic domain justifies oppression, and the interpersonal domain influences everyday lived experience and the individual consciousness that ensues."[53]

Power and the Powers

Collins's definition of power sounds very much like what Paul wrote to the church at Ephesus: "We aren't fighting against human enemies but against rulers, authorities, forces of cosmic darkness, and spiritual powers of evil in the heavens" (Eph. 6:12). If racism is the very powers and principalities—and I argue that it is—then the quest for racial reconciliation is part of a cosmic battle that has been ongoing since the creation of the world, since that moment in the garden when the serpent convinced Eve and Adam (who, as we know, was with her) to betray their God-given purpose in a quest for power (cf. Gen. 3:1–24). This battle cannot be reduced to the simplicity of how people treat those with whom they come into contact. In this war, the powers of evil can co-opt everyone and everything—every individual, community, and culture; every social structure, policy, and practice. This, again, is why reliance on social constructionist arguments is insufficient for "undoing" the problem of racism. Social constructionism, after all, can be employed to justify and enforce White supremacy in the same way that Christian doctrine and practice has been.

53. Collins, *Black Feminist Thought*, 276.

Racism Is Not One-Size-Fits-All

An important feature of White supremacy is that it rank-orders the value of humanity based on proximity to whiteness. The closer one is to whiteness, the more value she is believed to have. This rank ordering has taken various forms and rationales over time, evolving to incorporate newly immigrating ethnic groups. One thing that has remained constant in the racial hierarchy has been that Black identity is always on the bottom. This is why the Black-White binary is important in racial reconciliation. While people of color broadly are victimized by racism, the forms and degree of victimization vary based upon where each racial/ethnic group is grafted along the Black-White continuum.

The New Racial Caste System

Bonilla-Silva proposes that the US racial caste system is evolving from the simple biracial continuum (i.e., white and black) to a triracial stratification similar to that of many Latin American and Caribbean countries.[54] He categorizes US racial/ethnic groups into three strata: Whites, honorary Whites, and collective Black. Whites incorporates those traditionally included in this category (i.e., those of western European ancestry) as well as "new" Whites (e.g., Jews, Russians, Albanians), assimilated White Latinx, assimilated Native Americans, lighter-skinned multiracials, and some Asian subgroups. The intermediate group, honorary Whites, includes most light-skinned Latinx, select Asian American groups (i.e., Japanese Americans, Korean Americans, Chinese Americans, Asian Indians, and Middle Eastern Americans), and most multiracials. The collective Black group includes people typically identified as Black, that is, African Americans, Caribbean immigrants and their descendants, and African immigrants and their descendants. It also includes unassimilated (e.g., reservation-bound) Native Americans, dark-skinned Latinx, southeast Asian and Pacific Islander groups (i.e., Vietnamese, Cambodians, Filipinos, Laotians, and Hmongs).

54. Bonilla-Silva, *Racism without Racists*, 227–28.

Bonilla-Silva's concept of a triracial caste system is crucial to understanding race and racism in the United States for several reasons. First, it highlights the variability in experiences of racial privilege and oppression among nonwhite groups, even among those who might be broadly categorized in the same racial group. In other words, racism is not one-size-fits-all. It does not impact all people of color in the same way. Nor does it necessarily impact all people within one racial-ethnic group in the same way. A light-skinned Mexican American who can "pass" for White will likely have a quite different experience of racialization and racism than a dark-skinned Mexican American. "Racism deniers" will often use the relatively privileged racial perspectives of "honorary Whites" in order to dismiss claims of racism by those within the "collective Black" group. Second, Bonilla-Silva's hierarchy points out that while there is considerable fluidity within each caste, the overall positionality of whiteness and blackness remains fixed. Thus, non-Black groups may shift their position along the continuum over time, becoming inscribed into whiteness as they become more assimilated and advance in socioeconomic status. Those judged as Black, on the other hand, are perennially on the bottom of the racial hierarchy.

Bonilla-Silva's conceptualization has some distinct shortcomings. First, the term "honorary Whites" can be misleading and, as I have heard from several Asian American and Latinx women, quite frankly insulting. Notably, this is not Bonilla-Silva's intent. In a more recent publication, he clarifies that those in the second layer of this triracial system continue to be impacted by White supremacy. "Their standing and status will be ultimately dependent upon Whites' wishes and practices. 'Honorary' means they will remain secondary, will still face discrimination, and will not receive equal treatment in society."[55] Still, much like the problematic "model minority" label, the term "honorary Whites" appears to diminish the existence, nature, and severity of historical and contemporary racism experienced by these ethnic groups. It implies that those in the intermediate group have access to the privileges of whiteness without actually being White, an implication that is flatly contradicted by the microaggressions experienced regularly by many nonblack people of

55. Bonilla-Silva, *Racism without Racists,* 246.

I BRING THE VOICES OF MY PEOPLE

color. Many light-skinned Latinx and Asian Americans, for example, can attest to having their birthright citizenship questioned by others. *"Where are you from? ... No, where are you really from?"* is how the challenge is typically framed.

Second, Bonilla-Silva's framework compresses differences between experiences of race-based oppression and privilege within each caste. In particular, it ignores the uniqueness of antiblack racism, in fact, not just antiblack racism but anti–African American racism. A peculiar feature of US racism is that it exerts its power in unique and concentrated ways upon those who are "legacy African Americans"—that is, those who are the direct descendants of Africans who were enslaved in the United States. Take Jim Crow segregation, for example, which was applied universally to legacy African Americans, but discontinuously to other dark-skinned peoples who did not have the ancestral history of US chattel slavery.[56] A former coworker once shared with me the disparate treatment that his parents received when traveling through the southern states in the 1950s and 1960s. His father was a medium-brown complected Bahamian citizen with a heavy accent. His mother was similarly complected but was a southern-born African American. When they traveled, segregated hotels and restaurants would tell his father, "You can come in, but she cannot." Stories like this are common. Yet the uniqueness of antiblack racism is often overshadowed or ignored in antiracist organizing.

The Four Pillars of White Supremacy

The work of evangelical feminist scholar Andrea Smith is helpful in distinguishing between the unique ways in which racism is targeted toward various racial/ethnic groups. Smith points out that the as-

---

56. Lucas cautions against assuming that all people of a similar race have a similar history and thus should be treated the same in terms of discrimination claims (Lucas, "Functionally Suspect," 277). She alludes to different ethnicities within a racial group, for example, the distinction between "legacy Blacks" (defined as having four grandparents who were born in the United States and were descendants of American slaves), Caribbean-born Blacks, and those from Africa. This, however, does not appropriately handle the nuances between second-generation Blacks and those of mixed-ethnicity.

sumption behind the use of "women of color" as a collective label (and basis for organizing) for Native American, Latinx American, Asian American, African American, and Middle Eastern women is that these groups are equally victimized by White supremacy. In other words, it's symmetrical treatment. The same assumption undergirds the label "people of color." However, as Smith points out, "racism and white supremacy [are not] enacted in a singular fashion; rather, white supremacy is constituted by separate and distinct, but still interrelated, logics."[57] She identifies three such logics as the three "pillars" of White supremacy, in other words, the supportive structures that maintain White supremacy: slavery/capitalism, genocide/capitalism, and orientalism/war. With Smith's permission, in the space below I reformulate her concept of the pillars of White supremacy, renaming her three pillars by the operating principles that characterize them: commodification, extermination, and demonization. I also add a fourth pillar: indoctrination.

This reformulation of four pillars of White supremacy encompasses the shifting strategies that racial oppression takes. The pillars represent the various questions that White supremacy poses upon encountering nonwhite peoples of the world: *Should we exploit them (i.e., commodification)? Should we eradicate them (i.e., extermination)? Should we villify them (i.e., demonization)? Should we assimilate them (i.e., indoctrination)?*

Commodification. Commodification, which involves the control and exploitation of a people's labor, is the operating principle behind the slavery/capitalism pillar of White supremacy. It has been, and continues to be, the primary logic ascribed to Black bodies, especially the bodies of legacy African Americans. This pillar of White supremacy views blackness as "inherently slaveable—as nothing more than property."[58] Although the transatlantic slave trade did not introduce

---

57. Andrea Smith, "Heteropatriarchy and the Three Pillars of White Supremacy: Rethinking Women of Color Organizing," in *Color of Violence: The INCITE! Anthology*, ed. INCITE! Women of Color against Violence (Durham, NC: Duke University Press, 2016), 67.

58. Smith, "Heteropatriarchy and the Three Pillars," 67.

slavery to the world, it added an element that was previously unseen: slavery as a permanent condition of one's racial identity that was transmitted from mother to child. That is, slave status was determined by one's race. This was the law of the land. Whiteness was equated with freedom; to be Black was to be a slave or, at the very least, to be enslaveable.[59] "Free" papers were required to prove otherwise. My Trinidadian great-great-grandfather, John Greene, found this out the hard way when, in the nineteenth century, he landed in Charleston, South Carolina, as a ship's barber aboard a schooner. Ignoring the warnings of his White crewmembers, he dared to venture beyond the dock and was kidnapped and sold as a slave to the Sharpe Plantation. Fortunately, the nation was on the brink of the Civil War and he would be freed before the end of his life. This is why the Black-White dichotomy remains so important to this day. Since the introduction of race-based chattel slavery to the United States, the task of every immigrant group—sometimes including the descendants of the African Diaspora from the continent, the Caribbean, and Latin America—has been to prove themselves "not Black," or more specifically, not the kind of Black who could have been enslaved on US shores.

This pillar is foundational to capitalism, which endorses the commodification of Black bodies, indeed the valuing of all bodies based upon relationship to whiteness. (I will examine this more in the next chapter's discussion of colorism.) The cessation of chattel slavery within the United States did not demolish this pillar; it simply changed how it operated, evolving first into the sharecropping system and more recently into the prison industrial complex. Smith states:

> The logic of slavery can be seen clearly in the current prison industrial complex (PIC). While the PIC generally incarcerates communities of color, it seems to be structured primarily on an

---

59. One of the effects of equating whiteness with freedom is that it obfuscates the history of White indentured servitude. "The history of unfree white people slumbers in popular forgetfulness, although white slavery (like Black slavery) moved people around and mixed up human genes on a massive scale" (Neil Irvin Painter, *The History of White People* [New York: W. W. Norton, 2010], xi.).

anti-Black racism. That is, prior to the Civil War, most people in prison where white. However, after the thirteenth amendment was passed—which banned slavery, except for those in prison—Black people previously enslaved through the slavery system were reenslaved through the prison system. Black people who had been the property of slave owners became state property, through the convict leasing system. Thus, we can actually look at the criminalization of Blackness as a logical extension of Blackness as property.[60]

Not coincidentally, shortly after the fall of Jim Crow segregation, the United States became the world leader in rates of incarceration. Over the past forty years, the US prison population has increased 500 percent, with 2.2 million people currently housed in the nation's prisons and jails.[61] People of color account for two-thirds of people in state and federal prisons, with Black men being incarcerated at nearly six times the rate of White men and Latinx men at nearly three times the rate. And while women are frequently overlooked in conversations about mass incarceration, the racial disparities are nearly identical among women. Black women are incarcerated six times more often than White women and Latina women at more than twice the rate.[62] These numbers do not take into account the thirty-seven thousand people (disproportionately Black and Latinx) housed in immigration detention centers on any given day.[63]

Criminalizing and incarcerating the bodies of African American and Latinx women and men is a big business. In 2013, the United States spent $51.9 billion on corrections.[64] The explosion in the growth of prisons, including the seven hundred thousand people

60. Smith, "Heteropatriarchy and the Three Pillars," 67.

61. The Sentencing Project, *Fact Sheet: Trends in US Corrections* (Washington, DC: The Sentencing Project, 2015), http://www.sentencingproject.org/publications /trends-in-u-s-corrections/, 2.

62. The Sentencing Project, *Fact Sheet*, 5.

63. Carl Takei, Michael Tan, and Joanne Lin, *Shutting Down the Profiteers: Why and How the Department of Homeland Security Should Stop Using Private Prisons* (New York: ACLU Foundation, 2016), 7.

64. The Sentencing Project, *Fact Sheet*, 2.

they employ, has directly benefited many jurisdictions.[65] In her groundbreaking text, *The New Jim Crow*, Michelle Alexander points out that the number is even higher if we look at the criminal justice system as a whole, which is the second-highest federal budget expenditure behind Medicare.

> According to a report released by the U.S. Department of Justice's Bureau of Statistics in 2006, the U.S. spent a record $185 billion for police protection, detention, judicial, and legal activities in 2003. . . . The justice system employed almost 2.4 million people in 2003—58 percent of them at the local level and 31 percent at the state level. If four out of five people were released from prisons [the number necessary to return to the rate of incarceration of the 1970s], far more than a million people could lose their jobs.[66]

It is worth pointing out that prisoners are the one group exempt from the protections of the Thirteenth Amendment to the US Constitution, which abolished slavery but allowed forced labor as punishment for crime. Many prison inmates work for as little as 25 cents per hour, earnings that are then charged against expenses related to incarceration.[67] The logic of commodification continues to enslave Black, and increasingly Brown, bodies for the benefit of the state.

We also see commodification at work in the migrant farming system that employs between one and three million people annually, primarily Black and Brown natives of Mexico, South America, and the Caribbean.[68] Ironically, people on both sides of the political spectrum often cite the need for a low-cost labor force in farming and other industries in order to advance the cause of immigration reform. This argument reduces people of color from Latin America and the Caribbean

65. Michelle Alexander, *The New Jim Crow: Mass Incarceration in the Age of Color-blindness*, rev. ed. (New York: New Press, 2012), 230.

66. Alexander, *New Jim Crow*, 230.

67. Alexander, *New Jim Crow*, 157.

68. Eduardo González Jr., "Migrant Farm Workers: Our Nation's Invisible Population," http://articles.extension.org/pages/9960/migrant-farm-workers:-our-nations-invisible-population.

to their potential as laborers. On a more subtle level, this logic operates daily in employment settings where people of color are the minority, either numerically or in terms of power and influence. It operates in the corporate sector, academic institutions, professional sports, the Christian nonprofit community, and in every instance when a White person reaches a hand out, sans permission, to touch a Black woman's hair.

Extermination. Extermination is the operating principle undergirding the genocide/capitalism pillar of White supremacy. The logic that has been applied to the Indigenous peoples of America, it is heavily connected to land interests. When White Western expansionism encounters peoples of color with coveted land resources, those peoples become targets for extermination. Smith states:

> This logic holds that indigenous peoples must disappear. In fact, they must *always* be disappearing in order to allow nonindigenous peoples rightful claim over this land. Through this logic of genocide, non-Native peoples then become the rightful inheritors of all that was indigenous—land, resources, indigenous spirituality, or culture. . . . The pillar of genocide serves as the anchor for colonialism—it is what allows non-Native peoples to feel they can rightfully own indigenous peoples' land. It is okay to take land from indigenous peoples, because indigenous peoples have disappeared.[69]

Extermination takes multiple forms. At its most obvious extreme, it involves physical genocide, the literal slaughter of racial/ethnic groups in an attempt to take over their resources. At a more subtle level, it includes cultural genocide, the eradication of a group's cultural identity, history, and memory. A White male colleague once asked me, "When was the last time anyone saw a Native American? Do you even know any?" The statement was meant to be an indictment of the genocide of the Indigenous peoples of this land. However, it was also a form of genocide in itself, in that it erased the continuing existence and significance of Native peoples. The wide-

69. Smith, "Heteropatriarchy and the Three Pillars," 68.

spread appropriation of Indigenous symbols and land by individuals, corporations, and government also functions as cultural genocide.

In the US film industry, the practice of "whitewashing" exemplifies this. Whitewashing involves casting White actors to portray nonwhite characters, in some cases historical figures. It occurs most frequently when nonwhite persons are leading characters in a story. This practice was widespread in the pre–civil rights era, for example, when Yul Brynner donned yellowface to portray King Mongkut of Siam in the film adaptation of the musical *The King and I*. In the late twentieth century, the practice continued, often under the ruse of the limited pool of popular Indigenous and Asian American actors to portray leading roles. Yet while this pool has grown noticeably, we have seen several high-profile incidents of whitewashing in the first two decades of the twenty-first century: Johnny Depp's role as Tonto in *The Lone Ranger* (2013), Tilda Swinton's casting in a role meant to be played by an elderly Asian man in *Doctor Strange* (2016), and Scarlett Johansson being cast as the Japanese protagonist, Motoko Kusanagi, in *Ghost in the Shell* (2017). Each of these recent incidents has been justified as "color-blind" casting. In this case, color blindness is not really about making casting decisions without consideration of the actor's race (and even if it were, it's ironic that it only happens when the lead character is nonwhite); it is about making casting decisions with an eye on a presumably majority-White audience. It capitulates to White supremacy's insistence that whiteness be the center of the popular imagination while also refuting the legitimacy of Native American and Asian people and cultures.

Demonization. Demonization is the operating principle undergirding Smith's third pillar: orientalism/war. This logic is at work when the interests of White supremacy collide with a racial/ethnic group that it cannot—at least not immediately—assimilate, commodify, or exterminate. These groups, typically Middle Eastern and Asian cultures and nations, are consequently labeled as dangerous:

> Orientalism was defined by Edward Said as the process of the West defining itself as a superior civilization by constructing itself in opposition to an "exotic" but inferior "Orient." . . .

The logic of Orientalism marks certain peoples or nations as inferior and as posing a constant threat to the well-being of empire. These peoples are still seen as "civilizations"—they are not property or "disappeared"—however, they will always be imagined as permanent foreign threats to empire.[70]

Demonization is often employed to justify war and to destabilize attempts at peace making. Former president George W. Bush used this language often in the months prior to the US invasion of Iraq in 2003. In his 2002 State of the Union address following the attack on the World Trade Center and Pentagon on September 11, 2001, Mr. Bush described Iraq, Iran, and North Korea as the "axis of evil."

> States like these, and their terrorist allies, constitute an axis of evil, arming to threaten the peace of the world. By seeking weapons of mass destruction, these regimes pose a grave and growing danger. They could provide these arms to terrorists, giving them the means to match their hatred. They could attack our allies or attempt to blackmail the United States. In any of these cases, the price of indifference would be catastrophic.[71]

More than a clever turn of phrase, this ideology marked a significant turn in US foreign policy. It specified a new post–Cold War enemy—in this case, primarily the Muslim countries of Iraq and Iran and their allies—and it established the justification for military action against them. The term "axis of evil" implied that the problem was not merely a matter of the countries' policies or their alleged ties with Al-Qaeda. Rather, it was that the nations themselves—and by extension, their cultures and people—were inherently morally inferior to the United States and her "civilized" allies. The US approach to these countries, then, could require nothing less than military intervention, including pre-emptive strikes against those who had committed no acts of aggression toward the United States.

---

70. Smith, "Heteropatriarchy and the Three Pillars," 68.
71. "President Delivers State of the Union Address," January 29, 2002, https://georgewbush-whitehouse.archives.gov/news/releases/2002/01/20020129-11.html.

Demonization does not restrict its impact to foreign policy. Again, the film and television industry provides evidence of its far-reaching impact.

> The events of the day that Americans now call "9/11" created a rush to learn more about the Islamic community. Unfortunately, however, the intense media emphasis on the religious fanaticism of the protagonists resulted in stereotyping Americans of Middle Eastern heritage, and worse. Although the vast majority of Middle Eastern Americans are conventional practitioners of the Islamic faith—and share the national abhorrence to terrorism—general media reportage often failed to emphasize that distinction in public discourse. The result was that negative stereotypes across various media platforms in the first decade of the 21st century fostered an atmosphere that led to violence and other acts against fellow Americans who had the misfortune to be Muslim or descendants of Middle Eastern heritage.[72]

Prior to 9/11, media stereotypes of Middle Easterners were predominated by "what Arab American media scholar Jack Shaheen termed the 'three B syndrome'—bombers, belly dancers, and billionaires."[73] Afterwards—notwithstanding films such as *Kingdom of Heaven* (2005) and *The Kite Runner* (2007), which offered nuanced portrayals of Middle Eastern Muslim culture—television and film depictions largely leaned toward more sinister representations. For example, a 2004 study on diversity in prime-time television programming found that 46 percent of Arab/Middle Eastern roles were criminals.[74] It is no wonder, then, that many Trump supporters were attracted to his policy proposal to ban Muslim immigrants based solely upon their religion.[75]

---

72. Clint C. Wilson, Félix Gutiérrez, and Lena M. Chao, *Racism, Sexism, and Media*, 4th ed. (Los Angeles: Sage, 2013), 103.

73. Wilson et al., *Racism, Sexism, and Media,* 104.

74. Wilson et al., *Racism, Sexism, and Media,* 104.

75. John McCormick, "Bloomberg Politics Poll: Nearly Two-Thirds of Likely GOP Primary Voters Back Trump's Muslim Ban," *Bloomberg*, December 9, 2015, http://

Indoctrination. A continuing struggle in antiracist activism and organizing is the persistent refusal of many White (including "honorary White") allies to recognize themselves as products of a White supremacist system. People tend to think of racism as a set of behaviors that bad or sinful White people inflict against people of color. The implication of this is that good White people are not involved in this system. Here, we must return to Collins's conceptualization of oppression as a system of power to which all people are connected in various degrees. In other words, no one is untouched by White supremacy. As a facilitator in a cultural diversity workshop once told me, "Racism robs all of us of the ability to think for ourselves." Indoctrination, then, is the mechanism that White supremacy employs upon encounter with cultural groups that it wishes to assimilate into its logic, namely, Whites and honorary Whites. It is the means through which White supremacy enjoins the complicity, silence, and/or active support of those who benefit from it.

At the extreme level, indoctrination happens when nonwhite peoples are coerced, and sometimes even violently forced, to abdicate their native cultures and to adopt White cultural norms. Two examples of this in US history occurred during the slave trade and in the Native American boarding schools. Throughout the slaveholding era, newly enslaved Africans were often subjected to brutal punishment for speaking their native languages, engaging in native rituals (such as drumming), and practicing native religions. Other cultural practices, while not explicitly forbidden, were lost through the combination of geographical displacement, the working and living conditions of enslaved peoples, and the societal valorization of Eurocentric norms and beauty ideals. In their book, *Hair Story*, Ayana Byrd and Lori Tharps document the impact of this process upon African American hair care practices, an impact that persists today.[76]

Whereas cultural annihilation was one of the supportive legs of US chattel slavery, it was the *raison d'etre* for Native American

---

www.bloomberg.com/politics/articles/2015-12-09/bloomberg-politics-poll-trump
-muslim-ban-proposal.

76. Ayana Byrd and Lori Tharps, *Hair Story: Untangling the Roots of Black Hair in America* (New York: St. Martin's Press, 2014).

boarding schools. Beginning in the late eighteenth century and continuing well into the 1970s, the boarding schools were established by Christian denominations and the federal governments of Canada and the United States with the primary intention of assimilating Indigenous peoples into White culture. Most schools used the indoctrination model of the Carlisle Indian Industrial School, which was founded in 1879 by Richard Henry Pratt, an Army officer who had fought for the Union during the Civil War. By the standards of his day, Pratt was probably considered a "White liberal." He is the first person recorded as using the word "racism," which he invoked in 1902 to criticize the segregation and neglect of Indigenous peoples.[77] Instead, he proposed a plan of compulsory education designed to eradicate all traces of Native American culture. In a paper he presented at an 1892 convention, he began describing his approach to education by stating: "A great general has said that the only good Indian is a dead one, and that high sanction of his destruction has been an enormous factor in promoting Indian massacres. In a sense, I agree with the sentiment, but only in this: that all the Indian there is in the race should be dead. Kill the Indian in him, and save the man."[78] Using Pratt's model, the boarding schools forbade children to use Indigenous names, languages, rituals, religions, and hair customs, practices that were enforced through the use of physical punishment and abuse. Andrea Smith documents the lasting impact of the boarding schools on Native American women and communities in her text *Conquest*.[79]

Contemporary forms of indoctrination tend to be much subtler but no less supportive of White supremacy. They occur in classrooms on a regular basis when African American and Latinx students are deemed as less intelligent and less capable because they speak and write (and in seminaries, preach) in dialects

77. Gene Demby, "The Ugly, Fascinating History," *Code Switch*, January 6, 2014, http://www.npr.org/sections/codeswitch/2014/01/05/260006815/the-ugly-fascinating -history-of-the-word-racism.

78. Richard H. Pratt, "The Advantages of Mingling Indians with Whites," http:// historymatters.gmu.edu/d/4929/.

79. Andrea Smith, *Conquest: Sexual Violence and American Indian Genocide* (Durham, NC: Duke University Press, 2015).

deemed "non-standard English." It occurs when people of color learn to self-censure in order to gain acceptance or approval in predominantly White settings. Racial indoctrination often works by employing another form of systemic oppression: classism. It promises greater opportunity, power, and wealth to those who conform, and it excludes those who do not. By doing so, it elicits the cooperation of those who are its targets, so that assimilated people of color become critical of their own cultures. Far from having ended, indoctrination is the mechanism that holds the entire system together, the means by which racism continues to exert its power despite being denounced by most people in the United States.

Context Matters

It is important to note that the four pillars operate on a systemic level. In other words, these logics are applied to racial/ethnic groups, not merely to individuals. We can at times see how they exert their influence on the lives of individuals. But to focus at the individual level would cause us to ignore the larger patterns. For example, Tilda Swinton's portrayal of an elderly, Asian male character in *Doctor Strange* could be viewed as a unique experiment in race/gender bending. However, it cannot be separated from the film industry's longtime pattern of using White actors to portray Indigenous and Asian/Asian American characters while simultaneously relegating actors from those cultural groups to supporting roles that are often highly limited in scope. Restricting our focus to the individual level tends to overemphasize the exceptions to the rule or even to make comparisons between non-equivalent situations: "But Zendaya is playing the role of Mary Jane Watson in Spiderman." Context, both contemporary and historical, matters. In the context of an industry where people of color are grossly underrepresented and misrepresented, casting a person of color in a "White by default" role could be subversive. On the other hand, casting a White person in one of the few roles made available for people of color is simply another iteration of White supremacy.

Conclusion

At the outset of this chapter, I made the claim that the election of Barack Obama to the US presidency has exposed the myth of a postracial America. As shown by highly publicized incidents of antiblack police violence and the virulent expressions of racism associated with Donald Trump's 2016 presidential campaign, racism remains America's original sin. The need for Christians who are committed to God's mission of reconciliation could not be more pressing. But we cannot advance the movement for reconciliation if it is based upon faulty understandings of the construct of race and the dynamics of racism. While the shift to social constructionist theories of race has been a necessary and robust rejoinder against scientific racism, it is less capable of responding to twenty-first-century color-blind racism, with its call for the symmetrical treatment—and obliteration—of all racial identities.

It cannot be overstated: racism is about White supremacy and the complex, interlocking forms of power that maintain it. Racism is not "one-size-fits-all" but is meted out in distinct ways to nonwhite groups based on their position in the racial hierarchy and the degree to which they are viewed as threats or resources to the interests of White supremacy. This understanding of racism directly challenges the prevailing Christian paradigm for racial reconciliation, which assumes that increasing interpersonal contact between people of different races will reduce feelings of racial hostility. But racism is ultimately not about our relationships or our feelings. In the next chapter, I demonstrate this by examining several manifestations of racism that differentially impact women of color.

Chapter Two

Racism Is Not a Stand-Alone Issue

I have been woman for a long time
beware my smile
I am treacherous with old magic
and the noon's new fury
with all your wide futures
promised
I am
woman
and not white.

Audre Lorde, "A Woman Speaks"

In the summer of 1964, as thousands of Black Mississippians and out-of-state volunteers were embroiled in Freedom Summer, the US Congress passed the Civil Rights Act of 1964. It was a major victory for the civil rights movement and one of its pinnacle achievements. Finally, after decades of organizing and lobbying, and the murders of countless civil rights activists (including the killings of three Freedom Summer workers just two weeks earlier), race became a protected category, along with color, religion, sex, and national origin. The bill not only promised equal access based upon race; it paved the way for antidiscrimination legislation and lawsuits. A downside of the bill, however, was its decontextualization of race. Rather than attending to historical and contemporary patterns of White supremacy, the Civil Rights Act employed a color-blind logic that treated all racial identities as similarly constituted and thus equally protected. In the previous chapter, I discussed the problems with this approach as it relates to racial reconciliation. To reiterate, however, racism is not about race or racial difference. Racism is a complex matrix of power that is designed to protect and promulgate White supremacy. It is not meted out symmetrically to all racial-ethnic groups. Rather, it operates according to differing logics—commodification, extermination, demonization, and indoctrination—based on the particular challenge that each racial-ethnic group poses to the interests of White supremacy. Unfortunately, the language and interpretation (especially recent) of the Civil Rights Act of 1964 overshadowed these nuances. Consequently, the same bill that made discrimination illegal has also made it nearly impossible to rectify the damage of centuries of systemic racial discrimination. It overemphasizes intent rather than impact and individual behavior rather than systemic patterns.

Further, the bill's single-axis framework flattens identity into discrete categories: race, color, religion, sex, *or* national origin (notably, "sex" did not appear in the bill until the addition of Title VII, which protected against employment discrimination). The "or" language implies that oppressive structures work independently of one another. That is, it assumes that a person's disparate treatment is due to her or his race, *or* religious identity, *or* gender, *or* nationality, not any combination of these categories. Moreover, it assumes that we can tease apart those effects, as demonstrated by the question frequently posed to Black women who describe discriminatory treatment: "Do you think that you were treated that way because you're Black or because you're a woman?" When oppression is understood in this way, racism becomes identified with experiences and patterns that are gender-neutral, in other words, those that similarly impact people of color regardless of their gender identity or sexuality. In a patriarchal society, of course, "gender-neutral" really means "male."

This is precisely what has happened in the Christian racial reconciliation movement. Its disproportionately male leadership and emphasis upon personal experience have resulted in a single-axis understanding of racism, that is, one that ignores its interactions with other forms of oppression, especially gender oppression. Thus, the typical lineup at a Christian conference on racial justice features largely (often exclusively) male speakers, perhaps with a single (and usually White) female voice for the sake of gender diversity. The movement favors men's "race-talk" because it assumes that men's experiences of race, racism, and reconciliation are universal and comprehensive. Moreover, men's race-talk is more likely to be considered academically or theologically informed even when it is centered upon personal experience. In contrast, women's expertise is likely to be viewed as mere anecdote even when it substantially engages scholarship in critical race theory.

The patriarchy within Christian racial reconciliation has significantly shortchanged its advocates' understandings of racism and efforts toward racial justice. The assumption that men (specifically, cisgender heterosexual, or "cishet" men) know and experience all that there is to know and experience about racism obscures an important fact: oppression is intersectional. Racial identity and racism do not occur within a vacuum; they operate concurrently and in tandem with other layers of identity, including the patterns of privilege and oppression associated with those layers. In this chapter, therefore, I use intersectional theory to articulate how the location of women of color at the intersection of race and gender exposes them to forms of oppression that, while typically excluded in male-centered discussions, are critical to understanding how racism operates and how deeply entrenched it is in every aspect of US society. I begin by explaining intersectionality as a metaframework for organizing and scholarship among women of color. Then I offer three examples of gendered racism that are disproportionately experienced by women of color: colorism, mammification, and hypersexualization.

Getting Intersectional

Identity is always multilayered. That is, none of us exists as just a raced person. Our identities are complex combinations of race, class, gender identity, sexual orientation, nationality, geographic origin, dis/ability status, religion, and so on. In pastoral theology, we refer to this as multiplicity. Multiplicity argues that who I am culturally is a complex interplay of the various categories that make up my identity. In my case, for example, I am a middle-class, highly educated African American Christian woman who was raised in a working-class family in the Deep South. As I like to say, I can make a mean pot of greens and the best granola you have ever tasted. Multiplicity is a helpful tool for discerning the layers that make up one's cultural identity, including those layers that seem to oppose one another. Pamela Cooper-White uses the term "braided selves" to depict the idea that our identities are made up of discrete layers that are threaded together.[1]

Far too often, while multiplicity is meant to encompass the complexity of identity, it is used to imply that identity is additive. To return to the mathematical analogy that I used in the introduction to the text, this equation would look something like:

$$RacialGenderIdentity = Race + Gender$$

In other words, it posits that my experiences as an African American woman will be the sum total of my experiences as an African American and my experiences as a woman. Multiplicity recognizes that we are always raced and gendered, but also acknowledges that, in varying contexts, different aspects of our identity will be more salient. For example, in a predominantly White environment, my blackness may stand out and be the primary lens through which I interpret my experience. If I am in France, my Americanness may be the most salient factor. This approach to multiplicity is similar to the tendency in antiracist and antisexist organizing to treat race and gender as mutually exclusive domains that can be engaged separately from one another. When women of color are engaged in antiracist work with our male colleagues, we are often expected to assume a "race first, gender second" mentality, that is, to effectually relegate the non-raced layers of our identity to the background. When we are engaged in antisexist work with our White female peers, we are expected to do the same thing with respect to gender, focusing upon

1. Pamela Cooper-White, *Braided Selves: Collected Essays on God, Multiplicity, and Persons* (Eugene, OR: Cascade, 2011).

the *universal* experience of womanhood (as if such a thing exists). Both represent single-axis frameworks. And both are highly problematic for women of color.

The limitations of single-axis thinking about race and gender become clear in the following example shared by Kimberlé Crenshaw, the legal scholar and critical race theorist who introduced the term "intersectionality."

> I attempted to review Los Angeles Police Department statistics reflecting the rate of domestic violence interventions by precinct because such statistics can provide a rough picture of arrests by racial group, given the degree of racial segregation in Los Angeles. L.A.P.D., however, would not release the statistics. A representative explained that one reason the statistics were not released was that domestic violence activists both within and outside the Department feared that statistics reflecting the extent of domestic violence in minority communities might be selectively interpreted and publicized so as to undermine long-term efforts to force the Department to address domestic violence as a serious problem. I was told that activists were worried that the statistics might permit opponents to dismiss domestic violence as a minority problem and, therefore, not deserving of aggressive action. The informant also claimed that representatives from various minority communities opposed the release of these statistics. They were concerned, apparently, that the data would unfairly represent Black and Brown communities as unusually violent, potentially reinforcing stereotypes that might be used in attempts to justify oppressive police tactics and other discriminatory practices.[2]

In this case, the agendas of White antisexist activists and Black and Latinx antiracist activists colluded to prevent the release of data that would reveal the extent to which Black and Latinx women were victimized by

2. Kimberlé Crenshaw, "Mapping the Margins: Intersectionality, Identity Politics, and Violence against Women of Color," *Stanford Law Review* 43, no. 6 (July 1991): 1252–53.

domestic violence. By adopting a race-first or gender-first approach, both groups prevented the exposure of the unique needs of African American and Latinx women, or as Crenshaw put it, they "[relegated] the identity of women of color to a location that resists telling."[3]

In contrast, Crenshaw used the term "intersectionality" to describe how race and gender (and likewise, racism and sexism) uniquely interact to shape Black women's identities, experiences, and needs. Intersectionality recognizes that the layers of our identities are neither discrete nor separable; they are fused. Every layer is raced; every layer is gendered; and so on. Again, using the mathematical equation, we might represent this in the following way:

$$RacialGenderIdentity = Race + Gender + Race^*Gender$$

This is an oversimplification, but it demonstrates the idea that identity is not merely additive; it is also multiplicative. Indeed, it is even nonlinear (the statistics nerd within me really wants to add some quadratic functions to that equation). In other words, as an African American woman, I share some aspects of my experience with African American men and others with women of all races, but there are also unique experiences that are part of my Blackwomanness. This means that I am not only a target of racism and sexism; I am also a target of gendered racism and racialized sexism. Other layers of my identity—especially my class, sexuality, and nationality—further attenuate my experiences of oppression and privilege.

Intersectionality's core insight, then, is "that major axes of social divisions in a given society at a given time, for example, race, class, gender, sexuality, dis/ability, and age operate not as discrete and mutually exclusive entities, but build on each other and work together."[4] Inherently, then, intersectionality is about more than identity; it is about systemic inequality and the way in which oppressive structures intersect to uniquely impact the lives of those who exist at their intersections. As Collins and Bilge note, "When it comes to social inequality,

3. Crenshaw, "Mapping the Margins," 1242.
4. Patricia Hill Collins and Sirma Bilge, *Intersectionality: Key Concepts* (Cambridge: Polity Press, 2016), 4.

people's lives and the organization of power in a given society are better understood as being shaped not by a single axis of social division, be it race or gender or class, but by many axes that work together and influence each other. Intersectionality as an analytic tool gives people better access to the complexity of the world and of themselves."[5] With its genealogy in Black women's experiences and activism, intersectionality is not neutral; it is always concerned with and biased toward justice. "More than simply describe multiplicity, intersectional work takes a stand against inequality and harm and overtly aims for social transformation and meaningful change."[6] Consequently, Vivian May deems intersectionality "a form of resistant knowledge developed to unsettle conventional mindsets, challenge oppressive power, think through the full architecture of structural inequalities and asymmetrical life opportunities, and seek a more just world. It has been forged in the context of struggles for social justice as a means to challenge dominance, foster critical imaginaries, and craft collective models for change."[7]

Crenshaw identifies three forms of intersectionality: (1) structural intersectionality, the qualitative differences in the experiences of women of color relative to White women based upon their location at the intersection of race and gender; (2) political intersectionality, the ways in which feminist and antiracist organizing marginalizes the issues of women of color; and (3) representational intersectionality, the representation of women of color in popular culture.[8] The concept of political intersectionality is especially critical for racial reconciliation and gender egalitarian movements among Christians, as both movements tend to ignore or minimize the needs and experiences of women of color.

> The concept of political intersectionality highlights the fact that women of color are situated within at least two subordinated groups that frequently pursue conflicting political

5. Collins and Bilge, *Intersectionality*, 2.

6. Vivian M. May, *Pursuing Intersectionality, Unsettling Dominant Imaginaries* (New York: Routledge, 2015), 28–29.

7. May, *Pursuing Intersectionality*, xi.

8. Crenshaw, "Mapping the Margins," 1245.

agendas. The need to split one's political energies between two sometimes opposing groups is a dimension of intersectional disempowerment that men of color and white women seldom confront. Indeed, their specific raced *and* gendered experiences, although intersectional, often define as well as confine the interests of the entire group. . . . The problem is not simply that both discourses fail women of color by not acknowledging the "additional" issue of race or of patriarchy but that the discourses are often inadequate even to the discrete tasks of articulating the full dimensions of racism and sexism. Because women of color experience racism in ways not always the same as those experienced by men of color and sexism in ways not always parallel to experiences of white women, antiracism and feminism are limited, even on their own terms. . . . The failure of feminism to interrogate race means that the resistance strategies of feminism will often replicate and reinforce the subordination of people of color, and the failure of antiracism to interrogate patriarchy means that antiracism will frequently reproduce the subordination of women.[9]

Likewise, racial reconciliation's failure to interrogate patriarchy means that it will frequently reproduce the subordination of women. To put it bluntly, much of what passes for racial reconciliation among Christians is merely an exercise in making sure Black men and other men of color have the same access to male privilege as their White counterparts do. Racism and sexism, after all, have the same ultimate aim: the preservation of White supremacist heteropatriarchy. We cannot address one without the other. Intersectionality is the meta-framework that allows us to do this.

Intersectionality and Internalized Racism

Recall from the prior chapter that racism is designed to promote and maintain White supremacy, which is the belief that White people

9. Crenshaw, "Mapping the Margins," 1251–52.

are inherently superior to all other races in every respect, including their bodies, intellect, aesthetics, beliefs, values, behaviors, and customs. By design, White supremacy works by convincing all peoples—not just White people—of its truth. Recall again the diversity workshop facilitator's statement, "Racism robs all of us of the ability to think for ourselves." When people of color internalize the view that whiteness is superior to all other races (including their own), we call this *internalized oppression*. In a society where the superiority of whiteness is transmitted via multiple systems (e.g., mass media, educational institutions, corporate culture), internalized oppression is not an unusual occurrence or merely the "exception to the rule"; it is the rule. It is a universal phenomenon. It is not limited to childhood but extends throughout the life span. It is so ubiquitous that detecting and reconfiguring the ways in which we have internalized racism takes considerable, intentional effort. Cherríe Moraga, consequently, states that all members of oppressed groups must wrestle with the question, "How have I internalized my own oppression?" in their journeys to liberation.

> It is frightening to acknowledge that I have internalized a racism and classism, where the object of oppression is not only someone outside of my skin, but the someone inside my skin. In fact, to a large degree, the real battle with such oppression, for all of us, begins under the skin. I have had to confront the fact that much of what I value about being Chicana, about my family, has been subverted by anglo culture and my own cooperation with it. This realization did not occur to me overnight.[10]

The internalization of racism often means that people of color devalue our own bodies, our aesthetics, and our cultural and family values, norms, and beliefs. It also means that we tend to pathologize our own cultures, blaming them for anything that we see as a shortcoming in ourselves, our families, or our institutions. During

---

10. Cherríe Moraga, "La Güera," in *This Bridge Called My Back: Writings by Radical Women of Color*, ed. Cherríe Moraga and Gloría Anzaldúa, 4th ed. (Albany: State University of New York Press, 2015), 25.

my years on the faculty at a historically Black school, I was dismayed at how quickly and frequently Black students blamed the university's cultural heritage (and that of its leaders) for any and every shortcoming. No matter the issue (e.g., textbooks not being in the bookstore at the start of the semester, having no chalk in the classroom, the university network breaking down), students would exclaim, "Well, this is a Black school," as if predominantly White institutions never had similar problems. The internalization of racism means that people of color may simultaneously proclaim racial pride, makes jokes about or denigrate whiteness, and make jokes about or denigrate our own racial-ethnic group![11]

From birth, people of color are socialized into a world that affirms the beauty and value of whiteness. Children's décor, toys, books, and clothes routinely feature White faces, and parents of color can attest to the formidable work involved in finding consumer products with more diverse representation. Even for the most diligent parents, the message that "what's White is right" is ubiquitous and hard to counter. For the first few years of my son's life, for example, my partner and I followed a simple but stringent rule in selecting books for him: they had to feature nonwhite characters. We made a few exceptions for books that had highly compelling stories, especially classic books about families and love. It took quite a bit of research, but we eventually amassed a large collection of books featuring children of various races and ethnicities. Of course, we also ended up with a large collection of talking animal stories. The hardest task, though, was finding a children's Bible storybook. Our search had three requirements: (1) Jesus had to be nonwhite; (2) the other characters had to be diverse in skin tone and hair texture; and (3) the blame for the fall must not be put solely on Eve. It took over two years, but eventually we found one.

Our efforts notwithstanding, until he was five, my son often declared that he wished that he were White. Once, during a conversation in which I tried to affirm God's love for diversity, he went as far as to say: "God doesn't like brown skin. God likes white skin. His skin is white in my Bible." I was stunned. We had a long conver-

---

11. Andrea Canaan, "Brownness," in Moraga and Anzaldúa, *This Bridge*, 232.

sation about the biblical description of Jesus as having bronzed skin and woolly hair. I watched my son's caramel-colored face light up as he compared his own arm to our bronze stair rail and as he realized that "woolly" perfectly described his hair. We talked about how books are written and illustrated, and that they do not always represent the truth. Finally, I went to his room and grabbed the Bible storybook that my partner read to him nightly. As I had thought, Jesus and many of the other characters were clearly depicted with various shades of brown skin. It turned out to be a barely noticeable detail (at least to me) that had convinced my son of Jesus's whiteness: the illustrators had given many of the brown-skinned characters—including Jesus—rosy cheeks, an incongruous feature that my five-year-old had learned to associate with his White friends at school and church. Representation matters. Every detail of representation matters.

Intersectionality calls attention to the ways in which even those who are oppressed by racism are often complicit with it. This includes people of color accepting and articulating negative stereotypes about our own racial-ethnic group as well as our discriminating against members of other nonwhite ethnic groups using the logic of White supremacy. In her essay in *This Bridge Called My Back*, Barbara Cameron reveals the complex ways that racism inhabits the psyches of people of color, so that even as we recognize how racial oppression impacts our own racial/ethnic group, we may also be complicit in the oppression of others. As a Lakota and the only nonwhite person in her elementary school, Cameron experienced open racism at an early age and also witnessed firsthand the systemic impact that racism has upon a community. Yet she also internalized deep racism about other people of color.[12] She writes, "Racism is not easy for me to write about because of my own racism toward other people of color, and because of a complex set of 'racisms' within the Indian community. At times animosity exists between half-breed, full-blood, light-skinned Indians, dark-skinned Indians, and non-Indians who attempt to pass as Indians. . . . I've grown up with misconceptions

---

12. Barbara Cameron, "Gee, You Don't Seem like an Indian from the Reservation," in Moraga and Anzaldúa, *This Bridge*, 42–44.

about Blacks, Chicanos, and Asians. I'm still in the process of trying to eliminate my racist pictures of other people of color."[13]

Gendering Racism

One of intersectionality's core insights for racial reconciliation is that racism is gendered. That is to say, our gender identities dispose us to different manifestations of racism. Sometimes these differences take the form of experiences that are unique to certain racial-gender groups. Other times, they take the form of experiences that disproportionately impact a racial-gender group. The patriarchal bias of racial reconciliation and racial justice movements has meant that they have exclusively or disproportionately emphasized the forms of racism that are meted out against African American and Latinx men, including lynching, police brutality, and "driving while Black." In contrast, however, these movements often ignore forms of gendered racism that uniquely, differentially, or disproportionately impact African American, Latinx, Asian American, and Native American women.

To say that women and men of color experience differing forms of racism does not mean that either group is somehow more disadvantaged by racism than the other. Any form of oppression meted out against one segment of a racial/ethnic group necessarily affects, even indirectly, other members of that group, an issue that James Cone addresses in *The Cross and the Lynching Tree*. Cone notes that while Black women represented only 2 percent of Blacks killed by lynching, they were nevertheless targets of its impact.

> With many historians and sociologists writing about the lynching of black men, black women have objected to being invisible in lynching discourse, as if they were exempt from mob violence. Furthermore, when black men were lynched, black women not only suffered the loss of their sons, husbands,

13. Cameron, "Gee, You Don't Seem like an Indian," 44.

brothers, uncles, nephews, and cousins but also endured public insults and economic hardship as they tried to carry on, to take care of their fatherless children in a patriarchal and racist society in which Whites could lynch them or their children with impunity, at the slightest whim or smallest infraction of the southern racial etiquette. Such suffering created a deep religious paradox for black women, challenging their faith in the justice and love of God.[14]

Cone resists the common tendency to measure the comparative suffering of Black women and Black men, noting that while their experiences were different because of gender, neither was necessarily harder or easier than the other. "In a patriarchal white society, defined by lynching and state-sponsored executions, it was not easy for any black to survive with dignity, especially black men," he writes. "Yet, although black women's struggles for survival might have been somewhat different from those of men, they were not any easier."[15]

The aim of describing gendered racism is not to produce a sort of "oppression Olympics" in which groups jockey for the position of the most marginalized. Rather, considering how different groups experience racism gives us a more comprehensive understanding of how racism operates. Collins notes:

Ironically, by quantifying and ranking human oppressions, standpoint theorists invoke criteria for methodological adequacy that resemble those of positivism. Although it is tempting to claim that Black women are more oppressed than everyone else and therefore have the best standpoint from which to understand the mechanisms, processes, and effects of oppression, this is not the case. Instead, those ideas that are validated as true by African-American women, African-American men, Latina lesbians, Asian-American women, Puerto Rican

14. James H. Cone, *The Cross and the Lynching Tree* (Maryknoll, NY: Orbis Books, 2013), 122–23.
15. Cone, *The Cross and the Lynching Tree*, 139–40.

men, and other groups with distinctive standpoints, with each group using the epistemological approaches growing from its unique standpoint, become the most "objective" truths. Each group speaks from its own standpoint and shares its own partial, situated knowledge. But because each group perceives its own truth as partial, its knowledge is unfinished. Each group becomes better able to consider other groups' standpoints without relinquishing the uniqueness of its own standpoint or surprising other groups' partial perspectives.[16]

In contrast, then, to the symmetrical treatment approach to analyzing oppression, it is through perceiving and considering racism's partiality that we are better able to understand and combat it. This includes the forms of gendered racism that are commonly experienced by women of color.

What Does It Mean to Discuss "Women of Color"?

Even the "women of color" label is often inadequate in capturing a common identity for the diverse groups of women who are loosely bound together solely by the fact that we are not White and Anglo. Mirtha Quintanales points to this complexity when she states:

Not all Third World women are "women of color"—as if by this concept we mean exclusively "nonwhite." . . . And not all women of color are really Third World. . . . Yet, if we extend the concept of Third World to include internally "colonized" racial and ethnic minority groups in this country, so many different kinds of groups could be conceivably included, that the crucial issue of social and institutional racism and its historic tie to slavery in the US could get diluted, lost in the shuffle. The same thing would likely happen if we extended the meaning of "women of color" to include all those women in this

---

16. Patricia Hill Collins, *Black Feminist Thought: Knowledge, Consciousness, and the Politics of Empowerment* 2nd ed. (New York: Routledge, 2000), 270.

country who are victims of prejudice and discrimination (in many respects), but who nevertheless hold racial privileges and may even be racists.[17]

Intersectionality thus helps us to understand how our experiences of oppression vary based upon our complicated and multilayered identities, and it also points us to the fact that our understanding of what it means to seek liberation or to be "radical" also varies. It provides the interpretative framework for understanding, as Moraga and Anzaldúa note, that "how each of us perceives our ability to be radical against this oppressive state is largely affected by our economic privilege and our specific history of colonization in the US. Some of us were brought here centuries ago as slaves, others had our land of birthright taken away from us, some of us are the daughters and granddaughters of immigrants, others of us are still newly immigrated to the US."[18] These dynamics represent formidable challenges for coalition-building efforts among women of color.

A danger in using the "women of color" label is that it can obfuscate the distinctions between the forms of oppression experienced by women of different racial/ethnic identities and women of different hues. In short, it can glide over the fact that some of us are more "colored" than others, that we hold differing (and at times, competing) positions on the racial hierarchy, and that this shapes our experiences of racism and sexism in concrete and disparate ways. This is especially true for women and girls of African descent, who are often targeted by a highly specific form of racial-gender oppression known as misogynoir, wherein their bodies, behaviors, and traditions are denigrated even relative to other women of color. A clear example of this is the casting call for extras for *Straight Outta Compton*, the 2015 biopic of the rap group N.W.A. The casting call divided women into four categories that were largely determined by race/ethnicity, skin tone, hair, and body type.

---

17. Mirtha N. Quintanales, "I Paid Very Hard for My Immigrant Ignorance," in Moraga and Anzaldúa, *This Bridge*, 149.

18. Cherríe Moraga and Gloría Anzaldúa, "Between the Lines: On Culture, Class, and Homophobia," in Moraga and Anzaldúa, *This Bridge*, 101.

A GIRLS: These are the hottest of the hottest. Models. MUST have real hair—no extensions, very classy looking, great bodies. You can be black, white, asian, hispanic, mid eastern, or mixed race too. . . .

B GIRLS: These are fine girls, long natural hair, really nice bodies. Small waists, nice hips. You should be light-skinned. Beyoncé is a prototype here. . . .

C GIRLS: These are African American girls, medium- to light-skinned with a weave.

D GIRLS: These are African American girls. Poor, not in good shape. Medium to dark skin tone. Character types.[19]

If Beyoncé—with her blonde hair and creole heritage—is a type "B," it is probably safe to assume that "A" girls will be any race but Black.

In using the "women of color" framework, we must be careful not to jettison the particularity of our racial/ethnic identities in an effort to focus upon the universal. This, after all, would be a single-axis approach. An intersectional approach to women of color, in contrast, does not seek to flatten difference; rather, it examines the points at which the intersections collide—the interstices. "Interstitial spaces are possible sites within a defined context (a discipline, a practice, a culture) that are occupied by an actor/agent working as a 'carrier' of different cultural practices, knowledge, and theories. A 'carrier' can use the interstitial space to influence and challenge that context and thus loosen up boundaries."[20] In this case, I employ my own intersectional identity as an African American woman to interrogate the imagined spaces between boundaries, in other words, the commonalities that exist between and within the distinctive intersections of Indigenous, African American, Asian American, and Latinx female identities. This approach leads me to identify forms of

19. Danielle Cadet, "The 'Straight Outta Compton' Casting Call Is So Offensive It Will Make Your Jaw Drop," *Huffington Post*, July 17, 2014, https://www.huffington post.com/2014/07/17/straight-out-of-compton-casting-call_n_5597010.html.

20. Anita Hussenius et al., "Instital Spaces: A Model for Transgressive Processes," in *Illdisciplined Gender: Engaging Questions of Nature/Culture and Transgressive Encounters*, ed. Jacob Bull and Margaretha Fahlgren (Cham, CH: Springer International Publishing, 2015), 13.

gendered racism that are shared by women of color. In the remainder of this chapter, I explore three of these: colorism, mammification, and hypersexualization.

Colorism and the Politics of Beauty

One of the most pernicious examples of gendered racism is colorism, an extension of racism that measures beauty and worth based upon proximity to White aesthetic norms. Alice Walker may have been the first to use the term "colorism" in her 1982 text, *In Search of Our Mothers' Gardens*, in which she defined it as "prejudicial or preferential treatment of same-race people based solely on their color."[21] Rooted in European racial ideology, colorism confers privilege upon individuals and groups whose skin color, hair, and facial/body features more closely approximate whiteness. In many cultures, the association between light skin and social value began as a product of the association between class and outdoor labor. Individuals with class privilege, being exempt from manual and outdoor labor, tended to have fairer complexions than did those from the lower economic rungs of society. The use of the term "redneck" to refer to poor and working-class White people is rooted in this historic distinction, where a tanned and sunburned neck was a marker of someone who labored outside. Even prior to colonialism and slavery, western Europeans associated lightness with civility, intelligence, purity, and beauty. In contrast, darkness was associated with dirtiness, evil, and ugliness.[22] "Prior to the sixteenth century, the *Oxford English Dictionary* provided the following definition of the color 'black': 'Deeply stained with dirt; soiled, dirty, foul. . . . Having dark or deadly pur-

21. Alice Walker, *In Search of Our Mothers' Gardens: Womanist Prose* (San Diego: Harcourt Brace Jovanovich, 1983), 290.
22. Kellina M. Craig-Henderson, "Colorism and Interracial Intimacy: How Skin Color Matters," in *Color Matters: Skin Tone Bias and the Myth of a Postracial America*, ed. Kimberly Jade Norwood, New Directions in American History (London: Taylor and Francis, 2014), 270; Laura Quiros and Beverly Araujo Dawson, "The Color Paradigm: The Impact of Colorism on the Racial Identity and Identification of Latinas," *Journal of Human Behavior in the Social Environment* 23(April 2013): 288.

poses, malignant; pertaining to or involving death, deadly; baneful, disastrous, sinister. . . . Foul, iniquitous, atrocious, horrible, wicked. . . . Indicating disgrace, censure, liability to punishment, etc.' "[23] Given these associations, it is unsurprising that colorism most strongly manifests itself in the denigration of African hair and skin color.[24]

When colonialism and manifest destiny brought Europeans in contact with the Indigenous peoples of Africa and the Americas, colorism took on a new meaning. "Western colonization . . . used colorism to dehumanize enslaved populations, thus making discrimination based on skin color more than a class imperative, turning it instead into a system of hatred and denigration."[25] Slavery cemented the color hierarchy. From the late 1600s until the late 1800s, white skin in the United States was synonymous with freedom.[26] To be White was to be free; to be Black was to be enslaved or enslaveable. Thus, a racial hierarchy was established whereby racial groups and individuals within these groups are adjudicated based upon their proximity to whiteness. After the Civil War and the fall of slavery, skin color continued to determine life circumstances, from the quotidian experience of which water fountain to use to the larger issue of voting rights. "What makes America's preference for lighter skin colors distinctive from that which is apparent in other places in the world is the connection to a history in which a host of civil liberties and certain unalienable rights were legally and structurally linked to complexion."[27] Consequently, the task of every immigrant group to the Americas since the beginning of the Atlantic slave trade has been inscribing themselves closer to the White end of the color line. It is no coincidence, then, that eastern European immigrants have been the driving force behind the cosmetics industry, or that Black women spend more on cosmetics and hair care than do any other group.

23. Craig-Henderson, "Colorism and Interracial Intimacy," 269–70.

24. Quiros and Dawson, "The Color Paradigm," 288.

25. Kimberly Jade Norwood and Violeta Solonova Foreman, "The Ubiquitousness of Colorism: Then and Now," in Norwood, *Color Matters*, 29.

26. Norwood and Foreman, "The Ubiquitousness of Colorism," 38.

27. Craig-Henderson, "Colorism and Interracial Intimacy," 270.

When by accident of birth we fall far from the hegemonic beauty ideal, we are more likely, it seems, to use artificial means to approximate it.

Colorism's Trinity: Skin, Hair, and Body

Colorism is most strongly associated with skin tone. After all, it is usually through skin color that people infer or determine a person's racial identity. Colorism further distinguishes between members of the same racial group by making judgments about a person's beauty, personality, and behaviors based upon the lightness or darkness of her or his skin.

"Skin color is the most visible and noticeable aspect of racial status in the United States. It immediately cues thoughts about ancestry and heritage, as well as . . . activating the perceiver's stereotypes and expectations about behavior and competency," says Craig-Henderson. "Skin color differentiates members of different racial groups from one another, and it also serves to distinguish among members within racial groups."[28] Skin tone, of course, is highly subjective, even more than race. Skin tone judgments are relative and often egocentric, in that people judge the skin tone of others based upon their own.[29] Nevertheless, the relationship between perceived skin tone and objective markers of social prestige is so strong that many scholars argue that skin tone is becoming more important than racial identity. Banks, for example, argues that "conventional racial designations today may be less important than factors such as skin tone, especially when combined with traditional tropes of high-status whiteness like elite education, stable family structure, high socioeconomic status, and 'command of spoken English.' "[30] Craig-Henderson claims that "the tendency to use skin color as a moniker for other

28. Craig-Henderson, "Colorism and Interracial Intimacy," 262.

29. Taunya Lovell Banks, "A Darker Shade of Pale Revisited: Disaggregated Blackness and Colorism in the 'Post-Racial' Obama Era," in Norwood, *Color Matters*, 213–14.

30. Banks, "A Darker Shade of Pale Revisited," 209.

bases of judgment is so great that it may even be used independent of racial status."[31] Norwood and Foreman claim that today, "the closer one's skin color is to white, the closer one is to being treated with an elevated status: that of an 'honorary white person.'"[32]

These and other scholars conclude that skin tone is emerging as part of a set of new criteria for adjudicating distance from or closeness to White sensibilities. The other factors include earned education, occupational status, family structure, dialect, and so on. Together, they form a new system of racial inequality that is based upon racial stratification rather than racial difference per se.[33] This new system suggests an even more subtle racial hierarchy than Bonilla-Silva's proposed triracial order. The upper levels of the new racial caste system may well include individual Blacks who approximate White aesthetics and normative values. "Colorism practices, if not thwarted, will result in the United States becoming a pigmentocracy, where whiteness is on the top, and blackness, broadly defined to include other dark-skinned nonwhites, is on the bottom. In the middle will be a broad and changing group of nonwhites—light-skinned Asian, Latina/ o, black, and bi/ multiracial individuals—whose quest for whiteness will reinforce this country's persistent ideology of white privilege."[34] The irony of this new pigmentocracy is that it will reinforce the supremacy of whiteness even as the country becomes less White.[35] On the surface, it will appear that race is no longer a fundamental determinant of life chances and that class has a larger impact. The White supremacist underpinnings of the hierarchy will be obscured.

It is important to note that, while it is most strongly associated with skin tone, colorism also includes hair and facial/body features. As a function of White supremacy, "colorism elevates and values White and Anglo aesthetics so that positive traits are associated with

31. Craig-Henderson, "Colorism and Interracial Intimacy," 271.

32. Norwood and Foreman, "The Ubiquitousness of Colorism," 39.

33. Banks, "A Darker Shade of Pale Revisited," 217; Linda M. Burton et al., "Critical Race Theories, Colorism, and the Decade's Research on Families of Color," *Journal of Marriage and Family* 72 (June 2010): 441.

34. Banks, "A Darker Shade of Pale Revisited," 235.

35. Banks, "A Darker Shade of Pale Revisited," 210.

Whiteness and negative traits are associated with Blackness or Indigeneity."[36] Thus, colorism favors individuals whose hair and facial/body features approximate those of White, western European standards, particularly light skin tone, light eyes, aquiline noses, thin lips, and long, straight hair. At the opposite end of its hierarchy are individuals with dark skin, kinky hair, thick lips, and broad noses. Jill Nelson recalls that for her, "as a girl and young woman, hair, body, and color were society's trinity in determining female beauty and identity, the cultural and value-laden gang of three that formed the boundaries and determined the extent of women's visibility, influence, and importance."[37] Indeed, hair texture, eye color, and facial features often impact society's perceptions of who is considered light-skinned.[38] Under the apartheid system in South Africa, for example, hair texture was a key determinant in assigning people to the country's four recognized racial categories: native (i.e., Black Africans), coloured (i.e., people of mixed race), Indian (i.e., South Asians), or White. The "pencil test" was often used to determine whether a person was native or coloured. In an interview, Ahmed "Kathy" Kathrada, an antiapartheid activist and senior advisor to President Nelson Mandela, explains: "Ridiculous as it may sound . . . they would put a pencil through the hair. If the pencil sticks, African hair is curly, so it will hold the pencil. If the pencil drops, he or she can be classified as coloured because straight hair won't hold a pencil."[39]

In countries with long histories of light skin preferences (such as Japan and China), increasing commercial trade with the West has meant that colorism is not only about having light skin, but having western European features.

---

36. Margaret Hunter, "Colorism in the Classroom: How Skin Tone Stratifies African American and Latina/o Students," *Theory into Practice* 55, no. 1 (Winter 2016): 57.

37. Jill Nelson, *Straight, No Chaser: How I Became a Grown-Up Black Woman* (New York: Penguin, 1997), 35.

38. Burton et al., "Critical Race Theories," 441.

39. "Overcoming Apartheid: Building Democracy," African Online Digital Library, African Studies Center, Michigan State University, http://overcomingapartheid.msu.edu/video.php?id=65-24F-A3 (accessed February 22, 2018).

Increased globalization and the proliferation of Western mass-media notions of attractiveness have combined with the Asian cultural values associated with white skin to produce a new, heavily Westernized understanding of beauty. Today, European-like phenotypic traits are more desirable and whiter skin pigmentation and more angular facial structures abound. Virtually all advertisements in both countries are of Asian women who are not only pale in skin color, but who possess almost no hint of their Asian lineage. Surgically corrected eyes, lips, mouths, and noses are common. Cosmetic surgery is one of the most popular ways to spend one's discretionary income.[40]

Indeed, Asians and Asian Americans account for a large part of the growth in the plastic surgery market. Worldwide, the third-most-common procedure is blepharoplasty, which creates a double eyelid to make eyes appear larger.[41] Among immigrant women, broadly, attempting to reach the standards of feminine beauty often requires dieting, "nose bobbing, hair straightening, and bleaching. . . . Not only was the tall, slim Anglo-Saxon body preeminent, the body must look middle rather than working class."[42] Colorism, then, is about achieving the appearance of Western, White, middle-class status.

Colorism is both a between-group and within-group phenomenon. That is, it makes distinctions between nonwhite groups based upon their proximity to whiteness, judging those groups that are lighter in color as more intelligent, desirable, and civilized than those groups that are darker. Within racial-ethnic groups, it further distinguishes between individuals in much the same way.

40. Norwood and Foreman, "The Ubiquitousness of Colorism," 34.
41. Norwood and Foreman, "The Ubiquitousness of Colorism," 34.
42. Neil Irvin Painter, *The History of White People* (New York: Norton, 2010), 364.

A Global Phenomenon

Colorism is a global, mass-marketed phenomenon that has been spread through colonization and continues to be spread via the television, film, music, and advertising industries. In India, for example, there is a strong preference for light skin, or "fairness," which is often a marker of social caste. Notably, while skin color differences in social stratification in India are often attributed to the caste system, it was not until the fifteenth and sixteenth centuries—when contact with Europe increased—that the caste system incorporated skin color. "When the British colonized India, they not only used skin color to distinguish themselves physically, socially, and culturally from the Indians, but they also used skin color to distinguish the Aryan North and the high castes, from the Dravidian South and the lower castes. Following the Aryan conquest of the indigenous and darker-skinned Dravidians, society became segregated into castes."[43] Globalization has resulted in an even higher emphasis on "fairness" as a means of exclusion and of securing India's place in the world. Several national and international corporations exploit colorism for profit and reinforce it through advertisements that equate "light skin with beauty and success, with flight and fancy, with choice and empowerment."[44] Vaseline, L'Oreal, and Garnier all sell skin-lightening creams in India, which is the world's largest market for such products.[45] As Nadeem points out, the advertisements for "fairness" creams in India "do not whitewash inequalities and prejudices, they revel in them. The solution they offer is for you to 'whitewash' yourself and take advantage of those very social ills. They do not point to a post-color future; they tell us what to do to get ahead today. They are parables of darkness and light. They are tales of metamorphosis: the lowly caterpillar becomes a sprightly butterfly; the ugly duckling becomes the most beautiful bird of all."[46]

43. Norwood and Foreman, "The Ubiquitousness of Colorism," 32.
44. Shehzad Nadeem, "Fair and Anxious: On Mimicry and Skin-Lightening in India," *Social Identities* 20 (Mar/May 2014): 225.
45. Nadeem, "Fair and Anxious," 225, 227.
46. Nadeem, "Fair and Anxious," 225.

India is not alone in its valorization of whiteness. Skin-lightening creams rank among the top-selling cosmetic products throughout Africa, Latin America, East and Southeast Asia, and their diasporas.[47] Today, the preference for light skin in Africa is so pronounced that in many countries (including Nigeria, Zambia, Ghana, Dakar, Senegal, Mali, and South Africa), anywhere from one-third to one-half of adult women use skin-lightening creams. In some parts of Nigeria, the rate is estimated at 77 percent.[48] The prevalence of skin-bleaching products in Africa has become so common that a group of organizers in the Ivory Coast founded a new beauty pageant, "Miss Authentica," where the primary criterion for entry was having natural, unbleached skin![49]

It is especially crucial to understand colorism and its impact on racial stratification in Latin American countries and populations. Because many of these cultures have a concept of *mestizaje*, people do not make overt distinctions between races as we do in the United States. On the surface, then, national identity seems to eclipse racial identity. Closer examination, however, reveals that colorism runs rampant in these societies. People with lighter skin and Eurocentric facial features tend to dominate the upper economic strata: they have better educations, better jobs, higher incomes, and more prestige. In contrast, those with darker skin who have Indigenous and/or African features tend to be less educated, poorer, and marginalized.[50] For example, Norwood and Foreman allege that "Cuban society was . . . built with a strict code in which skin color placed human beings in certain social classes and even within varying degrees of humanity: Black, in many cases, was synonymous with beast."[51]

Indeed, many Latin American countries have openly advocated a process of "progressive mixture" to eradicate traces of their Indigenous and African heritage.

---

47. Nadeem, "Fair and Anxious," 228.

48. Norwood and Foreman, "The Ubiquitousness of Colorism," 36.

49. Margaret L. Hunter, "Buying Racial Capital: Skin-Bleaching and Cosmetic Surgery in a Globalized World," *Journal of Pan African Studies* 4, no. 4 (June 2011): 147.

50. Quiros and Dawson, "The Color Paradigm," 289.

51. Norwood and Foreman, "The Ubiquitousness of Colorism," 28.

During the postcolonial period, when most Latin American countries became independent republics, those in power had to reconcile the racial mixture of their populations with the popular theories about the inferiority of colored people. To solve this dilemma, some Latin Americans invoked the notion of "progressive mixture." . . . Unlike racial categories in the old American South . . . where one drop of black blood rendered an individual black, the Latino/a equivalent is almost the mirror opposite: One drop of white blood is a start on the path to whiteness. Moreover, appearance, gender, status, and social situation play a role in determining who is classified as black, mulatto, or white. Skin color, though, remains dominant and telling.[52]

The progressive mixture concept acknowledged the heterogeneity of races that made up Latinx identity but also assumed that the region would increasingly whiten. Some countries even encouraged European immigration in order to speed up the process of whitening, or "blanqueamiento." In the context of the United States, these distinctions are often obscured among the generalized "Latinx" or "Hispanic" labels that hardly recognize national origin differences, let alone distinctions based upon skin color. This does not mean, however, that they cease to be important. Indeed, differences in skin color probably account for some of the inconsistent findings regarding experiences of discrimination, racial attitudes, and even voting patterns among Latinx Americans.[53]

---

52. Norwood and Foreman, "The Ubiquitousness of Colorism," 30.

53. Quiros and Dawson, for example, argue that "research using umbrella terms such as *Latino/a* to study the experiences of such diverse groups have overlooked important differences in privilege and stigma experienced by white and dark-skinned Latino/as. . . . Based on phenotype variations, some lighter-skinned individuals are able to maintain an ambiguous racial identity and straddle the racial divide and are able to pass for White, while others are assigned a Black or Afro-Latino racial identity based on phenotypic features and, typically skin color. . . . The experience of stigma or privilege based on phenotype can affect the experiences of Latino/as in the United States, resulting in lighter-skinned Latino/as experiencing access and privilege while darker-skinned Latino/as experience marginalization and discrimination resulting

The New Racial Capital

While colorism's global presence can be traced to patterns of European colonization and US presence, its endurance persists because, in the context of global White supremacy, White or light aesthetics confer social and material privileges. Margaret Hunter, for example, argues that

> white or light skin is a form of "racial capital" gaining its status from existing racial hierarchies. Racial capital is a resource drawn from the body that can be related to skin tone, facial features, body shape, etc. . . . Both Anglo bodies and light or white skin confer status on people of color in an individualistic way. Light skin tone can be transformed into social capital (social networks), symbolic capital (esteem or status), or even economic capital (high-paying job or promotion).[54]

Research on colorism bears this out. Across the globe, skin tone has tangible impact upon educational and occupational opportunity, income, marital status, and disparate treatment in criminal justice systems.

Summarizing research on the impact of colorism on Blacks in America, Norwood and Foreman state that, overall, "lighter-skinned [B]lacks are often better educated, have higher occupational status (better jobs, careers, higher incomes), earn more money, have more overall wealth, tend to marry higher on the socioeconomic ladder, and are perceived as being more competent than darker-skinned blacks."[55] The findings of this research document the following disparities among African Americans:

- Darker-skinned Blacks have lower individual and family income, higher rates of unemployment and poverty, lower educational

---

in negative psychological and socioeconomic outcomes" (Quiros and Dawson, "The Color Paradigm," 287).

54. Hunter, "Buying Racial Capital," 145.

55. Norwood and Foreman, "The Ubiquitousness of Colorism," 41.

attainment, and lower occupational prestige than do lighter-skinned Blacks, even when studies control for factors that might account for the differences. For example, most Blacks in leadership roles within corporate and government institutions are light in skin tone, as are most tenured and tenure-track professors at US universities. Light skin is even preferred over academic credentials when it comes to employment interviews and callbacks.[56]

- Skin tone and Afrocentric features (skin color, hair texture, and lip shape/thickness) have been associated with disparate treatment in the criminal justice system for adults, increasing contact with law enforcement, rate of criminal convictions, and sentencing lengths. Darker-skinned Blacks are arrested, incarcerated, and even sentenced to death row at higher rates than lighter-skinned Blacks; they also serve more of their sentences. At least one study indicates that the colorism effect may partially, or perhaps even fully, account for racial disparities in sentencing lengths. Using data from the Georgia Department of Corrections, Burch found that while medium- and darker-skinned Blacks received sentences that were approximately 5 percent higher (translating to an average increase of two hundred days of incarceration) than Whites, the rates of lighter-skinned Blacks were statistically indistinguishable from those of Whites.[57]

- Colorism also accounts for disparities in school suspension rates between African American and White girls. Data from the US Department of Education indicate that African American girls in kindergarten through twelfth grade are suspended at almost three times the national average for all girls (12 percent versus 4.85 percent) and at twice the rate for White boys, a racial disparity that parallels that of African American boys. Data from

56. Ellis P. Monk Jr., "Skin Tone Stratification among Black Americans," *Social Forces* 92, no. 4 (June 2014): 1314, 1321–23; Norwood and Foreman, "The Ubiquitousness of Colorism," 40.

57. Jamilia J. Blake et al., "The Role of Colorism in Explaining African American Females' Suspension Risk," *School Psychology Quarterly* 31, no. 3 (Sept. 2016): 4; Norwood and Foreman, "The Ubiquitousness of Colorism," 40; Traci Burch, "Skin Color and the Criminal Justice System: Beyond Black-White Disparities in Sentencing," *Journal of Empirical Legal Studies* 12, no. 3 (Sept. 2015): 410.

the National Longitudinal Study of Adolescent to Adult Health (Add Health) indicates that colorism is a significant predictor of girls' risk for school suspension even when controlling for factors such as school setting (e.g., size, urban versus rural setting, diversity, disciplinary policies) and student characteristics (e.g., prior disciplinary history, behavioral and academic functioning, perceptions of teacher fairness). African American females with the darkest skin tone were suspended at twice the rate of White females, whereas there were no significant differences for lighter-skinned African American females.[58]

- The findings regarding the relationship between marital status and colorism are conflicting. Some researchers report that lighter-skinned Blacks, especially women, are more likely to marry than darker-skinned Blacks. Other studies have found no differences in rates of marriage between darker- and lighter-skinned Black women. The most consistent finding in this area is that lighter-skinned women marry higher-status partners, that is, men with higher educations and income, even after controlling for women's own socioeconomic status.[59]

- In the adoption market, potential parents express preferences for White over nonwhite children, and biracial over Black children, and lighter-skinned over darker-skinned children. In the private sector, these preferences translate to differences in adoption expenses. Adoption costs are highest for White children and lowest for Black children, with biracial children or non-Black children of color being at the midpoint.[60]

- Among Blacks in television, film, music, newscasting, dance, and print modeling, darker-skinned Blacks are vastly underrepresented in popular culture relative to their lighter-skinned counterparts. "Hollywood has long expressed its preference for light-skin women of color, and even today it is rare to find a

58. Blake et al., "The Role of Colorism," 1, 9.

59. Norwood and Foreman, "The Ubiquitousness of Colorism," 41; Monk, "Skin Tone Stratification," 1327–29.

60. Norwood and Foreman, "The Ubiquitousness of Colorism," 41.

dark-skin woman in a positive leading role or as a love interest."[61] Among African and African American women, much of the excitement over the film *Black Panther* had to do with the skin tones of the female characters, all of whom were dark-skinned and also depicted as beautiful, smart, and highly skilled (rather than subservient, tragic, or evil, as happens so frequently).

While much of the research on colorism has focused upon African Americans, social science research has documented a strong relationship between skin color and income among a wide variety of ethnic minority groups in the Americas, including Filipino Americans, Cuban Americans, and other Latinx groups. Within each of these groups, darker-skinned individuals tend to have lower wages than both their lighter-skinned racial/ethnic counterparts and Whites. Black or darker-skinned Latinx individuals have lower educational attainment, occupational status, and income compared to their lighter-skinned peers. In Brazil, for example, Black families earn less than Brown families, and both Black and Brown families earn less than White families. Lighter-skinned Asian Americans are more likely to be college-educated than are their darker-skinned counterparts.[62] And one study has revealed that among Korean and Vietnamese immigrants, a form of intraracial oppression known as "whitewashing" limits families' access to social capital that would enhance their economic standing.[63]

The Politics of Beauty

As the earlier story about my son reveals, colorism affects people of color regardless of their gender identity. However, because of its association with beauty, and the value placed upon wom-

61. Norwood and Foreman, "The Ubiquitousness of Colorism," 40–41.

62. Igor Ryabov, "Colorism and Educational Outcomes of Asian Americans: Evidence from the National Longitudinal Study of Adolescent Health," *Social Psychology of Education* 19 (2016): 303–24.

63. Norwood and Foreman, "The Ubiquitousness of Colorism," 30; Burton et al., "Critical Race Theories," 448–49.

en's beauty in a patriarchal society, it disproportionately impacts women of color. White supremacy, after all, does not only affirm whiteness as superior to all other racial-ethnic identities. It also maintains that a certain form of whiteness is the hegemonic standard, typically that associated with northern European countries. Thus, the iconic standard of beauty has been a White woman with fair skin, blue eyes, and long, blond, straight hair. All women, regardless of race, wrestle with this standard to some degree. Margot Starbuck has written about this in *Unsqueezed*, listing the negative and shaming messages that women receive about their bodies regardless of their race and ethnicity. These include the messages that "You're not quite right as you are" and "Refusing the world's image of beauty can threaten your career."[64] Cultural messages about and pressures to conform to beauty norms are not coincidental; rather, as Naomi Wolf argues persuasively in *The Beauty Myth*, they are designed to serve male institutions and reinforce male institutional power.[65]

The distinction for women of color is that our racial-ethnic skin tones, hair textures and lengths, and facial/body features often place us not just at a distance from the hegemonic ideal, but in an entirely different universe. In *More Than Serving Tea*, Kathy Khang writes: "We Asian American women wrestle with issues of body image and our identity as women. Western cultural ideals of beauty are voluptuous blondes. We will never be that. But Western cultural ideas of Asian American beauty are often linked to Lucy Liu or Zhang Ziyi. We may look more like them, but they still represent unattainable, airbrushed ideals."[66] The chasm is even wider for women of African descent, given the unique impact of antiblack racism. "Most women, white and black, are not comforted by the dominant myths of beauty. The difference for black women is that we do not feel simply ugly,

---

64. Margot Starbuck, *Unsqueezed: Springing Free from Skinny Jeans, Nose Jobs, Highlights, and Stilettos* (Downers Grove, IL: InterVarsity Press, 2010), 31.

65. Naomi Wolf, *The Beauty Myth: How Images of Beauty Are Used against Women* (New York: Anchor Books, 1991).

66. Kathy Khang, "Freedom in Sexuality," in *More Than Serving Tea: Asian American Women on Expectations, Relationships, Leadership, and Faith*, ed. Nikki A. Toyama and Tracey Gee (Downers Grove, IL: InterVarsity Press, 2006), 86–87.

but totally outside, irrelevant, invisible."[67] It makes sense, then, that Black women in America spend more per capita on cosmetics and hair products (including the weaves and wigs made from synthetic hair or from the hair of women in Malaysia, India, and Brazil) than any other racial-gender group. African American women spend $7.5 billion annually on beauty products, spending 80 percent more on cosmetics and twice as much on skin care as the general market.[68] While it would be overgeneralizing to state that all cosmetics are designed to approximate whiteness, it is probably safe to assume that many of us are trying to relax, weave, and makeup our way into some section of the hegemonic ideal.

We do this for good reason, too. In a patriarchal, capitalist society, conformity to hegemonic beauty ideals has tangible consequences across a wide variety of domains, including education, employment, marriage, and the criminal justice system. A large body of literature demonstrates that people perceived as physically attractive are considered more intelligent by their teachers, are more popular among their classmates, are more likely to be hired, have higher earnings, receive better performance evaluations, are promoted more often, and receive less severe punishments in criminal justice proceedings.[69] For example, data from the aforementioned Add Health study indicate that attractive individuals earn 11 percent more than "average" individuals, and very attractive individuals earn 20 percent more; this difference occurs even when controlling for factors such as race, personality, education, parental education, and childhood household income.[70] Further, while both women and men benefit from attractiveness, attractive women have the added advantage of marrying higher-status men.[71] Moreover, women who engage in "beauty work" (i.e., wearing makeup, choosing flattering outfits, di-

67. Nelson, *Straight, No Chaser*, 42.

68. Taylor Bryant, "How the Beauty Industry Has Failed Black Women," *REFINERY29*, February 27, 2016, http://www.refinery29.com/2016/02/103964/black-hair-care-makeup-business.

69. Jaclyn S. Wong and Andrew M. Penner, "Gender and the Returns to Attractiveness," *Research in Social Stratification and Mobility* 44 (June 2016): 113–14.

70. Wong and Penner, "Gender and the Returns," 118.

71. Wong and Penner, "Gender and the Returns" 114.

eting, undergoing cosmetic surgery) earn significantly higher wages (34 to 50 percent) than those who do not.[72]

When beauty results in tangible social and economic advantages and is also tied to ideals that are rooted in White supremacy, the impact upon women of color is striking. Women of color with light skin and European features have more racial and social capital. "Light skin operates as a form of social capital for women because it represents beauty and, conversely, beauty is a form of social capital. Light-skinned women convert their beauty, defined by European aesthetics, into social capital in the forms of economic, educational, and general prestige."[73] In contrast, women of color with darker skin and Indigenous features are more likely to experience more racial and gender hostility and oppression, even among their own people. In a study of the impact of colorism among women of color living in New York, Quiros and Dawson demonstrate its uniquely gendered role among Latinx women, who shared stories of having been negatively singled out for their dark skin and curly hair compared to their similarly complected brothers and fathers. Several women reported that they had to silently bear the ridicule of family and neighbors who openly and disparagingly referred to them as "Negrita," "La India," or even "fea" (ugly).[74]

The gendered nature of colorism and the particularity of anti-black racism mean that women and girls pay even higher penalties for having dark skin than do their male counterparts, and dark-skinned Black women and girls pay more than do women of other racial/ethnic groups.[75] Skin tone is often a central determinant of self-image for African American women across the color spectrum. Dark-skinned Black women have to grapple with not measuring up to the hegemonic ideal, whereas light-skinned women often experience shame and guilt about the fact that they do![76]

72. Wong and Penner, "Gender and the Returns," 119.
73. Quiros and Dawson, "The Color Paradigm," 289.
74. Quiros and Dawson, "The Color Paradigm," 292.
75. Monk, "Skin Tone Stratification," 1316.
76. Verna M. Keith, "A Colorstruck World: Skin Tone, Achievement, and Self-Esteem among African American Women," in *Shades of Difference: Why Skin Color Matters*, ed. Evelyn Nakato Glenn (Stanford: Stanford University Press, 2009), 32.

Yet, because stigmatized physical features weigh more heavily in the lives of black women than black men, skin tone gradations may be more relevant for women's self-esteem, suggesting an even greater advantage for black females compared with black males when complexion is taken into consideration. At the same time, light-skinned black women also face challenges to self-definition by having their parentage and ethnic identity questioned, and also express feelings of guilt and shame about their unfair advantages.[77]

One of the consequences of colorism is the backlash against light-complected women of color. The light-skinned Latinx women in the aforementioned study by Quiros and Dawson reported being constantly conscious of their racial identity and the ways in which they are perceived by others.[78] This is an experience that those who possess "genuine" White privilege do not have. Thus, even the privileges associated with colorism—that is, being light-skinned in a world that privileges whiteness—do not provide absolute protection from racial, gender, or class oppression. Moreover, for many women, these privileges come at the cost of isolation, invisibility, and loss of identity, an experience attested to by several of the writers in *This Bridge Called My Back*. Quintanales, for example, states: "Yes, lighter-than-black skin color *may* confer on some ethnic minority women the option of becoming 'assimilated,' 'integrated,' in mainstream American society. But is this really a privilege when it always means having to become invisible, those-like, identity-less, community-less, totally alienated? The perils of 'passing' as white Americans are perils indeed."[79] Moraga, moreover, describes how her sexuality mitigated whatever privilege she might have gained through colorism: "The joys of looking like a white girl ain't so great since I realized I could be beaten on the street for being a dyke. If my sister's being beaten because she's Black, it's pretty much the same principle. We're both getting beaten any way you look at it."[80]

77. Keith, "A Colorstruck World," 33–34.
78. Quiros and Dawson, "The Color Paradigm," 293.
79. Quintanales, "I Paid Very Hard," 152.
80. Moraga, "La Güera," 24.

In fact, misogynoir means that for Black and biracial women, lightness is sometimes not even enough. At a retreat focusing on race relations among women several years ago, a biracial woman asked if I could explain an experience that she had repeatedly. Her parents, an African American military man and an Italian woman, had met and married when her father was stationed in Italy. The woman, who was in her midtwenties and extremely fair-skinned, had been raised on military bases across Europe. Having recently moved to the United States for graduate school, she was still trying to navigate what it meant to be a "passable" biracial woman amid the country's racial politics. She was particularly puzzled because on two separate occasions, she had been approached by African American men who had seemed romantically interested in her. But when the topic of her background came up and she mentioned being partially Black, each man had responded, "Oh, I thought you were White," and then walked away. In a society structured by White supremacy, whiteness is still preferred over lightness, often even by people of color.

Colorism and Racial Reconciliation

Colorism has largely been treated as an intraethnic issue, a form of pathology created by ethnic minority groups and inflicted upon people of color themselves. Yet colorism is an extension of White supremacy that is produced and reinforced through social, educational, and economic systems that confer privilege to those with lighter skin and European features while simultaneously demonizing, punishing, and controlling those with darker skin and Indigenous features. Evidence indicates that the United States is well on its way to becoming a triracial pigmentocracy, with skin tone intersecting with race (and sometimes outweighing it) to impact educational achievement, occupational prestige, income, marriage patterns, and self-esteem. Despite the profound significance of colorism in the US racial hierarchy, the racial reconciliation movement has unilaterally ignored it, while at the same time celebrating interracial marriage as evidence of racial healing. What good are increased personal and ministry relationships between Whites and Blacks if colorism shapes our view of which

Blacks are deemed acceptable? Have we really made racial progress in the acceptance of Black women's natural hair when only women with naturally curly (and decidedly not kinky or African-textured) locks are featured in advertising? Is it actually a triumph when the Asian American women in television and film all appear to have had eyelid surgery, or when models from diverse ethnicities actually have the same phenotypically European features: light eyes, fair skin, aquiline noses, and long, straight hair? If racial reconciliation counts it as progress when a man of color loves whiteness more than his darker-skinned sister, it is not racial reconciliation at all, but rather a poorly disguised continuation of White patriarchal supremacy.

Mammies, Marianistas, Geishas, and Princesses

One of the primary ways in which White supremacy has impacted the material conditions of people of color is through the development and promulgation of negative stereotypes about various racial-ethnic groups. For example, the widespread myth of the violent, aggressive, and physically overdeveloped Black buck has been used for centuries in the United States to justify racist social control policies, including slavery, Jim Crow, lynching, and mass incarceration.[81] Likewise, the myth of the Indian savage has been used to justify the genocide and forced displacement of Indigenous peoples in the Americas. And Donald Trump's presidential campaign routinely invoked images of Mexican criminality to justify his push for harsh immigration laws, including the construction of an impenetrable wall along the United States–Mexico border and the deportation of young people raised in the United States who came to the country as children.

Like other elements of racism, however, racial stereotypes are gendered. The dominant images of women of color in the United States differ from those of men of color in significant ways. Yet while gendered stereotypes are racially/ethnically specific, there are some striking similarities in the ways that they are applied to women across

---

81. Patricia Hill Collins, *Black Sexual Politics: African Americans, Gender, and the New Racism* (New York: Routledge, 2004), 55–56, 152–54.

racial-ethnic groups. Specifically, African American, Asian American, Latinx, and Native American women's images are routinely subjected to similar processes of mammification and hypersexualization.

Ever the Mammy: Origins and Modern Conceptions

I use the term "mammification" to refer to the process of depicting women of color as servants. The clearest example of this, and the source of the term, is the Black mammy figure in the US cultural imagination. Originating during the US slaveholding era, the mammy was a romanticized depiction of enslaved Black women that was used to justify slavery and to disguise its horrors. In *Mammy*, Kimberly Wallace-Sanders offers the following description.

> I define the standard, most recognizable mammy character as a creative combination of extreme behavior and exaggerated features. Mammy's body is grotesquely marked by excess: she is usually extremely overweight, very tall, broad-shouldered; her skin is nearly black. She manages to be a jolly presence— she often sings or tells stories while she works—and a strict disciplinarian at the same time. First as slave, then as a free woman, the mammy is largely associated with the care of white children or depicted with noticeable attachment to white children. Her unprecedented devotion to her white family reflects her racial inferiority. *Mammy* is often both her title and the only name she has ever been given. She may also be a cook or personal maid to her mistress—a classic southern belle— whom she infantilizes. Her clothes are typical of a domestic: headscarf and apron, but she is especially attracted to brightly colored, elaborately tied scarves. Mammy speaks the ungrammatical "plantation dialect" made famous in the 1890s by popular white southern authors like Joel Chandler Harris and by subsequent minstrel shows. Her own children are usually dirty and ill mannered, yet they serve as suitable playmates for her white charges. She is typically depicted as impatient or brusque (sometimes even violent or abusive) with her own children,

in contrast to her lavish, affectionate patience for her white charges. Mammy wields considerable authority within the plantation household and consequently retains a measure of dubious, unreliable respect in the slave quarters; many slaves consider her untrustworthy because she allegedly identifies so completely with the culture that represses them.[82]

Mammy, then, represents the idealized Black caregiver for White families, at once affectionate and sassy, deferential and authoritative, amiable and asexual. She did not mind her enslavement because her highest aspiration was to serve Whites, whom she loved more than she did herself, her relatives, or her people.

The mammy stereotype had little basis in reality; nevertheless, it became a key part of White southern revisionist narratives of slavery post-Reconstruction, which attempted to portray the relationship between White slaveholders and enslaved Blacks as characterized by interracial harmony and loyalty. During the early part of the twentieth century, for example, White citizens installed plaques and monuments throughout the South that venerated "faithful slaves."[83] The United Daughters of the Confederacy (UDC) were especially strong advocates for statues dedicated to the mammy figure. In 1914, their advocacy helped to create the Confederate Memorial at Arlington National Cemetery, which included the figure of a weeping mammy and other loyal slaves, the sculptor's attempt to rectify what he and the UDC saw as the incorrect (and negative) image of slavery.[84] In 1923, the UDC proposed erecting a memorial statue for "The Black Mammy of the South" on the National Mall in Washington, DC.[85] Their proposal was ultimately unsuccessful, but by that time the mammy stereotype was so popular that "mammy" characters were frequently depicted in US literature (e.g., *Gone with the Wind*), television and film (e.g., the headless character in *Tom*

82. Kimberly Wallace-Sanders, *Mammy: A Century of Race, Gender, and Southern Memory* (Ann Arbor: University of Michigan Press, 2008), 5–6.

83. Wallace-Sanders, *Mammy*, 94–99.

84. Wallace-Sanders, *Mammy*, 97.

85. "Unique Monument for Commemorating Virtues of 'Mammy' Is Projected," *The Sunday Oregonian*, March 11, 1923.

and Jerry cartoons), and advertising (e.g., the trademarked Aunt Jemima logo, which was based upon a minstrel show character). And in a case of "life imitates art," many White families employing Black women as domestic servants referred to those women as "mammy"; in some cases, the children in those families did not realize that the women had actual names. It is a legacy that casts a shadow over dialogues about racism today. When I host these conversations in churches and other religious spaces, invariably a few older White Christians approach me afterward to "confess" that their first relationship with a Black woman was with the mammy who cared for their household.

Today, having become aware of the racist underpinnings of the stereotype, people are less likely to use the term "mammy." But the modern mammy remains a conspicuous figure in network television:

> These modern mammies are almost exclusively shown in the workplace. Many apparently either have no family life or such lives are clearly secondary to the requirements of their jobs. These women are tough, independent, smart, and asexual. But they are also devoted to their organizations, their jobs, and upon occasion, their White male bosses. They are team players and their participation on the team is predicated upon their willingness to lack ambition for running the team and never to put family ahead of the team.[86]

Given that the majority of US Whites live, go to school, and worship in highly segregated environments, media representations of the mammy strongly shape their understandings of how "real" Black women are expected to function and assimilate into racially integrated environments.[87] Having been socialized that Black women's roles are to serve and care for them, White Americans force these same expectations upon the Black women with

86. Collins, *Black Sexual Politics*, 140–41.
87. Collins states, "The representations developed for domestic servants foreshadowed contemporary understandings of assimilation and the skills needed for racial integration" (Collins, *Black Sexual Politics*, 57).

whom they work. In *Presumed Incompetent,* an edited collection of first-person testimonies by female faculty of color about their challenges in higher education settings, Angela Mae Kupenda describes an explicit instance of this in her relationship with an older White female colleague:

> After she helped me, she expressed an interest in our being close friends. I was delighted and reached out to her often. When she became distant and disrespectful, I realized our friendship would never be close and equal, but I remained professionally respectful and appreciative of her. I then received a letter from this white female describing a wall she perceived as dividing us. She went on to tell me that I should be more like Lulu. Lulu had been her black nanny and later her maid for many years, and she was the best Christian the woman had ever met. My white female acquaintance wondered aloud why I could not be just like Lulu for her.[88]

Mammification, consequently, remains a common experience among Black women who work and minister in predominantly White contexts, including corporations, churches and parachurch organizations, and colleges and universities.

Mammy by Another Name?

A woman-of-color framework reveals that mammification—while more historically entrenched and explicit for African American women—is not limited to Black women in the United States. Other women of color are also plagued by stereotypes that depict them as overly subservient, unthinking, and loyal to male and/or White authority, in other words, as "the help." For Asian American women, the representations of the China doll or geisha girl perform similar

---

88. Angela Mae Kupenda, "Facing Down the Spooks," in *Presumed Incompetent: The Intersections of Race and Class for Women in Academia,* ed. Gabriella Gutiérrez y Muhs et al. (Boulder: University Press of Colorado, 2012), 27.

functions. "The China doll and the geisha girl evoke pictures of quiet, docile, overly feminine women whose main role is to please and serve men. These images emphasize the physical body over intelligence or voice. What is conveyed is that Asian women are useful only to serve, to be looked at or to be sexually exploited."[89] Mihee Kim-Kort describes how even the model minority myth carries the expectation of servitude and submission: "Yet, as the model minority, besides the expectations for having a high standard of intelligence and musical ability, Asian American women encounter the expectation for their unwavering subordination."[90]

For Latina women, we see the mammification process at work in the Marianismo ideal. Patriarchal gender role expectations about women in Hispanic and Latino cultures dichotomize women into two categories: "the good woman" (Marianismo) and "the bad woman" (Malinchismo). In the context of White supremacy's logics of commodification and demonization, these images become further concretized in the US popular imagination, where Latinx femininity becomes imagined through the lenses of classist, racist, and xenophobic power structures. Thus, mass media commonly represents Latinx women as domestic servants (maids, housekeepers, nannies, etc.) and "as submissive and obedient women who can do anything for their families and jobs."[91] As educational leadership researcher Johana Lopez explains:

> The Marianista perspective claims that women are seen as mothers, nurturers, care givers, and willing to serve. . . . As a consequence of the qualities associated with Marianismo, Latina women are perceived as submissive, emotional, and weak, making them more vulnerable to mistreatment and abuse not only by their family members, but also by individ-

89. Christie Heller de Leon, "Sticks, Stones, and Stereotypes," in Toyoma and Gee, *More Than Serving Tea*, 22.

90. Mihee Kim-Kort, *Making Paper Cranes: Toward an Asian American Feminist Theology* (St. Louis: Chalice Press, 2012), 21.

91. Johana P. Lopez, "Speaking with Them or Speaking for Them: A Conversation about the Effect of Stereotypes in the Latina/Hispanic Women's Experiences in the United States," *New Horizons in Adult Education & Human Resource Development* 25, no. 2 (Spring 2013): 100–101.

uals outside of their family. . . . [In] the American workplace
Mexican women are seen as passive employees willing to work
in positions that offer low salaries, usually without benefits
and with inconsistent periods of employment. Thus, the stereotype of Latina women as submissive is transferred from
patriarchal Latino households to organizations where Latina
women workers may be seen as submissive employees that can
do whatever employers ask.[92]

In professional contexts, the Marianista is expected to be willing to
take on more difficult workloads without complaining. Whether she
is a recent immigrant or a fourth-generation American, xenophobic
views of Latinx workers render her disposable. Thus, she may suffer unfair work conditions because of an ever-present threat, spoken or unspoken, that she can be easily replaced.[93] She is expected
to be motherly, offering care and compassion to everyone around
her, without exerting her own thoughts, opinions, or desires. At the
same time, she is viewed as being unsuitable for leadership because
of her strong commitments to family or her presumedly excessive
emotionality.

For Native American women, mammification occurs through
the Indian princess stereotype. Like the mammy, the Indian princess is a mythic figure whose fascination with and loyalty to White
people and White culture overshadow her cultural identity. The
myth is steeped in Eurocentric assumptions about gender relations
among Native Americans. "Early Euro-centric accounts portrayed
American Indian women as being forced to do all the work and being treated very much worse than an animal. It is almost a universal
belief perpetrated by literature, movies, and pictures that the American Indian woman was the abject slave and drudge of men in her
tribe, a heavyset workhorse, dragging a travois, trudging along a trail
behind her swarthy warrior husband, who was riding a horse."[94] In
this distorted view, elite status was bestowed upon Native American

92. Lopez, "Speaking with Them," 102.
93. Lopez, "Speaking with Them," 102–3.
94. Denise K. Lajimodiere, "American Indian Females and Stereotypes: Warriors,

women who betrayed their communities to collaborate with White conquerors and settlers. The Indian princess, then, "is defined in terms of her relationships with White male figures. If she wishes to be called a Princess, she must save or give aid to White men."[95] This stereotype looms large in the White American fascination with and Disney-fication of Pocahontas. The Indian princess stereotype both misconstrues and reshapes reality, as Native American women must constantly live and labor under its shadow. Denise Lajimodiere, an Ojibwe activist and professor of Critical Indigenous Feminist Theory, describes an encounter with a nonnative male colleague during a faculty orientation meeting. " 'Good for you on your accomplishment,' he said referring to my recent doctorate and dissertation on American Indian women leaders, 'because traditionally, weren't Indian women mostly drudges?' " It is not unreasonable to think that someone who expects Native American women to be drudges might actually treat them as such. This presents an insurmountable dilemma for Indigenous women. On the one hand, because Indigenous cultural values about the primacy of leaders providing care runs counter to the individualist perspective required for success in many professions, Native American women who embrace these values will likely end up with excessive workloads but little opportunity for advancement.

> A common result of embracing Native cultural values in academia means Native women become overburdened by carrying heavy service loads (which the academy largely fails to recognize or reward). Native women I interviewed spoke of being overloaded because—in addition to the care work they perform for Native students and communities—they also have their regular duties in the (white) academy. This extra work takes a very personal toll on the women because they are not merely laboring more but are trying to help their culture survive. Underlying all of their extra work is a sense of urgency:

Leaders, Healers, Feminists; Not Drudges, Princesses, Prostitutes," *Multicultural Perspectives* 15, no. 2 (May 2013): 105.

95. Lajimodiere, "American Indian Females," 105.

if the women do not assume these burdens, then their culture
and people will suffer and perhaps die (within the academy).[96]

On the other hand, those who do not assume such responsibilities
may be accused of betraying their communities and collaborating
with White power figures.

Again and again, these stereotypes exert real effects upon the
professional and personal experiences of women of color, as they are
compelled and pressured to shoulder additional service obligations
on all fronts. Whether it is the stereotype of the caring mammy (or
her modern counterpart, the StrongBlackWoman), the domestic
Marianista, the subservient China doll or geisha, or the collabora-
tionist Indian princess, romanticized images of African American,
Asian American, Native American, and Latinx women shape expectations about their behavior, performance, and relationships.
These expectations become the measure by which they are gauged
in intraethnic and interethnic relationships, in professional and personal settings. It is not surprising, then, that in *Presumed Incompetent*,
multiple writers—across race and ethnicity—attest to the burden of
dealing with White colleagues' and administrators' expectations that
they will assume caretaking responsibilities for students, for their
colleagues, and for the institution, in addition to their formal teaching, research, and service obligations. Kupenda, for example, reports
an encounter with an administrator who explicitly states that her
role is to "nurture, mother, feed, and nurse all the students."[97] The
reports are frequent enough that in the concluding chapter, Yolanda
Flores Niemann provides the following feedback as part of a "road
map" to help women of color navigate racial and gender challenges
in academic settings:

> Faculty, staff, and students may have particularly adverse re-
> actions—conscious and unconscious—toward women of color
> who are not perceived as adequately nurturing or feminine.

96. Michelle M. Jacob, "Native Women Maintaining Their Culture in the White
Academy," in Gutiérrez y Muhs et al., *Presumed Incompetent*, 244.
97. Kupenda, "Facing Down the Spooks," 23.

The stereotype of the mammy and the motherly Latina are particularly strong. Women who do not meet stereotypical expectations that they will nurture students arouse anger, distrust, and feelings of betrayal. Be aware of these different expectations—not only from students but often from faculty colleagues—and their harmful impact on evaluating women faculty members.[98]

Indeed, women of color who resist mammification are often subjected to the disciplinary power of structural racism. In academic settings, this often comes in the form of lower student evaluations for faculty who are women of color.[99] During my first few years as an academic in a predominantly White institution, I consistently received low marks on the survey item, "My professor cares about me." After getting the feedback in an undergraduate psychology course where I had literally restructured the entire class midsemester to improve students' performances on exams, I began talking about it to other colleagues. A clear pattern quickly emerged: it was Black women, across a variety of institutions and disciplines, who consistently received similar feedback even when it contradicted the extraordinary effort that they put into helping students do well. Some of us reached the consensus that students at both predominantly White and historically Black institutions had unrealistically high expectations that we would nurture and support them, that we would, in essence, be their mammies. When we did not meet those expectations, they reciprocated with lower evaluations. Women of color in corporate, nonprofit, and ministry contexts often narrate similar experiences.

---

98. Yolanda Flores Niemann, "Lessons from the Experiences of Women of Color Working in Academia," in Gutiérrez y Muhs et al., *Presumed Incompetent*, 469.

99. Sherrée Wilson, "They Forgot Mammy Had a Brain," in Gutiérrez y Muhs et al., *Presumed Incompetent*, 66.

Racism Is Not a Stand-Alone Issue

Better a Mammy Than a Jezebel?

The impact of mammification can be understood only when we view the mammified stereotypes of women of color in conjunction with their photonegatives. The caring, doting, and loyal mammy, Marianista, China doll/geisha, and Indian princess each represent the antithesis to what White supremacist patriarchy frames as "bad" femininity among women of color: the Jezebel, the spicy Latina, the dragon lady, and the squaw, respectively. The central characteristic of each of these figures is her hypersexuality. Mammification demands that women of color be asexual (and thus not a threat to White women) or passively sexual (and thus not a threat to male power). In contrast, the Jezebel, the spicy Latina, the dragon lady, and the squaw evidence aggressive (and therefore deviant) hypersexualities. Moreover, they are usually represented as cunning, dishonest, manipulative, and domineering, much like the biblical character Jezebel.

In the Hebrew canon, Jezebel was a Phoenician princess who married Ahab, the king of Israel. Perhaps the preeminent "bad girl" of the Bible, Jezebel was notorious for her cunning, deceit, and immorality. Under her influence, Scripture notes, Ahab did more evil than any other Israelite king: "Indeed, there was no one like Ahab, who sold himself to do what was evil in the sight of the Lord, urged on by his wife Jezebel" (1 Kgs 21:25). Not content to maintain her cultural worship of Baal as an individual, she led the king, and hence all of Israel, to do the same. Further, she directly challenged the authority of YHWH, killing the Lord's prophets, likely instigating the epic battle between Elijah and the prophets of Baal, and defying the divinely instituted rules surrounding land ownership (1 Kgs 18:4; 18:15–46; 21:1–16). Jezebel remained unrepentant to the point of death; she confronted her death by painting her eyes and adorning her head and taunting Jehu, then king of Israel (2 Kgs 9:30–37).[100]

---

100. Chanequa Walker-Barnes, *Too Heavy a Yoke: Black Women and the Burden of Strength* (Eugene, OR: Cascade, 2014), 83.

It is noteworthy that while the scriptural narrative lacks any mention of Jezebel's sexuality (with the exception of her painted eyes and adorned head), the character has become almost synonymous with sexual deviancy. Within Christian cultural contexts, women are labeled "jezebels" when their sexuality defies social norms. The label has functioned as a form of social control, meant to shame women into conformity with the expectations of true womanhood. Today, the purity subculture within evangelical Christianity exercises this shaming function. "Good" Christian girls celebrate and mark their piety and virginity by attending father-daughter purity balls. Girls pledge to remain abstinent until marriage and fathers promise to protect their daughters' moral and sexual chastity. They seal the covenant with a promise ring, which daughters wear as a reminder of their pledge. The rings serve as a sign (and perhaps warning) to boys who would dare violate the psychologically incestuous covenant between girls and their fathers. They also serve as ever-present markers of shame for girls who break their pledge, a modern-day scarlet letter.

Notably, purity culture has no parallel for boys, and it is a largely White movement. This raises a peculiar dilemma. If "good" Christian White girls and women are expected to remain pure until marriage but "good" Christian White boys and men are permitted to be sexually active, with whom are these boys supposed to engage in premarital sex? The stereotypes that exaggerate and demonize the sexuality of women of color provide the solution to this dilemma. Hypersexualizing women of color renders them perpetually sexually available to, as well as inviolable by, White males. It, in essence, sanctions institutionalized rape. Nowhere is this more evident in US history than in slavery.

> Institutionalized rape, a form of sexual violence whose aim is to dominate or control its female (and male) victims, permeated chattel slavery. Rape served the specific purpose of political and/or economic domination of enslaved African women, and by extension, African Americans as a collectivity. . . . Sexual stereotypes of women of African descent as jezebels not only justified rape, medical experimentation, and unwanted

childbearing inflicted upon Black women but it covered up Black women's protests as well.[101]

Throughout the slaveholding era, antirape laws in the United States did not apply to Black women, particularly those who were enslaved. Enslaved women were considered chattel and not people in their own right; thus, it was not a crime for either a White or Black man to sexually assault a Black woman, unless the attack somehow threatened the economic interests of her owner by limiting her capacity to work or bear children. Collins argues that Black women were even more vulnerable to rape after emancipation: "No longer the property of a *few* White men, African American women became sexually available to *all* White men."[102] Thus, myths about the hypersexuality of women of color have functioned to allow White men to rape them with impunity, providing White men with socially sanctioned outlets for exercising sexual power while also allowing White women to adhere to cultural expectations about purity.

Moreover, the notion of the unrapeability of women of color is inherently linked to myths about the proclivities of men of color (especially Black and Latinx men) toward rape. When Donald Trump, upon announcing his bid for the US presidency on June 15, 2015, characterized Mexican immigrants as rapists, he was invoking the trope of Black and Latinx men as dangerous to White women. The following day, after sitting through a Bible study with African Americans at Emanuel AME Church in Charleston, South Carolina, Dylann Roof pulled out a gun and began shooting, killing nine African American women and men. At Roof's trial, one of the surviving victims testified that when Tywanza Sanders told Roof that he did not have to hurt people, Roof replied, "Y'all are raping our white women. Y'all are taking over the world," before fatally shooting Sanders.[103] While Roof's allegation was made against

---

101. Collins, *Black Sexual Politics*, 58–59.

102. Collins, *Black Sexual Politics*, 65.

103. Kristen McFann, Steve Osunsami, and Emily Shapiro, "Prosecutor: Accused Charleston Church Shooter Dylann Roof Stood Over Victims, Shooting Repeatedly," ABCNews.com, Dec. 7, 2016, http://abcnews.go.com/US/prosecutor-accused-charles ton-church-shooter-dylann-roof-stood/story?id=44031417.

Black men, it was both Black men and women who were punished in his extrajudicial "sentencing."

Many African Americans are well acquainted with the consequences of false allegations of rape against Black men, whether it be through exposure to high-profile cases like those of the Scottsboro Boys and the Central Park Five or through firsthand experience of being falsely accused (or being in close relationship with someone who has been). Such allegations have at times led to the violent destruction of entire African American communities, as in the cases of the Tulsa Massacre of 1921 and the Rosewood Massacre of 1923. Consequently, much of the discussion about race and rape has focused upon such allegations and the resultant implications for the lynching of African American men.

In *Against Our Will*, White feminist author and activist Susan Brownmiller describes a disturbing encounter with an older African American male librarian at the Schomburg Center for Research in Black Culture that demonstrates how single-axis thinking about race and rape fails African American women. When Brownmiller asked the librarian to direct her to any special resources that the library might have about rape and Black women, he corrected her with a look of displeasure, telling her that she must "mean to ask about the lynching of Black men."

> "Sir, I know about that," I answered, "and I know where to find the material when I'm ready for it. At this point I really need to know about the rape of black women."
>
> "I'm sorry, young lady. If you're serious about your subject you need to start with the historic injustice to black men. That must be your approach."
>
> "That has been your approach, sir. I'm interested in the historic injustice to women."
>
> "To black people, rape has meant the lynching of the black man," he said with his voice rising.[104]

104. Susan Brownmiller, *Against Our Will: Men, Women, and Rape* (New York: Ballantine, 1993), 455–56.

Many discussions about rape and race follow much the same script. Consequently, women of color who experience rape are silenced, and White women remain the iconic victim. "The historical experience of Black men has so completely occupied the dominant conceptions of racism and rape that there is little room to squeeze in the experiences of Black women. . . . The fact that Black men have often been falsely accused of raping white women underlies the antiracist defense of Black men accused of rape even when the accuser herself is a Black woman."[105] This patriarchal bias has led many antiracist advocates to overlook the fact that depictions of sexual aggression among both men and women of color have been critical to defending systems of social control such as slavery, mass incarceration, and anti-immigration laws. It is certainly true that accusations of rape have been used as a form of social control and a tool of terror against men of color. But it is also true that actual rape has been (and continues to be) used by men to police, punish, and control the bodies of women of color.

Mammification, Hypersexualization, and Racial Reconciliation

Stereotypical images of women of color—whether mammified or hypersexualized—cast an ominous shadow over the lived reality of African American, Native American, Asian American, and Latinx women. To be a woman of color in predominantly White spaces means grappling with the impact of these images on others' expectations in some way. This happens for all people of color, to some extent. If one of racism's consequences is that people of color must continually appraise whether their experiences are impacted by racism, gendered racism adds another layer for women of color, who must continually gauge whether people view them as mammies or jezebels, that is, as subservient race traitors or as sexual deviants. "I am not your mammy!" is the internal cry of Black women in work and ministry settings where women of color are expected to carry a heavier load than their White and/or male peers, where they are

105. Crenshaw, "Mapping the Margins," 1273.

expected to give sacrificially without recompense, and where they are judged for their failure to perform caregiving duties that are not part of their job description. At the same time, women of color must walk the tightrope of proving their femininity while remaining sufficiently desexualized to avoid being labeled jezebels.

For many women of color, these stereotypes present a no-win situation. If they are guarded and reluctant to share details about their personal lives with White colleagues who have not proven their trustworthiness (or worse, who have proved their untrustworthiness), their failure to live up to mammified expectations may lead to accusations of being unfriendly, difficult, or selfish. At the same time, those who decide to conform to the mammy ideal may be seen as insufficiently dedicated to their "real" work. If they use makeup and jewelry to level the racial-gender playing field or to subvert normative ideas about who is considered beautiful, they may be rendered invisible, invalidated, or chastised as unprofessional and overly sexual. Yet if they eschew makeup and jewelry and wear ankle-length skirts, they may be viewed as uptight, sexually repressed, and provincial.

Always and everywhere, the bodies and behavior of women of color are judged by standards that are neither of their making nor of their choosing, standards that maintain and reinforce White supremacist heteropatriarchy. Meanwhile, those who claim to be ambassadors in God's mission of racial reconciliation remain silent about their oppression. Indeed, with its demand that the oppressed be "in relationship" with their oppressors, the racial reconciliation movement may expose vulnerable women of color to even greater abuse and mistreatment.

Conclusion

If the racial reconciliation movement is to move beyond its complicity with White supremacist heteropatriarchy, it must get intersectional. Drawing on May's aforementioned definition of intersectionality, we clearly can see that an intersectional approach to racial reconciliation that is centered upon the experiences of women of color:

(1) will view identity and systems of oppression as interlaced and inseparable;

(2) will be particularly attentive to gendered racism and racialized sexism, and how those shape issues of sexuality, disability, nationality, and/or class;

(3) will use a nodal approach in which it probes lived experience and examines what is needed to effect change from the position of the interstices, the points where the lived identities and systems of oppression hinge or touch;

(4) will expose how privilege and oppression co-occur to produce both between-group power dynamics (such as those between Whites and people of color) and within-group inequities (such as those between women of color and men of color); and

(5) will be both pragmatic and idealistic, focused upon the racial-gender realities of the here and now and also upon the possibilities of eradicating injustice at the micro- and macro-levels.[106]

Theologically speaking, an intersectional approach to racial reconciliation is prophetic and pastoral, incarnational and eschatological, systemic and practical, sacred and profane.

An intersectional understanding of racial reconciliation rejects outright the lie that reconciliation is about relationship. It instead centers upon dismantling White supremacy and White power structures. This understanding requires far more of White people than making a Black friend; indeed, it requires more of White people than it does people of color. But can the people who embody the very construct—whiteness—responsible for racism really be expected to dismantle it? Or does White racial identity pose an insurmountable obstacle to racial justice? I turn my attention to those questions in the next chapter.

106. May, *Pursuing Intersectionality*, 3–5.

Chapter Three

The Unbearable Whiteness of Being

One of the primary issues we must face, especially in this sociopolitical climate, is the need for white people to do the hard work of wrestling with what it really means to be white. . . . The poisonous impact of the narrative of racial difference does not land solely on people of color. The narrative of racial difference has also profoundly affected white people. But unlike people of color, most white people remain completely unaware of the ways this narrative has affected their sense of identity.

Brenda Salter McNeil,
preface to Daniel Hill, *White Awake:
An Honest Look at What It Means to Be White*

A great shortcoming of the Christian racial reconciliation movement is its failure to fully engage the problem of whiteness. With their symmetrical treatment approach to race relations, many racial reconciliation efforts have advocated a mutual and equal obligations perspective, which assumes that White people and people of color are equally responsible for the sin of racial division. Even antiracist communities increasingly tend to simply dismiss whiteness as an illegitimate racial category. However, as I have explained, just because something is socially constructed does not mean that it is not real or that it is inconsequential. And whiteness is both very real and very consequential. After all, whiteness—what it means, who gets to be part of it, and what advantages it accrues to its bearers—is precisely what global racism is about. Recall that a central claim of this book is that racism is a complex system of power designed to promote and maintain White supremacy, the belief that White cultural values, beliefs, aesthetics, and yes, even people are inherently superior to those of all other people groups. At the heart of racism is the intention of ensuring that people who fit into the category of whiteness receive special advantages over and above all other racial/ethnic groups. In fact, US history is littered with legal cases in which individuals have attempted to argue their way into whiteness. It is ironic, then, that given the centuries of policies designed to protect whiteness, there is so much resistance to naming it. Yet it is impossible to address issues of racism and reconciliation without broaching the issue of whiteness.

To be clear: it is true that all racial identities are constructed, but they were not constructed equally. Whiteness was created as a way of determining who got to partake of the benefits of White supremacy. All other racial identities are, more or less, survival strategies of nonwhite people in a White supremacist world. Blackness, for example, was birthed somewhere between the slave dungeons on the West African coast and the auction blocks in the Americas. It was somewhere during that process that my African ancestors realized that the tribal affiliations and enmities that had defined their entire realities no longer mattered. To survive this hostile new world necessitated learning to see former friends, foes, and strangers as one's kinfolk. Every people group that has suffered the brunt of European and North American imperialism has had to shift its self-definition to accommodate White supremacy. Thus, any effort to dismantle racism and White supremacy must always begin by wrestling with, not simply dismissing, the peculiar problem of whiteness. It must interrogate the ways in which White racial identity is intrinsically tied to the system of White supremacy. And it must illuminate the ways in which ordinary White people, including those interested in racial justice and reconciliation, reinforce White supremacy through their everyday embodiment of White cultural norms.

My objective in this chapter, therefore, is to wrestle with the problem of whiteness from my unique vantage point as a pastoral theologian and a licensed psychologist. I will not attempt to provide a history of the construction of whiteness, nor will I spend time trying to prove the existence and impact of "White privilege." Instead, as someone trained in the diagnosis and treatment of mental illness and dysfunctional family systems, I want to explore the notion of whiteness as a sociocultural system, indeed as a condition of moral injury, into which all White Americans—regardless of their particular ethnic heritage or immigration history—are socialized and in which they participate daily in ways that continuously reinforce White supremacy and undermine racial justice.

Slavery and the Making of Whiteness

In addressing whiteness, I am primarily focusing upon racial identity as it is constructed and conceptualized in the United States. I use the term "whiteness" rather than "White privilege" intentionally. The term "White privilege" is often used in ways that imply that it is distinct from one's racial identity, akin to a benefits package that a person can relinquish or control. It is common, for example, to hear White people engaged in antiracism to talk about "giving up," "unlearning," or even "leveraging" their privilege. While there may be some aspects of White privilege that operate in this way, whiteness is not just something that people possess; it is something that possesses them. Whiteness is a sociocultural identity bestowed (or imposed) upon individuals and ethnocultural groups based upon their presumed distance from blackness and their assumed access to the racial power matrix of domination (see chapter 1). Whiteness is a matter of heritage in that various ethnocultural groups (i.e., Germans, Italians, Irish, Jews, etc.) have been formally or informally inscribed into the category at varying points in US history. Whiteness is only partially determined by self-identification; it is mainly a matter of perception. Thus, an individual who looks (and perhaps also acts) White may be considered White, regardless of whether that person overtly identifies as such; further, she or he will have access to the privileges and advantages that are accorded by White supremacy.

The Unbearable Whiteness of Being

To Be White and Free

Historically, the primary advantage of whiteness was freedom. In *The History of White People*, Nell Painter effectively demonstrates that while the concept of whiteness is relatively new in human history, it has antecedents in antiquity, specifically in the ways that Greek philosophers, historians, and scientists categorized the differing European races. As far back as four hundred years before the Christian era, figures such as Herodotous and Hippocrates were making distinctions between the Scythians (an amorphous area that included northeastern Europe), Greeks, and Asians (not the continent we know today, but the area around Persia and Babylonia) based upon categories such as purity (bodily cleanness and sexual chastity), temperament, warfare, physique, and intelligence. (Of course, they consistently judged Greek aesthetics and norms as superior.)[1] Throughout most of history, people believed that there were multiple White "races," in contrast to our modern-day tendency to collapse all descendants of western Europeans into a single White race.[2] The system of race-based chattel slavery changed all that.

When the transatlantic slave trade began in the early sixteenth century, slavery was neither a new human invention nor a uniquely European one. Some version of treating people as property to be bought or sold has existed throughout human history. For example, European slavery was widespread from the fifth through eleventh centuries, largely as a result of Viking raids on northern Europe and Russia. That those enslaved were White was considered unremarkable. However, during this period a characterization of slaves as morally and physically inferior to free people begins to emerge. Anglo-Saxon and Norse literature from the period describes slaves as ugly, dirty people who were prone to drunkenness, physical and sexual aggression, and laziness.[3] The early American colonizers initially tried exploiting two other sources for unpaid labor: White in-

1. Nell Irvin Painter, *The History of White People* (New York: Norton, 2010), 1–12.

2. Painter, *The History of White People*, ix.

3. Painter, *The History of White People*, 34–35.

dentured servants and Indigenous Native Americans. Both groups proved unsustainable over the long term in a rapidly developing system of hyper-capitalism that sought to minimize labor costs and maximize profit as much as possible. White indentured servants, who accounted for 50 to 67 percent of immigrants to America during the eighteenth century, could still claim some rights as citizens of England or other European countries, and after their period of service ended, they usually sought paid employment under better conditions.[4] Indigenous peoples were familiar with the territory and, at first opportunity, could escape and blend in with free Native American communities. Turning to Africa for a permanently enslaved labor pool helped solve both problems. Since enslaved Africans were not citizens of European nations, they had no legal rights that had to be respected. Thus, not only could they be enslaved for life, but also their status was automatically transferred to each descendant generation. But perhaps more important for the sustainability of the system, their skin color made them highly identifiable, which in turn made escape exceedingly difficult.

Notably, from the initial contact with the Indigenous peoples of America and Africa until the mid-1600s, the English most frequently used the term "Christian" to identify their racial-ethnic identity and to differentiate themselves from the "heathen" and "savage" Natives and Africans. It was not until after 1680, following the displacement and genocide of Indigenous Americans and the institutionalization of African enslavement, that the use of the term "White" commenced.[5] It was the need to justify and sustain the economy of slavery that led to the formalization of racial categories and the differential application of the four pillars of White supremacy: commodification, extermination, demonization, and indoctrination. African peoples were subjected to the logic of commodification, changing their legal status from human beings to chattel. Indeed, the default status of Black people was enslaved or enslaveable; hence, free papers were required on demand of any Black person claiming to be free, or that person

---

4. Painter, *The History of White People*, 42.
5. Jennifer Harvey, *Dear White Christians: For Those Still Longing for Racial Reconciliation* (Grand Rapids: Eerdmans, 2014), 51.

could be taken to the auction block. Native peoples were targeted for extermination, as the British determined they were "not able to enslave the Indians, and not able to live with them."[6] The category of whiteness—previously reserved for Anglo-Saxon regions such as Britain and Scandinavia—underwent one of several periods of enlargement as European immigrant groups that had formerly been demonized were indoctrinated into Anglo-Saxon cultural standards, values, and beliefs.[7] By the end of the nineteenth century, US racial ideology generally used what Painter calls a "four and a half part scheme." This scheme actually had four levels: (1) Anglo-Saxons; (2) German and Irish Catholics, who were moving toward the top strata; (3) other Europeans; and (4) African Americans. Asians and Native Americans were omitted from the racial stratification.[8] By the turn of the twentieth century, Catholic Irish and Germans were "old" immigrants who had been fully absorbed into whiteness; the new immigrant classes were Hungarians, Russian and Polish Jews, and Italians.[9] Eventually, all Europeans were subsumed into whiteness, as were people from the Middle East.

As a socially constructed category, whiteness has always been in a constant state of flux as its boundaries expanded to include new immigrant groups or contracted to exclude those who had previously been included. One constant, however, has been the relationship between the racial hierarchy and freedom. To be White in America was—and still is—at the top of the racial hierarchy and thus automatically eligible for the full rights and benefits of American citizenship. As Painter notes, "A notion of freedom lies at the core of the American idea of whiteness. Accordingly, the concept of slavery—at any time in any society—calls up racial difference, carving a permanent chasm of race between the free and the enslaved."[10] In other words, to be White was, and is still, to be free. In contrast, to be any other race is to have one's rights and freedoms diminished. To be

6. Howard Zinn, *A People's History of the United States* (New York: HarperCollins, 2003), 13.

7. Painter, *The History of White People*, 201–2.

8. Painter, *The History of White People*, 256.

9. Painter, *The History of White People*, 206.

10. Painter, *The History of White People*, 34.

Black, in particular, is to be at the bottom of the racial hierarchy and to have one's very humanity called into question. This is the essence of White supremacy and White racial ideology.

Slaveholding Religion

Slavery, and later lynching and Jim Crow segregation, did more than to set up a hierarchy of racial labels; it profoundly shaped the cultures and identities of the groups within it. Considerable attention has been given to the historical and contemporary impact of slavery on African Americans, especially as it pertains to family formation and child-rearing, educational and economic inequalities, confinement in the criminal justice system, and political disenfranchisement. Black religious scholars have astutely analyzed how the experiences of slavery and dehumanization shaped African American Christianity in nearly every aspect, including biblical interpretation, preaching, hymnody, worship, and social ethics. Little attention, however, has been given to the impact of slavery upon the cultures, identities, and functioning of White people. The underlying assumption has been that White people—including White Christianity—have remained more or less unaffected by their participation in or compliance with a system that brutalized millions of Africans. This assumption has remained intact despite the fact that the construction of whiteness itself was dependent upon slavery and other White supremacist institutions. As Harvey states:

> "Whiteness" emerged as people of European descent flourished by largely complying with supremacist social processes and reaping the wealth that came from that compliance. . . . Although a majority of whites on this land base were not slaveholders themselves, all occupied Native land, and most refused to disrupt the institution of slavery. Even those whose economic interests were harmed by the existence of slavery benefited from it in various ways. Moreover, slavery could not have functioned were not most whites—rich or poor, third generation or new immigrant—willing to allow it to continue.

> As long as the system could rely on [white] people to choose
> not to be a safe haven when African peoples ran away, and
> to choose to serve as overseers, to mill the cotton that moved
> from South to North, to rely on wages earned in that produc-
> tion to feed their families, and on a myriad of other similar
> behaviors that ensured slavery functioned, it did not matter
> that most whites did not themselves own slaves.[11]

The pre–Civil War American economy was dependent upon slavery, and the maintenance of slavery depended upon White acquiescence. How is it, then, that many (if not most) White people consider themselves to be unaffected by any lingering consequences of slavery? How is it that White theologians and ethicists have not taken up this question as *the* existential conundrum facing White Americans, particularly White Christians?

White supremacy, in all its variations, is an evil ideology that relies upon brute power to enforce and maintain itself. Violence is inherent in the system: in the land theft, slaughter, and forced displacement of Native Americans, and in the kidnapping, enslavement, and lynching of African peoples and their descendants. It was not merely that the system used its structural power to create laws classifying African people as property. It also employed its disciplinary power to brutally enforce those laws. Chains, whips, beatings, rape, cutting off limbs of runaways, threatened and actual separation from family, armed slave patrols and their hunting dogs: the system used all of these mechanisms to terrorize enslaved Africans into submission *on a daily basis*. This real and threatened violence was in addition to the brutality of the work that enslaved Africans did. But make no mistake: living with quotidian violence did not render it any less evil, either for its Black victims or its White perpetrators. A poignant moment in Katrina Browne's documentary, *Traces of the Trade*, demonstrates this point.[12] Descendants of the New England DeWolf family, the largest slave-trading

---

11. Harvey, *Dear White Christians*, 54.

12. *Traces of the Trade: A Story from the Deep North*, produced and directed by Katrina Browne (Washington, DC: Ebb Pod Productions, 2008), DVD, 86 min.

family in US history, Browne and nine of her family members undertake a three-week journey retracing the Triangle Trade from their ancestral Rhode Island hometown to the slave forts in Ghana to a former family sugar plantation in Cuba. After visiting Elmina Castle in Ghana, one of the slave forts where their ancestor James DeWolf may have negotiated for captured Africans, Tom DeWolf says: "We've talked when we were in Bristol and when we were in Providence and we're listening to historians and scholars. We've heard people talk about, 'You know, you've got to place it in the context of the times. And this is the way things were done. And this is how, you know, life was.' And I sit in that dungeon and I say bullshit. It was an evil thing and they knew it was an evil thing and they did it anyway." Wendell Berry echoes this sentiment in *The Hidden Wound* when he confesses that chattel slavery was an inherently violent system: "For if there was any kindness in slavery it was dependent on the docility of the slaves; any slave who was *unwilling* to be a slave broke through the myth of paternalism and benevolence, and brought down on himself the violence inherent in the system."[13] Berry, moreover, acknowledges that the violence and evil of the system was so readily apparent that those involved in it had to know their own complicity. "In spite of the self-defensive myth of benevolence, it was impossible for the slave owner to secure any limit to the depth or the extent of his complicity; as soon as he found it necessary to deal with the slave as property he was in as deep as he could go."[14]

The church, unfortunately, was neither an innocent bystander nor a conscientious objector to the horrors of White supremacy. If anything, the church was the prime wielder of the slaveholding economy's hegemonic power, cultivating and disseminating the theology that undergirded White supremacy. In 1493, the Catholic Church, after all, developed and disseminated the ideology that came to be known as the Doctrine of Discovery, which declared that since all of the earth belonged to God, and by extension to the Pope, any land that was not inhabited by Christians could be discovered, claimed,

13. Wendell Berry, *The Hidden Wound* (New York: North Point Press, 1989), 6.
14. Berry, *The Hidden Wound*, 7.

and exploited by Christian explorers.[15] In *The Christian Imagination,* Willie Jennings argues that the construction of race was an essentially theological enterprise.

> Europeans enacted racial agency as a theologically articulated way of understanding their bodies in relation to new spaces and new peoples and to their new power over those spaces and peoples. Before this agency would yield the "idea of race," "the scientific concept of race," "the social principle of race," or even a fully formed "racial optic" on the world, it was a theological form—an inverted, distorted vision of creation that reduced theological anthropology to commodified bodies. In this inversion, whiteness replaced the earth as the signifier of identities.[16]

The US church's participation in slavery is writ large. While there were notable exceptions—denominations (such as the Quaker church) and pastors who consistently opposed slavery—initial Christian opposition to slavery quickly gave way to silent acceptance, at best, and rabid support, at worst. In *The Cross and the Lynching Tree,* James Cone observes, "White ministers sometimes served as mob leaders, blessing lynchings, or citing the stories of Ham and Cain to justify white supremacy as a divine right."[17] Writings and testimonies from formerly enslaved Blacks reveal how White pastors preached in ways that encouraged them to obey their masters. Peter Randolph, who became a licensed Baptist minister after being emancipated upon the death of his master in 1847, describes:

> The prominent preaching to the slaves was, " 'Servants, obey your masters.' Do not *steal* or *lie,* for this is very wrong. Such conduct is sinning against the Holy Ghost, *and is base ingrat-*

---

15. Pope Alexander VI, "Demarcation Bull Granting Spain Possession of Lands Discovered by Columbus," May 4, 1493, https://www.gilderlehrman.org/sites/default /files/inline-pdfs/T-04093.pdf.

16. Willie James Jennings, *The Christian Imagination: Theology and the Origins of Race* (New Haven: Yale University Press, 2010), 58.

17. James H. Cone, *The Cross and the Lynching Tree,* reprint ed. (Maryknoll, NY: Orbis Books, 2013), 76.

itude to your kind masters, who feed, clothe, and protect you." . . .
Shame! Shame! to take upon yourselves the name of Christ,
with all that blackness of heart. I should think, when making
such statements, the slave-holders would feel the rebuke of
the Apostle, and fall down and be carried out from the face of
day, as were Ananias and Sapphira, when they betrayed the
trust committed to them, or refused to bear true testimony in
regard to that trust.[18]

Frederick Douglass, moreover, described southern religion as:

a mere covering for the most horrid crimes,—a justifier of the
most appalling barbarity,—a sanctifier of the most hateful
frauds,—and a dark shelter under, which the darkest, foul-
est, grossest, and most infernal deeds of slaveholders find the
strongest protection. Were I to be again reduced to the chains
of slavery, next to that enslavement, I should regard being the
slave of a religious master the greatest calamity that could be-
fall me. For of all slaveholders with whom I have ever met,
religious slaveholders are the worst. I have ever found them the
meanest and basest, the most cruel and cowardly, of all others.[19]

Thus, as James Cone argued in *The Cross and the Lynching Tree*,
the failure to grapple with White supremacy, including its past and
contemporary expressions, is at the heart of the failure of White
Christianity. Christian seminaries continue to replicate this failure
through their teaching. The idea that "Whites could claim a Christian identity without feeling the need to oppose slavery, segregation,
and lynching as a contradiction of the gospel for America" ought
to astound modern Christians and send them running back to the

18. Peter Randolph, "Plantation Churches: Visible and Invisible," in *African
American Religious History*, 2nd ed., ed. Milton C. Sernett (Durham, NC: Duke University Press, 1999), 64.

19. Frederick Douglass, "Slaveholding Religion and the Christianity of Christ,"
in *African American Religious History*, 2nd ed., ed. Milton C. Sernett (Durham, NC:
Duke University Press, 1999), 103.

drawing board to rethink White theology.[20] But White Christians have not, in large measure, grappled with the ways in which slavery has shaped the identity and cultures of White people in ways that continue to present themselves today. They have not wrestled with the moral injuriousness of slavery.

Whiteness as Moral Injury

Over the past two decades, there has been growing scholarly and clinical attentiveness to the psychospiritual impact of participating in the subjugation, abuse, and murder of other human beings. Even when these acts come as a result of one's adherence to social norms or duty to governmental authorities, they violate core beliefs about what it means to be human, to be moral, and to be Christian. To return to Tom DeWolf's statement in *Traces of the Trade*, the question that White Americans must ask themselves is: *What does it mean to know that a system is evil and to participate in it anyway?* Moral injury, further, asks the question: *How does it affect a person to participate in a system that that person knows or believes to be evil?*

The term "moral injury" has emerged to describe this phenomenon, which can be distinct from posttraumatic stress. The concept of moral injury emerged through awareness of the moral burdens of military war veterans. In the context of war, soldiers are required to engage in acts that often go against their moral compasses, the internalized rules and societal expectations about what constitutes right and wrong. For Christians and most other religious people, this includes some version of the commandment "Thou shalt not kill." As part of their combat duties, soldiers may kill other people, or participate in other acts that would be considered criminal, unethical, or immoral if committed in the routine course of civilian life. Historically, the expectation was that, as long as these acts were justified and in accordance with military orders, soldiers would be able to "leave it on the battlefield," in essence, be able to reckon with their actions as the consequences of war conditions and to be unaffected by them.

20. Cone, *The Cross and the Lynching Tree*, 159.

Since the Persian Gulf War in the mid-1990s, however, therapists and other professionals working with combat veterans have recognized that some individuals returning from war are deeply conflicted about their actions on the battlefield and unable to integrate their wartime experience with post-war life. Some even experienced some of the hallmark symptoms associated with a trauma diagnosis, including avoidance behaviors, re-experiencing the event, and problems with mood and cognition. In many cases, however, a diagnosis of posttraumatic stress disorder (PTSD) was inappropriate because the triggering event did not meet the clinically accepted definition of a trauma, which is an event in which a person's own life is harmed or threatened. To be sure, combat also routinely exposes soldiers to these sorts of events, and many veterans struggle with PTSD. But therapists were struggling to name the experiences in which soldiers were the perpetrators, rather than the victims, of harm against other people.

A term originally used by Jonathan Shay in 2002, "moral injury" occurs when three conditions are met: (1) "a betrayal of what's right" (2) "by someone who holds legitimate authority" (3) "in a high stakes situation."[21] Others have expanded Shay's definition to encompass a person's response to her or his own participation in acts that violate the conscience. Pastoral theologian Larry Kent Graham has defined moral injury more broadly "as the failure to live in accordance with our deepest moral aspirations and as the diminishment that comes from our own actions as well as the actions of those against us."[22] In other words, moral injury consists of how we are impacted when our actions violate our beliefs about what it means to be a good person. Morally injurious behaviors can involve acts of commission (i.e., doing the wrong thing), acts of omission (i.e., failing to do the right thing), or actions that lead to unintentional harm upon others.[23] They may be discrete, onetime events or ongoing situations.

21. Jonathan Shay, "Moral Injury," *Intertexts* 16, no. 1 (2012): 59. Shay initially used the term in his 2002 book, *Odysseus in America*.

22. Larry Kent Graham, *Moral Injury: Restoring Wounded Souls* (Nashville: Abingdon, 2017), 24.

23. Graham, *Moral Injury*, 27.

Graham's definition of moral injury has broader applicability to situations of moral dissonance, that is, situations that call people to behave, think, and feel in ways that run counter to their moral beliefs, ethics, and values. This, I believe, would include the US system of chattel slavery. Slavery, in all its forms, is a crime against humanity. As South African psychologist and Truth and Reconciliation Commission member Pumla Gobodo-Madikizela notes:

> Like sin, crime that is a gross violation of human rights almost always hides its true nature from its own self. It is by its very nature delusional: perpetrators of human rights violations redefine morality and start believing that they can commit systematic murder and other atrocities "for the greater good." The distance between evil and sickness is not that great. The evil component of crimes against humanity is the moral failing. The sickness aspect is the defect in perspective, the distortion in mental processing that both precedes the evil and is intensified by it.[24]

In other words, the moral injuriousness of slavery is not merely that to participate in, acquiesce to, or condone it was to commit a moral failing. Rather, it was that committing such a moral failing in the first place required one to distort one's cognitive and moral processing, one's "Christian imagination," as Jennings has argued. Further, the very act of participation intensified the distortion that enabled it to begin with. At its most basic level, slavery was enabled by the beliefs that White people were superior to all other peoples, that Black people were inferior to all others, and that human beings could be treated as property to be exploited, bought, and sold. Endorsing and acting upon these beliefs further intensified them; it also opened the door for committing countless other moral failings in order to sustain the original sin of enslavement. In the midst of this vicious cycle, the entire cognitive structure of White Americans was distorted.

---

24. Pumla Gobodo-Madikizela, *A Human Being Died That Night: A South African Woman Confronts the Legacy of Apartheid* (New York: Houghton Mifflin, 2003), 58–59.

At the heart of whiteness, then, is a great moral injury. The justification and maintenance of a slave economy required the construction and defense of an elaborate cultural system. Literally everything—laws, religious beliefs and practices, educational systems—had to be carefully organized in order to maintain a brutal and utterly unnatural system. This included the careful cultivation of the White psyche so that White people could accept the brutality with which they were surrounded and in which they participated on a regular basis. In other words, to accept what was going on around them, White people had to be formed in a very particular way, that is, they had to be enculturated into whiteness. This enculturation did not end post–Civil War; rather, it continued in some capacity through the dismantling of legalized segregation and racial discrimination in the 1960s and 1970s. With the rise of color-blind racial ideology, many people stopped using overtly racial language, but the culture into which they were assimilated remained the same in every other way. After all, at no point in the history of this country have White people on a societal level asked the questions, "Who have we become? How do we need to transform ourselves and our culture?"

A few authors have attempted to name the impact of racism upon the collective identity and personality of White people. Wendell Berry, for example, states:

> If white people have suffered less obviously from racism than black people, they have nevertheless suffered greatly; the cost has been greater perhaps than we can yet know. If the white man has inflicted the wound of racism upon black men, the cost has been that he would receive the mirror image of that wound into himself. As the master, or as a member of the dominant race, he has felt little compulsion to acknowledge it or speak of it; the more painful it has grown the more deeply he has hidden it within himself. But the wound is there, and it is a profound disorder, as great a damage in his mind as it is in his society.[25]

25. Berry, *The Hidden Wound*, 3–4.

Berry shares that while he has long known that both sides of his family were slaveholders and he has felt a sense of personal connection to this historical scandal, it has taken considerable time and effort "to finally realize that in owning slaves my ancestors assumed limitations and implicated themselves in troubles that have lived on to afflict me."[26]

In *White Awake*, Pastor Daniel Hill uses the language of *sickness* to characterize the condition of white America:

> Once you realize you're sick, you stop trying to act healthy. And you go on the search for the cure. When you discover that the cure was already searching for you, an explosion of gratitude makes sense. That's why I so regularly and comfortably repent for the sins of white Christians—both for mine and for the sins of my community. It isn't because I think I'm better than everybody else or that I'm trying to prove that some bad white Christians out there need to be chastised. No, I repent all the time because I believe I'm surrounded by the sickness of racism. I see the sickness in the ideology of white supremacy and have no doubt that it has infected me. I see the sickness in the narrative of racial difference and have no doubt it has infected me. I see the sickness of systemic racism and have no doubt that I contribute to it in ways I'm not aware of. I am surrounded by sickness, and I *am* sick. I am in need of the great Physician. It's the only hope I have to be healthy.[27]

To say that the souls and psyches of White Americans are afflicted with moral injury is not to cast them as victims of trauma. Indeed, I adamantly reject the racial reconciliation movement's increasing appropriation of trauma language to categorize the effects of racism upon White identity. Even scholars who conceptualize moral injury as a form of trauma are careful to distinguish it from PTSD. Jinkerson, for example, defines moral injury as "a particular

26. Berry, *The Hidden Wound*, 6.
27. Daniel Hill, *White Awake: An Honest Look at What It Means to Be White* (Downers Grove, IL: InterVarsity Press, 2017), 139.

type of psychological trauma characterized by intense guilt, shame, and spiritual crisis, which can develop when one violates his or her moral beliefs, is betrayed, or witnesses trusted individuals committing atrocities."[28] However, even while using the word "trauma" in his definition, he is clear to note that the two concepts are distinct both in etiology and symptomatology. As defined in the *Diagnostic and Statistical Manual of Mental Disorders (DSM-5)*, the precipitating event for PTSD is "exposure to a traumatic event, where trauma is defined as a perceived threat to self or others, sexual violence, or witnessing harmful acts." Moral injury, in contrast, "develops through a moral conflict in which one's actions, or the actions of one's peers or leaders, are demonstrably inconsistent with one's moral code."[29] Further, while there are several similarities in the clinical presentation of moral injury and PTSD, there are some key symptomological differences. Namely, moral injury does not typically involve physiological hyperarousal, the conditioned anxiety response that is associated with experiencing a threat to one's life. In contrast, PTSD does not necessarily involve guilt and shame, which are predominant in moral injury.[30] Consequently, Brock and Lettini argue that, whereas trauma is a "fear-victim reaction to danger," moral injury is a shame-perpetrator reaction.[31] Moral injury and PTSD can co-occur, but it also possible to have one without the other.[32]

Ultimately, I reject the language of trauma to characterize the condition of White racial identity because to use such language would be to use the symmetrical treatment approach, in essence, to argue that White and Black people are similarly and perhaps equally impacted by the ongoing legacy of slavery. I agree with Shannon Sullivan, who is careful to note that understanding racism's harm upon White people is not "a reason to feel sorry for white people or to view them as 'victims' of white domination, as if white domination harmed

28. Jeremy D. Jinkerson, "Defining and Assessing Moral Injury: A Syndrome Perspective," *Traumatology* 22, no. 2 (2016): 122.

29. Jinkerson, "Defining and Assessing Moral Injury," 125.

30. Jinkerson, "Defining and Assessing Moral Injury," 125.

31. Rita Nakashima Brock and Gabriella Lettini, *Soul Repair: Recovering from Moral Injury after War* (Boston: Beacon Press, 2012), xiii.

32. Brock and Lettini, *Soul Repair*, xiii.

and/or benefited everyone equally. To recognize the spiritual damage done to white people by white racism is instead to acknowledge that one of the messes of white racism for which white people need to take responsibility is white people themselves."[33] Taking responsibility for the way in which White culture and White racial identity have been formed and distorted ought to be the primary work of White Christians who claim to desire racial reconciliation and racial justice. Instead, the prevailing strategies of White Christians have been to diminish the horrors of slavery, to ignore the involvement of the church and its leaders, to demonize and distance themselves from their White slaveholding ancestors, or to resist being labeled "White" altogether.

Resisting Whiteness

Over the past two decades, I have had the opportunity to teach about issues of race, racism, and cultural diversity in a wide range of academic settings. But whether I am teaching in a clinical psychology doctoral program at a Research 1 public university, an undergraduate gender studies course at one of the "southern Ivies," or a masters-level theology course at a Baptist seminary, one experience remains constant: the reluctance, and in many cases the outright refusal, of White American students to identify as White. More often than not, it is a passive resistance. White students simply let the matter of their racial identities go unmentioned even in class activities that require its identification. When the students in my "Cultural Intelligence" course present their cultural autobiographies, the vast majority of my White students omit mentioning their race—even in a passing way—as they describe the multiple components of their cultural identities. They will name gender identity, sexual orientation, and often nationality, but rarely race, even though the assignment guidelines explicitly call for it. In contrast, none of my Black students have ever neglected to mention their racial identity, not even the African

---

33. Shannon Sullivan, *Good White People: The Problem with Middle-Class White Anti-Racism* (Albany, NY: SUNY Press, 2014), 13.

and Afro-Caribbean students hailing from predominantly Black countries where race is a less prominent social category.

In some cases, the resistance is more pronounced. Every other year, I teach a course entitled Christian Formation for Racial Reconciliation. The course, which is spread over two semesters, requires students to grapple deeply with the relationship between their own histories and the complex realities of structural racism before we begin to broach the discussion of what justice and reconciliation might look like. It generally takes a full semester for students to understand the complexities of racism. It usually also takes about that much time for my White students to recognize their whiteness and to confess how it benefits them in a White supremacist society. Only when we reach that point will I allow the class to begin to discuss the concept of reconciliation.

A few months into the course, after students have adjusted to having hard, honest conversations about race, I conduct an exercise that I adapted from Harvey's *Dear White Christians*.[34] I divide the students into small groups based upon their racial/ethnic identity. In my context, that usually ends up being White and Black. I give each group the same task: identify five distinct and positive characteristics that they associate with their racial identity. The characteristics must be those they could wholeheartedly celebrate, not negative traits or those associated with unjust privilege or dominance. The Black students—who include African-, Caribbean-, and US-born Blacks—quickly and easily generate long lists of positive features such as "faith," "creative," "resilience," "survivors," and "making a way out of no way." The White students, in contrast, have considerable difficulty with this exercise. They spend a great deal of time critiquing the exercise itself, often asking me if they can modify the instructions.

Student: "Can we modify the instructions?"

Me: "No. Stick to the directions."

34. Harvey, *Dear White Christians*, 43–45. The experience that I describe here is consistent with Harvey's description of her experience in using this exercise with White students.

Student: "We can't do this exercise because whiteness is not really a racial identity. It's a social construct."

Me: "So is blackness. Stick to the directions."

Student: "I never really grew up thinking of myself as White. I'm just American."

Me: "There's a lot of privilege in who gets to be considered 'just American.'"

Student: "What we're trying to say is that nobody is really White. That's a socially constructed identity, not a real identity like being Scottish or British or German or Irish or Italian, or something like that."

Me: "National identities are also socially constructed. Nations and their boundaries exist because humans say that they do."

Student: "But Europe is a huge continent with a lot of diverse cultures, whereas Africa is . . . Africa."

Me: "Africa is considerably larger geographically than Europe, and it's every bit as diverse. Most Africans probably don't think of themselves primarily as Africans. They think of themselves as Igbo or Xhosa or Massai or Yoruba or whatever their tribal identities are. Then they probably think of themselves in terms of their national identities. The term 'African' usually isn't very meaningful until someone leaves Africa."

Eventually, the students acquiesce, recognizing that I will not allow them to escape the assignment's demands. They manage to identify a few characteristics (e.g., "productive," "conquerors," "wealthy," and "powerful") that they associate with White culture, even as they admit that many of those are tied to histories of White supremacy.

What is striking about their resistance to and difficulty in doing the exercise is that, while whiteness is invisible and undetectable to those who possess it, to nonwhite people who contend with it, it is palpably oppressive. Merely to exist as a person of color—especially as a woman of color—within a culturally White organizational or relational context requires an incredible amount of labor. The term "code-switching" is often used to describe the cognitive, behavioral, linguistic, and affective shifts that African Americans and other people of color undergo when they transition from spaces dominated by people from their ethnocultural group to spaces that are culturally White, even when those spaces are filled with people from similar socioeconomic classes. Whiteness is real, even if White people have difficulty naming it. The very difficulty of naming whiteness is a marker of White moral injury.

Hallmarks of White Moral Injury

The hallmarks of White moral injury become especially clear when it comes to engaging the issues of race and racism. No matter the audience or the setting, White people tend to react in highly similar ways when the topics of race and racism arise. White antiracist activist and educator Robin DiAngelo confirms this in her book, *White Fragility*. DiAngelo notes that in the early years of her work as a diversity trainer working with primarily White audiences in educational and corporate settings, she was astonished by the anger, defensiveness, and disinterest that White people demonstrated in addressing issues of race.

> The very idea that they would be required to attend a workshop on racism outraged them. They entered the room angry and made that feeling clear to us throughout the day as they slammed their notebooks down on the table, refused to participate in exercises, and argued against any and all points. I couldn't understand their resentment or disinterest in learning more about such a complex social dynamic as racism. These reactions were especially perplexing when there were few or no people of color in their workplace, and they had the opportunity to learn from my cofacilitators of color. I assumed that

in these circumstances, an educational workshop on racism would be appreciated. After all, didn't the lack of diversity indicate a problem or at least suggest that some perspectives were missing? Or that the participants might be undereducated about race because of scant cross-racial interactions? . . .There was both knee-jerk defensiveness about any suggestion that being white had meaning and a refusal to acknowledge any advantage to being white. Many participants claimed white people were now the oppressed group, and they deeply resented anything perceived to be a form of affirmative action. These responses were so predictable—so consistent and reliable—I was able to stop taking the resistance personally, get past my own conflict avoidance, and reflect on what was behind them.[35]

What is particularly striking about DiAngelo's experience is that these workshop participants were attending a training that their companies had paid her to do! My experience in the classroom and at seminars and conferences on racism has been similar. I am frequently dumbstruck by the number of occasions that White students complain about the degree to which I talk about race in classes where the official course description, listed both in the university catalog and on the syllabus, centers upon race. It is not merely that White people become resistant in these settings. It is that the forms of resistance are highly consistent and often evidence a superficiality that belies the intelligence of the people complaining. It is as if the capacity for critical thinking and reflective discussion disappears among many White people when the topic of racism comes up, replaced by tropes involving minimization, denial, blame, and defensiveness: "I don't see race." "Black people are really the racists because they're the ones who talk about it all the time." "We really need to be talking about class." "My family didn't own slaves." "My best friend is Black." "But what about Obama?" And so on and so on.

I contend that these similarities are not merely coincidental; neither are they harmless. Instead, they are culturally inscribed pat-

---

35. Robin DiAngelo, *White Fragility: Why It's So Hard for White People to Talk about Racism* (Boston: Beacon Press, 2018), 2–3.

terns that prevent White people from recognizing, caring about, responding to, and combating racial inequity. They are, in essence, manifestations of the moral injury that White supremacy continues to impact upon the collective and individual personalities of White people. In the following sections, I identify four hallmarks of White moral injury: conformity, trust in authority, selective sight, and egoethnocentrism.

A Culture of Conformity

First, whiteness demands conformity. As I have noted repeatedly, and as other scholars have demonstrated quite convincingly, from the colonial period until today, whiteness has been a key marker of fitness for US citizenship. During the slaveholding era, new arrivals onto the shores of the United States had to prove themselves "not Black" in order to escape being condemned to intergenerational involuntary servitude. Once they passed the enslaveability litmus test, they faced an additional hurdle: that of proving themselves white in order to enjoy the full rights of citizenship. Drawing upon the work of Ian Hack, Omi and Winant describe race as a process of "making up people."[36] "Race is a fundamental organizing principle of social stratification. It has influenced the definition of rights and privileges, the distribution of resources, and the ideologies and practices of subordination and oppression."[37] As European immigrants entered the United States, they underwent a process of racial formation that transformed their sociocultural identities; in other words, they were made White. The process of racial formation was both a macro-level social process and a micro-level individual process.[38] At the macro level, it included leg-

36. Michael Omi and Howard Winant, *Racial Formation in the United States*, 3rd ed. (New York: Routledge, 2015), 105.

37. Omi and Winant, *Racial Formation*, 107.

38. Defining racialization as "the extension of racial meaning to a previously racially unclassified relationship, social practice, or group," Omi and Winant argue that it occurs "in large-scale and small-scale ways, macro- and micro-socially. In large-scale, even world-historical settings, racialization can be observed in the foundation and consolidation of the modern world-system: The conquest and settlement of the

islation that determined who met the qualification of whiteness and what consequent rights they could enjoy. Whites (or specifically, White men) could own land and businesses, become citizens, vote, and self-govern. They could receive land grants, whereby they were given (free of charge) land that had been stolen from Native Americans. Far from being a matter of self-perception, classification as White was often an issue determined through the legal system. For example, the Naturalization Law of 1790 restricted citizenship in the newly forming United States to free White immigrants.[39] While the passage of the Fourteenth Amendment in 1868 expanded citizenship to include people of African descent, both birthright citizenship and naturalization remained limited to Whites and Blacks.[40] When non-white immigrants frequently petitioned the courts to contest their denial of citizenship, they used the argument that they were, in fact, White. Native American, Chinese, Japanese, Indian, Korean, Mexican, Armenian, Syrian, and Filipino petitioners—all of them claimed that they were White.[41] The courts decided the cases based on social knowledge and scientific ideas about who was White.

Western Hemisphere, the development of African slavery, and the rise of abolitionism, all involved profuse and profound extension of racial meanings into new social terrain. In smaller-scale settings as well, "making up people" or racial interpellation also operates as a quotidian form of racialization: Racial profiling, for example, may be understood as a form of racialization. Racial categories, and the meanings attached to them, are often constructed from pre-existing conceptual or discursive elements that have crystallized through the genealogies of competing religious, scientific, and political ideologies and projects. These are so to speak the raw materials of racialization" (Omi and Winant, *Racial Formation*, 111).

39. Omi and Winant, *Racial Formation,* 142.

40. Tonya Golash-Boza, *Race and Racisms: A Critical Approach* (New York: Oxford University Press, 2015), 45–46.

41. Golash-Boza notes that "Between 1878 and 1952, US courts considered fifty-one cases in which a non-citizen contested his denial of citizenship on the basis of his race. In all but one case, the non-citizen claimed that he was in fact white and therefore should be granted citizenship. These petitioners were Native American, Chinese, Hawaiian, Burmese, Japanese, Indian, Syrian, Armenian, Filipino, Korean, Arabian, Mexican, and mixed race. The courts were not consistent in their determinations: one court declared Syrians to be not white, whereas an appeal court ruled that they were. Most of the claims to whiteness were denied with the exception of those of Mexicans (1897), Armenians (1909 and 1925), and Syrians (1910 and 1915)" (Golash-Boza, *Race and Racisms*, 46).

Determined in this way, whiteness became a matter not only of skin color and heritage, but also of conformity to community recognition and racial performance, particularly conformity to White middle-class ideals.[42] As a performative identity, whiteness became "something that [had] to be acted out and constantly reproduced in everyday life."[43] At the microlevel, therefore, European immigrants engaged in the quotidian project of proving themselves White by conforming to White cultural aesthetics, norms, interests, patterns of communication, dietary preferences, and so on. In other words, they proved themselves White by acting White. This required conforming to what Charles W. Mills has termed "the racial contract," that is, the global agreement, spoken and unspoken, between Western nation-states to differentially privilege Whites with respect to nonwhites, allowing the former to exploit the latter's bodies, lands, and resources and to deny them equal socioeconomic opportunity.[44] Moreover, it required conformity to a very specific cultural ideal: that of middle-class, Anglo-Saxon Protestant whiteness. Painter observes that "To be American American [as opposed to hyphenated American] had rapidly come to mean being 'middle class' and therefore white, as in the facile equation of 'white' with 'middle-class.' It was as though to be the one was automatically to be the other."[45]

In essence, White culture is deeply concerned about fitting in both racially and socioeconomically. Failure to conform to the hegemonic ideals, after all, would jeopardize one's racial categorization, possibly putting one on the "wrong" side of the racial contract. The pressure to conform becomes obvious when we consider two terms

42. The US legal system uses four indicators to determine race: physical appearance (or phenotype), ancestry, community recognition, and racial performance. Of course, these are highly malleable criteria that depend as much upon the person applying them as they do upon the object of evaluation (Lauren Sudeall Lucas, "Functionally Suspect: Reconceptualizing 'Race' as a Suspect Classification," *Michigan Journal of Race & Law* 20, no. 2 [Spring 2015]:262).

43. John Clammer, "Performing Ethnicity: Performance, Gender, Body and Belief in the Construction and Signalling of Identity," *Ethnic & Racial Studies* 38, no. 13 (2015): 2159.

44. Charles W. Mills, *The Racial Contract* (Ithaca, NY: Cornell University Press, 2014), 12.

45. Painter, *The History of White People*, 370.

used to label White people who are judged by other Whites as having failed to conform: "White trash" and "race traitors." Poor Whites are labeled "White trash" for having failed to conform to middle-class standards of achievement, success, and productivity; and they are frequently made scapegoats for the racial failings of White Americans broadly.[46] And Whites who are perceived to be too similar or sympathetic to Blacks or other people of color are labeled as traitors to their own kind. In both cases, the message is clear: "real" White people behave as other White people do. They conform.

The pressure to conform makes it very difficult for White Americans, especially White Christians, to engage in discourse related to race and racism. Whites who enter these conversations without critical awareness of their own cultural socialization tend to project their values onto others and to expect that antiracist dialogue will conform to the hallmarks of White middle-class propriety. In *Waking Up White,* Debby Irving identifies these as avoiding conflict; being judgmental, defensive, competitive, and status oriented; valuing formal education over life experience; having a perceived right to comfort or entitlement, a sense of time urgency, and a belief that there is one right way; valuing emotional restraint; and engaging in either/or thinking.[47] To these, I would add adhering to social etiquette and "being nice."

As a matter of course, conformity requires vigilant attention to how one is perceived by other people. After all, conformity is ulti-

---

46. Shannon Sullivan identifies demonizing poor Whites as a specific racial strategy employed by middle-class Whites to deflect attention from their own complicity with racism. "When middle-class white people attempt to draw a sharp line between themselves and lower-class white people, they engage in a process of othering that replicates white slaveholders' attitude toward Black slaves. They also reenact what historian Joel Williamson has called the 'grits thesis,' which is a view of politics and race strongly promoted by white elites in the turn of the century South that blamed racial violence on poor Whites rather than examine racism as an institutional problem. . . . Just as in 1900, contemporary white middle-class people who demonize white trash as intrinsically racist mask the pervasiveness of white racism, including their own role in it. The damnableness of slavery lives on, compulsively repeating itself in the unexamined habits of good white people" (Sullivan, *Good White People*, 81).

47. Debby Irving, *Waking Up White, and Finding Myself in the Story of Race* (Cambridge, MA: Elephant Room Press, 2014), 194.

mately about pleasing other people and making them comfortable. When many Whites enter conversations about race, their concern over being seen as nice, good, and nonracist makes them preoccupied with saying the "wrong thing." In describing the socialization of her middle-class New England family, Irving states, "I had never been socialized to say what I thought or felt. Instead I had been trained to say what I imagined the other person wanted to hear."[48] Consequently, Whites become guarded and refrain from the type of conversational risk-taking, open dialogue, and confrontational truth-telling (I will say more about this in the next chapter) that genuine racial justice and reconciliation efforts require. Irving affirms this when she states:

> Because my main objective was to learn how not to screw up around people of color, my mind was trained away from what I really needed to learn. Had I understood racism as a social system, or explored the way race had shaped my identity, my perspective, my values, and my achievements, I would have made more progress sooner. Instead, I made the mistake of overlaying my cultural values, such as "Say the right thing" and "Be a good person," on a new, markedly different social situation. I now understand that fear of doing or saying something offensive perpetuated my cultural incompetence.[49]

Further, because they have been taught that "productive" dialogue is objective, logical, and non-emotional, Whites quickly become uncomfortable with the high emotional content of antiracist dialogue; indeed, they often view it as actually running counter to progress. Thus, they will rather quickly focus upon critiquing the process of dialogue as too conflictual, too emotional, and too unsafe. The frequent result is that dialogue efforts become stalled, either remaining at the level of superficiality that is comfortable to White participants or breaking off altogether.

48. Irving, *Waking Up White*, 127.
49. Irving, *Waking Up White*, 129.

Trust in the System

The widespread willingness of White Americans to conform to the culture created by White supremacy is no doubt predicated upon a second hallmark of White moral injury: trust in the authority of the social order, especially its legislative, economic, and judicial systems. Trusting in authority is not inherently negative, but uncritical and unwavering trust in a rigged system is. White supremacy means that, more often than not, US structures and systems—and the authorities who govern them—were designed to protect White interests and to maintain White dominance in all areas of society. Thus, White Americans are more likely to trust the system because they have been able to count on the fact that it will work in their favor. Moreover, in the cases where the system does not work in their favor, they could assume that it was due to some factor other than their race. To trust in the system means to trust the myths that the system tells about itself, for example, that the United States is a country that offers equal opportunity for all, a casteless social system, and protection of liberty and personal rights. It means trusting that the system is fair and just; that those who wield power and authority will use it to act in your best interest, and that they will be accountable to you if they do not; and that people get what they deserve. Reflecting upon the advantages that she received as a result of living in a White town with well-resourced parents, Irving states:

> The thing of it is, I didn't just experience tangible benefits like easier-to-get jobs, a home near a vibrant town center, fully stocked classroom, and hassle-free transportation. I received a whole host of intangible benefits. In addition to developing a sense of optimism and confidence, I developed an unshakable faith in the idea that anyone could make it with hard work, in the freedom that comes with choice, and in the thrill that comes with high expectations. And I developed a sense of trust in American institutions and the belief that the future was mine for the taking. My life had been built on more than a diploma, a paycheck, fresh fruit, or medicine when I needed

it; it had been cemented with a sense of access, belonging, and optimism.[50]

Those who trust in the system expect that if you follow the rules, you will succeed; conversely, they believe that bad things happen only to people who do not follow the rules. Achievement and success, then, are predicated upon individual conformity and effort.

Critical to the US narrative of fairness and opportunity is the ideology of the self-made man, "a model of manhood that derives identity entirely from a man's activities in the public sphere, measured by accumulated wealth and status, by geographic and social mobility."[51] The ideology of the self-made man was critical to the formation of the United States as a nation-state. It positioned US masculinity—characterized by independence, control, dominance, heroism, success in the marketplace, and self-acquired (rather than inherited) wealth—over and against that of the genteel (read: feminized) British aristocracy.[52] Though it remains the hegemonic ideal for US masculinity, being self-made has become an important social expectation for women as well as men. It has become such a critical narrative for political candidates that even Donald Trump leveraged it in his 2016 presidential campaign, repeatedly downplaying the wealth that he inherited from his father, Fred Trump, a real-estate investor and one of the richest men in the country in the 1970s. Trump routinely portrayed himself as a business genius who had independently amassed his own fortune.[53] Ideologies such as these have a strong self-protection element, both for the individuals who employ them and for the culture of White supremacy as a whole. Drawing upon sociologist Max Weber, Painter notes that a peculiar feature of privilege is that no one wants to admit that they possess it

50. Irving, *Waking Up White*, 58–59.

51. Michael S. Kimmel, *Manhood in America: A Cultural History*, 2nd ed. (New York: Oxford University Press, 2006), 13.

52. Kimmel, *Manhood in America*, 13–17.

53. Ana Swanson, "The Myth and the Reality of Donald Trump's Business Empire," *The Washington Post*, February 29, 2016, https://www.washingtonpost.com /news/wonk/wp/2016/02/29/the-myth-and-the-reality-of-donald-trumps-business -empire/?noredirect=on&utm_term=.f0bc914e50aa.

or that it is linked to their success. The privileged, in essence, want to be viewed as having a legitimate right to their privilege.[54] The narrative of being self-made, in turn, reinforces the myth that the system works fairly and equitably. It prevents looking beneath the surface of racial inequities to examine the foundation of White supremacy that props them up.

Like conformity, White America's trust in the system and related belief in its own merit pose a frequent roadblock in racial reconciliation. Many Whites in these settings are fine with discussing White supremacy as an abstract principle, or a historical artifact, or even as an ongoing reality in the lives of people of color. But they are highly resistant to examining their own privilege or to the suggestion that any element of their success may be the product of racial privilege. We see this resistance at work in another powerful moment in *Traces of the Trade* when the DeWolf descendants discuss their next steps following their pilgrimage across their ancestral slaveholding journey. Despite the fact that nine of the ten family members are multiple-generation legacy graduates of Ivy League schools (meaning they attended the same school as at least one parent), one member insists that their family's racial and class privilege is unrelated to his attendance at an Ivy League school. "My going to Harvard wasn't about privilege. I earned my way to privilege. . . . I'd have gone to Harvard if I had grown up in a very different family."[55] His denial of privilege is especially striking given the widespread knowledge that legacy students have a massive advantage when they apply, with one study estimating that it is equivalent to 160 points on the SAT.[56] Reflecting on the tension that arose among her family members when the topic of privilege arises, Browne states: "Nothing like having to look at ourselves in the mirror. It's not surprising we're getting nervous about our privilege, how to own up to it, what to do with it. The truth is, none of us inherited money directly from the slave

---

54. Painter, *The History of White People*, 193–94.

55. *Traces of the Trade*.

56. Max Nisen, "Legacies Still Get a Staggeringly Unfair College Admissions Advantage," *Business Insider*, June 5, 2013, https://www.businessinsider.com/legacy-kids-have-an-admissions-advantage-2013-6.

trade. That was squandered long ago. But some in the family do have other inherited wealth: railroad money, cotton money, coal, steel. And money or no money, we've stayed in the elite."[57]

Even when they are willing to acknowledge personal and systemic privilege, White Americans' trust in the system often deeply constrains their capacity to respond to systemic injustice. Their belief that the system is fair and just often means that they see injustice as accidental, temporary, and a product of ignorance, rather than as an intentional, enduring, and willful act. In other words, they believe that racism exists because White people do not know what is going on. Remarkably, even White progressives who are well educated about systemic racism manage to hold on to this rather positive view. Irving, for example, states: "I believe most white people would take a stand against racism if only they knew how, or even imagined they had a role."[58] Belief in the inherent goodness of the system often translates to a resistance to direct action and civil disobedience. After all, if the system is inherently good, then any injustice will naturally resolve over time as people become more aware. It is no coincidence, then, that it has often been moderate or progressive Whites who have levied the harshest criticisms against campaigns of civil disobedience such as Black Lives Matter. Recall that it was the resistance of moderate Christians and Jews who issued the critical statements resulting in Martin Luther King Jr.'s "Letter from a Birmingham Jail." King's letter was a response to two statements published in the *Birmingham News* on January 16, 1963, by prominent White clergymen in Alabama. The first letter, "An Appeal for Law and Order and Common Sense," appealed to "all people of goodwill" in Alabama to peacefully and legally submit to the anticipated court-ordered desegregation of public schools. Three months later, on Good Friday, the group published a second letter, "A Call for Unity," which condemned a planned march by King, Ralph Abernathy, and Fred Shuttlesworth, and appealed to Birmingham's African American citizens to avoid the march and to instead use "proper channels" (i.e., private meetings and the le-

57. Browne, *Traces of the Trade.*
58. Irving, *Waking Up White*, xii.

gal process) to argue for their rights.[59] It made no difference to the White clergymen whether laws were just or unjust, or whether the protest was peaceful or violent; in either case, they believed that the righteous act was to obey them. Fifty years later, Whites supposedly engaged in racial reconciliation are often deeply critical of antiracist strategies that use civil disobedience, often labeling them as self-serving and even inconsistent with the aims of reconciliation.

For example, in an article for *Christianity Today*, Tony Carnes described the work of and tension between two pastors following the April 2001 riots in Cincinnati that resulted from a fatal shooting of a nineteen-year-old Black man by police. The two pastors were Damon Lynch III, a forty-one-year-old African American Baptist, and Phil Heimlich, a forty-nine-year-old White evangelical pastor and conservative city council member. Although both had worked together on racial reconciliation, their responses to the shooting and the riots demonstrated significant differences in their approaches. Lynch, more activist-oriented, went to police headquarters the morning after the shooting and demanded answers. After the riots, he led a series of sit-ins and nonviolent protests. Heimlich, a former city prosecutor, criticized Lynch's behavior as being self-serving and inconsistent with racial reconciliation, arguing that one "cannot be a reconciler at the same time he is engaging in civil disobedience."[60] Ironically, Heimlich considered Dr. Martin Luther King Jr. "a hero and a role model for racial reconciliation."[61]

59. King's letter (Martin Luther King Jr., "Letter from a Birmingham Jail," *The Atlantic*, https://www.theatlantic.com/magazine/archive/2018/02/letter-from -birmingham-jail/552461/) was a response to an initial statement by eleven prominent white clergymen in Alabama ("An Appeal for Law and Order and Common Sense," *Birmingham News,* January 16, 1963). The signatories were broadly ecumenical, including seven senior level officers (bishops, moderators, or regional directors) of Catholic, Methodist, Presbyterian, Episcopal, and Christian churches as well as three Jewish rabbis, a Greek Orthodox priest, and a pastor of a prominent Baptist church. Eight of the eleven (including the six Catholic, Methodist, Presbyterian, and Episcopal bishops/moderators, one rabbi, and the Baptist pastor) signed the second letter ("A Call for Unity," *Birmingham News*, April 12, 1963, https://swap.stanford.edu/20141218230016/http://mlk-kpp01 .stanford.edu/kingweb/popular_requests/frequentdocs/clergy.pdf).

60. Tony Carnes, "Lost Common Cause," *Christianity Today*, July 9, 2001, 16.
61. Carnes, "Lost Common Cause," 16.

The Problem of Selective Sight

During my second year in seminary, I participated in a yearlong racial reconciliation group. For the first few weeks, students were asked to introduce themselves by telling the story of when they first became aware of racism. The assumption was that each of us would be able to identify a discrete event or situation when we recognized that some people were treated unfairly due to their race. For my White classmates, that turned out to be true. Over the next few weeks each of them related some story—often taking place during adolescence or adulthood—when they realized that racism existed. As I listened to each of them, I struggled to find my own story. No matter how far back I went in my history, I could not recall a moment when I was not aware that racism existed.

One of the challenges in antiracist dialogue is the vast difference in awareness of racism that exists between people of color and White people. Conformity to the racial contract requires being silent about its sins. During slavery, to maintain their self-images as good, morally upright Christians, White Americans learned to repress any awareness of the racial evil that surrounded them. They developed a cultural capacity for selective sight that shielded them from knowledge of what was happening (what they were doing) to enslaved Africans while also preserving their sense of moral superiority. Irving refers to this as inattentional blindness but attributes it to her preoccupation with the urgencies of daily life.[62] Berry, in contrast, calls it a "peculiar muteness" and explicitly connects it with the institution of slavery:

---

62. Irving, *Waking Up White*, 69. Irving asks herself, "What was I so busy keeping my eye on that I hadn't noticed my white privilege? Keeping myself and my family fed, getting myself and my kids to where we needed to be on time, making sure there was enough money in the bank, paying the bills on time, keeping in touch with friends and family—these were the things that occupied my attention in a way that allowed the rest of the world and other people's problems to remain background noise" (Irving, *Waking Up White*, 70). This explanation, however, falls short in that people of color are also concerned with and focused upon those things on a day-to-day basis, but that concern does not automatically eliminate their awareness of the reality of racial injustice.

First, consider the moral predicament of the master who sat in church with his slaves, thus attesting his belief in the immortality of the souls of people whose bodies he owned and used. He thus placed his body, if not his mind, at the very crux of the deepest contradiction of his life. How could he presume to own the body of a man whose soul he considered as worthy of salvation as his own? To keep this question from articulating itself in his thoughts and demanding an answer, he had to perfect an empty space in his mind, a silence, between heavenly concerns and earthly concerns, between body and spirit. If there had ever opened a conscious connection between the two claims, if the two sides of his mind had ever touched, it would have been like building a fire in a house full of gunpowder: somewhere down deep in his mind he always knew of the danger, and his nerves were always alert to it.[63]

Moreover, as Berry points out, far from calling attention to this split, the church aided and abetted it.

If a man wanted to remain a preacher he would have to honor that division in the minds of the congregation between earth and heaven, body and soul. His concern obviously had to be with things heavenly; unless he was a saint or a fool he would leave earthly things to the care of those who stood to benefit from them. The moral obligation was cleanly excerpted from the religion. The question of how best to live on the earth, among one's fellow creatures, was permitted to atrophy, and the churches devoted themselves exclusively and obsessively with the question of salvation.[64]

Thus, one of the legacies of slavery in White racial ideology is the widespread use of splitting, a psychological defense mechanism in which people separate the positive and negative aspects of their personalities. Splitting is the answer to the question, "How could

63. Berry, *The Hidden Wound*, 16.
64. Berry, *The Hidden Wound*, 17.

White people consider themselves Christian while engaging in the daily horrors of slavery, especially when those horrors were targeted toward their supposed brothers and sisters in Christ?" Essentially, White Christians learned to separate their personal ethics from their social ethics. In order to preserve their self-images as good people, they had to minimize, repress, and deny their sinfulness—their active participation in racial oppression or silent complicity with it. Further, they had to create theologies and ecclesiologies that supported this minimization, repression, and denial. Thus, Christian identity became a matter of orthodoxy rather than orthopraxy. In other words, believing in God and feeling good about one's personal relationship with God became more critical in defining Christian identity than did acting in a manner consistent with Christian social ethics. Confession was relegated to a private matter that took place in one's personal prayer time with God. Meanwhile, denominational doctrine redefined slavery so that it no longer constituted a sin. Confession in Protestant worship was watered down to liturgies that included general statements of failing to be obedient with little reflection upon and no spoken acknowledgment of one's specific sinfulness.

The cessation of US chattel slavery did not put an end to this. Over time, however, White Americans began to shift not just how they talked about race, but whether they talked about it at all. As late as the 1920s, scientists continued to rely upon hereditary race to explain all manner of human variation and to justify the continued oppression of African Americans.[65] Only after the rise of the Nazi party and the atrocities of the Holocaust was racial science widely rejected. Subsequently, many earlier proponents of racial science began to retract or modify the claims of their previous work, and by the end of World War II, scholarly interest in race had shifted from "proving" the science of race to challenging its ontology and examining the root of racial prejudice.[66] Then, in the 1960s, as the civil rights movement drew widespread visibility to southern racism, many Whites attempted to distance themselves from the image of the "mean racist" by abandoning any mention of race altogether.

65. Painter, *The History of White People*, 311–12.
66. Painter, *The History of White People*, 327–31, 341.

This was especially the case with respect to whiteness. Having thoroughly identified whiteness with White supremacists, many Whites simply stopped thinking of themselves as White.[67] They crafted a color-blind racial ideology that reinforced the idea that noticing, acknowledging, or talking about race was undesirable. Likewise, noticing, acknowledging, or talking about racism was also undesirable.

As Sullivan points out, however, color blindness often coexists with racist worldviews; thus, it is not an effective strategy for combating racial inequality and injustice. "Hiding behind color blindness makes it difficult, if not impossible, to see how white privileged beliefs and habits continue to function in one's life. The result is a strange kind of pride in one's interpersonal cluelessness. . . . White people's epistemic failure is simultaneously spiritual because of the hubristic pride taken in white ignorance, camouflaged as moral innocence and goodness."[68] Indeed, a consequence of color-blind racial ideology is that, because it implies that race is a bad thing, it also implies that those who identify as raced—that is, people of color—are thus morally inferior to those who do not—that is, White people. Thus it reinforces the supremacy of whiteness even as it renders whiteness invisible.[69]

It is not only that selective sight diminishes the capacity of White people to acknowledge racism; it also provides them with distorted information about race, and it constrains the intellectual curiosity that would impel them to seek more complete and accurate information. Irving identifies this in a moment from her childhood when an innocent fascination with Native American culture led her to ask her mother where Native Americans were. Her mother responded by telling her, "They were lovely people . . . who became dangerous when they drank liquor," and then proceeded to tell her a story involving drunken Native Americans slaughtering children.[70] Irving notes that she, most likely like her mother, never questioned the truthfulness of the narrative, simply accepting it as accurate.[71]

---

67. Painter, *The History of White People*, 383.
68. Sullivan, *Good White People*, 86.
69. Sullivan, *Good White People*, 91.
70. Irving, *Waking Up White*, 4.
71. Irving, *Waking Up White*, 4.

"Waking up white has been an unexpected journey that's required me to dig back into childhood memories to recall when, how, and why I developed such distorted ideas about race, racism, and the dominant culture in which I soaked."[72] For Irving, those distortions include the ideas that (1) race, culture, and ethnicity are pertinent to only nonwhite people; (2) race is biologically determined; (3) racism consists of making derogatory comments or engaging in intentionally cruel acts against nonwhite people; and (4) "If the cause of racial inequity were understood, it would be solved by now."[73]

In racial reconciliation, selective sight often means that White people enter antiracist spaces with serious deficiencies in racial knowledge. They often do not understand how the historical construction of whiteness implicates them; they are usually unaware of the material impact that racism has on the lives of people of color in their immediate contexts; and they frequently lack even rudimentary vocabulary to engage in sustained conversation about race. At the same time, however, their sense of superiority often makes them more confident in their own ill-informed opinions than they should be, or it causes them to expect people of color to do the work of teaching them about racism.[74]

Egoethnocentrism and White Fragility

The final hallmark of White moral injury is egoethnocentrism, the tendency to view oneself and one's racial-ethnic group as the

---

72. Irving, *Waking Up White*, xii.

73. Irving, *Waking Up White*, xii.

74. Many authors have described this tendency within antiracist dialogue. Austin Channing Brown, for example, asserts that the myth of White innocence enables White people to believe that people of color have the same perspectives on race that they do, to be unfamiliar with the lexicon and ideology of racism, and to nevertheless be convinced of their rightness about race (Austin Channing Brown, *I'm Still Here: Black Dignity in a World Made for Whiteness* [New York: Convergent Books, 2018], 105–6). Likewise, DiAngelo notes that while most White people have strong opinions about racism, those opinions are often uninformed and ignorant (DiAngelo, *White Fragility*, 8).

moral and cultural center of all things. This is the cornerstone of White supremacy, the notion that White people (and the culture that they produce) are the hegemonic ideal and thus represent the gold standard by which all other peoples and cultures should be adjudicated. White supremacy posits that because White people are the most beautiful and talented, they should be the faces that we see in magazines, on television, and in film; because they are the most intelligent, their books and theories (the "classics") should be the focal point of our educations; because they are the most authoritative, they should be the people in charge of . . . well, everything. White supremacy tells us that what is White is universally right and that any departure from the norm is a deficiency to be remedied. And because the majority of US Whites live, work, and worship in social isolation from people of color, they rarely have the opportunity for the kind of meaningful cross-cultural exchange that might occasion them to question their internalized sense of superiority. What limited cross-cultural engagement they do have (such as on mission trips) occurs in the context of such an enormous power imbalance that it usually affirms, rather than challenges, their cultural comfort.

Many White people engaged in racial reconciliation understand this, at least at a theoretical level. But because whiteness remains unnamed and unseen in their day-to-day lives, they have a difficult time understanding that their culture is, in essence, White culture. They have a hard time recognizing that the capacity to see themselves as "just regular Americans" is itself a sign that the dominant culture has been designed to center them. Daniel Hill affirms this by describing the moment of awakening that occurred when, at the wedding reception for an American Indian friend whose ceremony he had just conducted, he expressed jealousy about his friend having a culture. The friend, in turn, corrected his view, telling Hill that he needed to learn about his own culture, particularly given its domineering impact upon other cultures.[75] It is the classic "fish don't know they're in water" analogy. Being White in America is akin to being a fish that, having lived its entire life in water, is unable to describe water or even to understand that water exists. It cannot

75. Hill, *White Awake*, 4.

imagine "wet" because it has never experienced "dry." Likewise, most White Americans cannot describe "White" because they have never experienced "not White." In fact, White supremacy means that even when they do experience "not White," they think of it as "wrong."

A consequence of egoethnocentrism is that White people often feel extremely uncomfortable when they are racially named, that is, "being seen racially or having to proceed as if [their] race matters."[76] The sense of discomfort is so strong that the authors of *Being White* explain to their anticipated White readership that they use lowercase letters for "White" because most White people are uncomfortable with claiming that label. "In white culture, as you may have observed, it's fairly unusual to call attention to the fact that someone is white. In this book we will use a small *w* for white because that is most comfortable. We don't want the way the word is typed to shout *WHITE* at you."[77] If simply being named as White is discomfiting for White people, then it is not difficult to foresee that the lifelong experience of being centered racially also means that White people have a diminished capacity to deal with racial stress. In fact, DiAngelo posits that White people are generally unable to tolerate even the smallest amount of racial stress. "White equilibrium is a cocoon of racial comfort, centrality, superiority, entitlement, racial apathy, and obliviousness, all rooted in an identity of being good people free of racism. Challenging this cocoon throws off our racial balance. Because being racially off balance is so rare, we have not had to build the capacity to sustain the discomfort. Thus, Whites find these challenges unbearable and want them to stop."[78] Drawing upon DiAngelo's work, Hill notes that "white people tend to confuse comfort with safety. . . . Because our stamina is low and tolerance for racial stress is weak, we often have conversations about racial justice being unsafe."[79]

In antiracist spaces, White Americans tend to do more than label conversations unsafe. Their corresponding emotional and behavioral

---

76. DiAngelo, *White Fragility*, 7.

77. Paula Harris and Doug Schaupp, *Being White: Finding Our Place in a Multiethnic World* (Downers Grove, IL: InterVarsity Press, 2004), 13.

78. DiAngelo, *White Fragility*, 112.

79. Hill, *White Awake,* 90–91.

responses often include anger, fear, guilt, argumentativeness, silence, and withdrawal—in essence, White fragility. Importantly, however, though White fragility results from an incapacity to handle racial stress, it is not a mark of powerlessness. DiAngelo posits, "These responses work to reinstate white equilibrium as they repel the challenge, return our racial comfort, and maintain our dominance within the racial hierarchy. I conceptualize this process as *white fragility*. Though white fragility is triggered by discomfort and anxiety, it is born of superiority and entitlement. White fragility is not weakness per se. In fact, it is a powerful means of white racial control and the protection of white advantage."[80]

One of the ways that Whites protect themselves in racial discourse is by evoking language of violence to portray themselves as victims in need of defense. That is, they describe being "attacked," "slammed," or "blamed." This language works because it draws upon stereotypical images of people of color, especially Black people, as dangerous. It places White people in the role of victim and moral superior while relegating people of color, who have less social power, to that of moral inferior.[81] White women are especially likely to evoke the language of violence. The manifestations of White fragility often vary by gender; men are more likely to evince anger, argumentativeness, and aggression, whereas women are more likely to employ tears and proclamations of fear and helplessness.

White women's tears are especially potent tools in disrupting antiracist discourse. Mamta Accapadi notes that White women's tears take advantage of their "one up/one down" position, that is, their simultaneous wielding of racial power with gender oppression.[82] When antiracist conversation makes White women confront their privilege, they "toggle" their identities, drawing upon long-standing racialized ideas of White women as damsels in distress who need to be rescued from Black violence. White women do not just cry;

80. DiAngelo, *White Fragility*, 2.

81. DiAngelo, *White Fragility*, 109–10.

82. Mamta Motwani Accapadi, "When White Women Cry: How White Women's Tears Oppress Women of Color," *The College Student Affairs Journal* 26, no. 2 (Spring 2007): 210.

they weaponize their tears against Black people and other people of color. And as in eras past when White women's tears and allegations of Black violence provoked White men to murder Black people and destroy Black communities (think Emmett Till, Rosewood, Tulsa), White women's tears have an important effect upon White men.

> White men also get to authorize what constitutes pain and whose pain is legitimate. When white men come to the rescue of white women in cross-racial settings, patriarchy is reinforced as they play savior to our damsel in distress. By legitimating white women as the targets of harm, both white men and women accrue social capital. People of color are abandoned and left to bear witness as the resources meted out to white people actually increase—yet again—on their backs.[83]

Indeed, White fragility as a whole frequently turns the tide of antiracist discourse so that the needs of White people become the central concern. "Whether intended or not, when a white woman cries over some aspect of racism, all the attention immediately goes to her, demanding time, energy, and attention from everyone in the room when they should be focused on ameliorating racism. . . . In a common but particularly subversive move, racism becomes about white distress, white suffering, and white victimization."[84] An unfortunate consequence of this is that conversations about racial reconciliation are frequently structured around White participants' desire for racial safety.[85] This often includes establishing ground rules for dialogue

83. DiAngelo, *White Fragility*, 137. DiAngelo also recognizes that men of color, responding to a similar patriarchal impulse, may feel the need to protect White women's fragility in cross-racial spaces. She cautions, however, that their rescue attempts may also be driven by the specter of the harm that comes to men of color when White women cry. Nevertheless, she notes, these rescue attempts have the impact of driving a wedge between men and women of color (DiAngelo, *White Fragility*, 137).

84. DiAngelo, *White Fragility*, 134.

85. Harvey argues that even when activists, scholars, and laity from nonwhite backgrounds are involved in reconciliation efforts, those efforts often become dictated by White concerns and interests. "Even when reconciliation is nuanced and addresses social power so as to work against privileging white concerns—and even in the rare cases when reconciliation is being worked on together by activists, thinkers, and com-

that focus upon building White participants' sense of safety and trust, discussing race and racism in general terms rather than specifying White supremacy as the cause of racism, and using symmetrical treatment approaches that position racism as a social problem for which all people share similar responsibility.[86]

Yes, All White People

To speak of culture in any sense is to attempt to make broad generalizations about a group comprised of diverse people. Throughout this chapter, I have employed generalized language to paint with a broad brush what I allege to be the hallmarks of White moral injury that remain from the legacy of slavery, lynching, and Jim Crow segregation, and from the ongoing system of White supremacy. Likely a question that arises from readers (at least White readers) is: "But do you mean all White people?" After all, not everyone in the United States who is considered White is wealthy; some are not even the descendants of slaveholders; some of their families arrived in the United States after the end of slavery. In a nutshell, my response to that question is, "Yes, all White people." My argument is that as an identity predicated upon the oppression of nonwhite peoples, the moral injuriousness of whiteness extends to all those who identify (or are identified by others) as White. Different White people and families may be affected differently, but all are affected.

To understand this, imagine living in a frozen tundra, an environment that is so hostile to human flourishing that merely existing takes a Herculean effort. Now, imagine that the tundra has a small patch of highly fertile, mineral rich soil that is not covered by the ice. Six hundred years ago, some explorers from another world— let's call them the Architects—found the patch and decided to settle

---

munities in ways that can be described as truly multiracial—the reconciliation paradigm often succumbs and becomes overly attentive to white concerns at the expense of the concerns and needs of communities of color" (Harvey, *Dear White Christians,* 68).

86. DiAngelo critiques the ground rules and guidelines that frame diversity and antiracist dialogue as being driven by the impulse to "coddle white fragility" (DiAngelo, *White Fragility,* 127).

there. The first thing that they did was to build a huge bonfire using a magical fire starter that had been given to them by the highest officials of the church in their homeland. The fire starter was given to the Architects both as a sign of the church's blessing upon their travels and also as a symbol of its power to those who might dare to challenge their rights to the land. Its magic power was its provision of eternal heat: a person who experienced the warmth of the flames kindled by this fire starter never experienced cold again. While the heat lessened as they move further away from the flames, their body chemistry was changed such that they always retain a comfortable level of warmth. Because of this, the tundra that was hostile to others became a sanctuary for the Architects and their descendants.

Six hundred years later, both the fire starter and the Architects are long gone. But the fire remains and an independent nation (let's call it the Society) has developed around it. The Society is governed by the Potentates, a group of extremely wealthy and politically connected people who are responsible for tending the fire and making sure that it never goes out. The Potentates—many of whom are direct descendants of the Architects—spend most of their time producing the goods that feed the fire, developing legislation to maintain the fire and their access to it, and identifying and neutralizing threats to the Society's social order. They also oversee the Bureau, which regulates the Society's schools, media, healthcare and legal systems, and the corporations. It is the Bureau's job to ensure that everyone in the Society plays a part in keeping it going. For example, everyone in the Society has been educated and socialized by the Bureau's schools, publishers, and news media. Most of the people in the Society work for some part of the Bureau, as well.

At the furthest edge of the Society, the point where the bonfire's magical heat fades away, the Architects constructed a heavily fortified wall, one so tall that its top cannot be seen from the ground. The wall has a few heavily guarded gates. People who are born into the Society can freely traverse the borders, coming and going through the gates as they please. The fire's eternal warmth provides them with some protection even as they venture into the coldest parts of the tundra. Despite this, few citizens of the Society ever leave its borders. There are some people appointed by the church (the same one that provided the magical fire starter) and the Potentates to operate charities and foreign aid missions to the people outside the wall (the Beyonders).

There are the rare few who, having genuinely been gripped by the cries and pleas of those outside the wall, travel beyond the wall to stand in solidarity with the Beyonders. As best they can, they try to use the eternal heat that they have gained from the fire to warm the less fortunate. There are also, unfortunately, people who travel outside the wall to take advantage of the fact that there are few laws protecting the Beyonders from exploitation. The Patrollers who guard the wall are especially prone to brutalizing the Beyonders. The Patrollers themselves are usually from the lowest-ranked families in the Society, those who have lived just inside the wall for generations and are thus not quite as warm as the others. Some Patrollers used to be high ranked, but they committed an act that resulted in their banishment to the edges of society (but never to the Beyond). In either case, the Patrollers tend to be an angry bunch. And while the cause of their anger is the Society, they usually vent their rage at the Beyonders.

No one knows where exactly the Beyonders come from. Some say that they are the descendants of the original inhabitants of the land that the Society now occupies and they were expelled by the Architects. Others say that their ancestors were indentured servants whom the Architects abducted from yet another world and forced to build the wall. The land now occupied by the Beyonders (rather, the land that Society allows them to occupy) is largely incapable of sustaining an independent nation. Most Beyonders have work permits that allow them to travel through the gates for employment, mainly in menial (or sometimes mid-level) work just inside the wall. When they enter the Society gates, they are forced to don special uniforms that identify them as Beyonders. The uniforms have the added feature of being completely heat blocking, preventing the Beyonders from benefiting from the warmth of the bonfire. Occasionally, the church and the Rulers decide that new people can enter the Society. Most of these are immigrants from the homeland who will readily adapt to the Society's cultural rules and norms. Every once in a while, though, one of the Beyonders is granted entry as a reward for hard work on behalf of the Society. This also works as a form of social control because it helps Beyonders think that they, too, can be part of the Society if they just work hard enough.

Most of the people in the Society, however, neither work to maintain the fire nor to guard the wall. They have no idea, perhaps, how the fire started, why it works, or why some people are warmed while others are not. They do not know that their own warmth is actually a result of its magical power. They may have never seen the actual fire; they have only heard about it in their Bureau-created curriculum at school. They do not actually understand the concept called "warm" at all. After all, they have never been not "warm." They know that the Beyonders exist, but the Beyonders they know are those who were admitted entrance to the Society. That in itself is proof that the Society is fair and just and its warmth available to all those who deserve it.

This sounds like something out of a dystopian novel, but living as a nonwhite person in a world is a lot like trying to survive in a frozen tundra without the protection of heat. In this case, it is White racial identity that qualifies one for membership in the privileged group, the group with access to the bonfire. Notice in this analogy that while the system is structured to benefit White people, only a small percentage of them are directly and actively involved in its construction and maintenance. These are the gatekeepers who wield the disciplinary power of racism, which controls who can benefit from the system, rewards those who conform to the system, and punishes those who deviate from it. They create, pass, and enforce the policies that produce and maintain racial inequalities.

Most White people are not in this group. They are not actively trying to subordinate nonwhite peoples. They are just living their lives. This does not mean, however, that they are non-complicit in the racial order. They help to reinforce the system through their adherence to (and failure to question) the hegemonic ideals and ideologies that define what and who is valued, desirable, and deserving. The professors in this society, for example, do this by loading their course syllabi with "the classics," texts written by White men. Those working in mass media contribute by inundating the public with movies and television shows that disproportionately feature White people. Children's ministry leaders play their part by painting murals and using books and other media that routinely depict Jesus as White. And nearly all White people structure their interpersonal relationships around race, including where they live, work, and worship, and whom they befriend. They may not have created the system of White supremacy, but they all are possessed by whiteness and they all possess its benefits.

Conclusion

By now, I hope that this text has lived up to its goal of disrupting racial reconciliation. In these first three chapters, I have attempted to bring the voices of my people—my southern African American relatives, my womanist and feminist colleagues, and my fellow women of color who traverse White Christian environments—to bear in naming and disrupting some of the core assumptions of the racial reconciliation paradigm that is so prominent among evangelicals and other Christians. In particular, I have disrupted the movement's reliance upon symmetrical treatment approaches to race and racism that attempt to lay blame, and thus responsibility, for racism at the feet of Blacks and Whites equally. Moreover, I have disrupted the notion that the system of racism can be dismantled without addressing other systems of oppression, especially gender and class oppression. Centering the experiences of women of color, I have disrupted the notion that racism is "one-size-fits-all," in other words, that the racial experiences of men of color are identical to those of women of color, and even that the experiences of nonblack women of color are identical to those of Black women. And finally, in this chapter, I have disrupted the notion that racial reconciliation can take place without deconstructing White racial identity.

Like Jennifer Harvey, I believe that the racial reconciliation movement has failed to grapple with the peculiar problem of whiteness through "direct and unflinching recognition of the relationship all white people have to white supremacy, along with the many ways this relationship affects those . . . who are racialized as white."[87] Be-

87. Harvey, *Dear White Christians*, 43.

cause the US is a White supremacist society in which whiteness is considered both normative and superior, White people can—and most often do—live free from daily awareness of race and racism. Consequently, they lack (1) an awareness of how their own personalities, identities, and cultural preferences have been shaped by whiteness; (2) the vocabulary and rudimentary knowledge base needed to discuss structural racism competently; and (3) the biopsychosocial stamina to withstand racial stress. Their solutions to racism, then, tend to emphasize efforts that remain within their comfort zone: establishing cross-racial friendships and multicultural congregations. This, however, is not reconciliation. It does nothing to repair the harm of systemic racism or to dismantle the system of White supremacy. It is a therapeutic approach designed to make White people feel better about the unjust system in which they live and with which they are complicit. In that sense, it is a continuation of White supremacy, one that caters to the needs of White people while relegating the needs of people of color to the background.

If race and racism are far more complex than the dominant racial reconciliation paradigm allows, then so too is genuine racial reconciliation. But what might this look like? Again, I believe that women of color—especially Black women—can help to illuminate this. In the next chapter, therefore, I draw upon the voices of womanists, Black feminists, and Black liberation theologians to construct a womanist theology of racial reconciliation.

Chapter Four

Reconciliation Begins with a Curse

I curse you, I say.

What that mean? he say.

I say, Until you do right by me, everything you touch will crumble.

He laugh. Who you think you is? he say. You can't curse nobody. Look at you. You black, you pore, you ugly, you a woman. Goddam, he say, you nothing at all.

Until you do right by me, I say, everything you even dream about will fail. I give it to him straight, just like it come to me. And it seem to come to me from the trees. . . . I'm pore, I'm black, I may be ugly and can't cook, a voice say to everything listening. But I'm here.

Amen, say Shug. Amen, amen.

Alice Walker, The Color Purple

In 1982, Alice Walker published her now-classic book *The Color Purple*, which chronicles the life of a young Black woman in Macon, Georgia.[1] Caught between White supremacy and Black patriarchy,

---

1. Alice Walker, *The Color Purple* (Boston: Mariner Books, 1982). While *The Color Purple* contains no dates or references to factual events, its historical setting is consistent with the first half of the twentieth century. Subsequent references to this book will be given parenthetically in the text.

Celie is subjected to decades of sexual, emotional, and physical abuse by her stepfather and her husband. Walker's stark depiction of relational and systemic violence against Black women, by the men in their families and by White power structures, is masterful. The success of the 1985 film adaptation by Stephen Spielberg has often overshadowed the novel itself, which differs from the film in substantive ways. Most notably, popular commentary often overlooks that *The Color Purple* is a deeply spiritual story that is ultimately centered upon issues of faith, liberation, and reconciliation. The book takes the form of a collection of letters written to God. It is not only a story of a woman's experience of abuse; it is the story of her communication with God about the abuse that she witnesses and experiences in her home and community. The changing nature of Celie's view of and relationship with God is a critical element in her transformation, as well as in that of other members of her family. It is an allegory of Walker's own faith journey from the dogmatic Christianity of her youth to the more expansive, heavily Buddhist spirituality that she has embraced as an adult. In the original preface, Walker notes that *The Color Purple* is fundamentally "the theological work examining the journey from the religious back to the spiritual. . . . This is the book in which I was able to express a new spiritual awareness, a rebirth into strong feelings of Oneness I realized I had experienced and taken for granted as a child; a chance for me as well as the main character, Celie, to encounter That Which Is Beyond Understanding But Not Beyond Loving and to say: I see and hear you clearly, Great Mystery, now that I expect to see and hear you everywhere I am, which is the right place" (preface).

The Color Purple is a narrative about women and men finding liberation and becoming their authentic selves in the midst of an oppressive culture. Celie, Albert, Sofia, Harpo, and Shug are people whose self-images and relationships are broken by the deeply racist and patriarchal context in which they live: Celie, whose survival depends upon making others happy so that they will not abuse her; Albert and Harpo, who try to prove their manhood by exacting violence and domination over the women in their lives; Sofia, the strong woman who uses marriage as a means of escape from her father's abusive household; and Shug, the sexually liberated woman whose attempts to transcend the limitations of patriarchy have filled her with resentment.[2] Over the course of the narrative, each of them breaks free from the ideological prisons that have bound them and begins to recover the *imago Dei*, the image and likeness of God that is stamped upon all humans. In this chapter, therefore, I draw upon the depiction of the transformed relationship between an abused woman and her abuser in *The Color Purple* to describe a womanist vision of reconciliation. The relationship between Celie and Albert reveals that reconciliation is not a destination or a fixed point in time, but is rather a developmental process—a journey—that requires (1) confrontational truth-telling; (2) liberation and healing for the oppressed; (3) repentance and conversion for the oppressor; and (4) building beloved community.

First, a note on language is necessary. Throughout this chapter, I will use victim/perpetrator and oppressed/oppressor language to describe different figures in the reconciliation process. Victim/oppressed generally refers to the individuals, groups, communities, and institutions that are the targets of oppression, whereas perpetrator/oppressor refers to those who are the primary enactors and beneficiaries. Because my focus here is upon racial reconciliation, these two groups generally break down into people of color and White people. I recognize, however, that even in the case of racism there is not always a clear bifurcation between agents and targets of oppression. For example, as noted in chapter 2, people of color can internalize racism so much that they become its enforcers. And within the broad category "people of color," various ethnic groups can engage in acts of racism toward one another, as is the case when an African American comedian performs stereotypic caricatures of Latinx peoples, or when an Asian American family in Birmingham mounts a Confederate flag outside their home. These acts, though, still serve to affirm White supremacy in that they are based upon White supremacist notions of African American, Latinx, Native American, and Asian American

---

2. Notably, in the first half of the narrative, the three central female characters—Celie, Sofia, and Shug—embody the stereotypic figures of the mammy, the sapphire, and the Jezebel, respectively (cf. Chanequa Walker-Barnes, *Too Heavy a Yoke: Black Women and the Burden of Strength* [Eugene, OR: Cascade, 2014], 82–90).

bodies. Moreover, even though people can be both victims and per-petrators, those roles usually pertain to two different acts. In other words, as Margaret Urban Walker explains: "That person is a victim of some *particular* wrong and a perpetrator of *another* distinct one."[3] In this chapter, my use of dichotomous language is an intentional strategy for moving beyond passive or "politically correct" language that diffuses responsibility for oppression. In racism, as in other forms of oppression, there are victims and there are perpetrators; there are people and institutions who inflict racial harm (or, at the least, benefit from it) and those who suffer from it. Naming this explicitly is critical to a model of reconciliation that begins with truth-telling.

Getting Confrontational

The journey of reconciliation begins with confrontational truth-telling that lays bare the complex horrors of oppression. *The Color Purple* embodies this dramatically. There is no slow transition into Celie's story, no easing into or circumnavigating the painful details: sexual, physical, and emotional abuse by her stepfather and mother; the births and disappearances of the two children born of rape; and an abusive husband. Celie's initial letter to God recounts the first time that she is raped by her stepfather, Alphonso, whom at that point she believes to be her biological father. Her mother, who re-mains unnamed throughout the book, has fallen ill after giving birth and resists her husband's sexual advances. When she goes to town to visit a doctor, Alphonso turns his sexual predilections toward fourteen-year-old Celie, raping her for the first time and telling her that it will not be the last. "He start to choke me, saying You better shut up and git used to it" (1). He threatens her not to reveal the abuse, telling her that the truth would kill her mother. He even pre-pares for the eventuality that she will reveal the truth to others by publicly labeling her as untrustworthy. When he gives her away to Albert to marry, he provides a warning: "She tell lies" (8).

3. Margaret Urban Walker, *Moral Repair: Reconstructing Moral Relations after Wrongdoing* (Cambridge: Cambridge University Press, 2006), 7.

Her mother, as well as the community, is also complicit in forcing Celie's silence. When her mother asks, about the first pregnancy,
"Whose it is?" Celie responds simply, "God's" (2). Her mother men-
tions the pregnancy only once more, asking about the baby's where-
abouts after Celie gives birth. When Celie becomes pregnant for the
second time, her mother does not mention it at all; she subsequently
dies before Celie gives birth. Likewise, the people in Celie's community, including those in her congregation, pretend not to see or know
what is happening in her household even as her belly grows large
from her two pregnancies. After the babies are born, no one comes
to see Celie. And when each baby disappears immediately after birth,
no one ever acknowledges that they ever existed.

Eventually, Celie is forced not only to silently comply with the
abuse, but also to solicit it in order to protect her younger sister, Nettie. When her new teenage stepmother gets sick, Celie worries that
Alphonso will turn his attentions to Nettie. She tries to preempt it
by offering herself as a willing sacrifice: "Dear God, I ast him to take
me instead of Nettie while our new mammy sick. But he just ast me
what I'm talking bout. I tell him I can fix myself up for him. I duck
into my room and come out wearing horsehair, feathers, and a pair
of our new mammy high heel shoes. He beat me for dressing trampy
but he do it to me anyway" (7). Alphonso's behavior is gaslighting at
its finest.[4] He feigns ignorance about the reason for Celie's behavior
and punishes her for being sexually provocative but then has sex with
her nevertheless.

It is important to note that despite Celie's "provocative" behavior, this is still nonconsensual sex, that is, rape. Celie is not engaging in intercourse of her own volition. She has wittingly assessed
the facts of her household and has realized that her father's inces-
tuously pedophiliac nature will inevitably lead him to raping one
of his daughters (she still believes Alphonso to be her and Nettie's
biological father at this point) while his new teenage wife is sick.

---

4. Gaslighting is a form of psychological manipulation in which a perpetrator employs tactics such as denial, deception, and misdirection to make a victim question her
own memory, perception, sanity, and/or morality ("Gaslighting," *Wikipedia*, https://
en.wikipedia.org/wiki/Gaslighting).

Celie does what victims of oppression are often forced to do: she makes a choice between the lesser of two evils. She sacrifices herself for the chance to save her sister. This remains the pattern of Celie's life after she is transferred to Albert's household. Celie learns that the best way to survive is to be silent and unseen while taking care of the needs of Albert, his children, and his guests. As in her stepfather's household, she passively endures abuse in order to protect herself and also to protect her sister. She even internalizes her abuse so much that when her stepson Harpo asks her how to make Sofia behave like a proper wife, Celie responds, "Beat her" (36).

The Conspiracy of Silence

In chapter 1, I reviewed Patricia Hill Collins's concept of the four domains of power through which oppression operates: structural, disciplinary, hegemonic, and interpersonal. In its depiction of Celie's attempts to cope with and survive the violent patriarchal abuse that she experiences, *The Color Purple* demonstrates how these forms of power collude to silence victims of oppression. At the structural level, which includes the way in which societal systems and institutions are structured to create and reproduce patterns of injustice, Celie is silenced by a social order that is designed to maintain White patriarchal supremacy. In this system, men—specifically fathers and husbands—have complete legal authority over girls and women. There are no legal authorities or social service agencies concerned with the treatment of Black women and girls in the rural Jim Crow South. In essence, her abuse is legally sanctioned by a system that views Black women valuable only inasmuch as they benefit White male economic interests. At the disciplinary domain, which includes the regulations and practices that sustain bureaucratic systems, Celie is silenced by the strong message that women who exert agency and resist their subjugation are to be punished. The threat of punishment is ever-present for "uppity" women who dare to speak out against oppressive powers. In reflecting on how she learned to self-silence as a form of submission to patriarchal authority, bell hooks states, "Questioning authority, raising issues that were not deemed appropriate subjects brought pain, punishments."[5] We see this in Sofia, who is sentenced to twelve years of imprisonment after defending herself against a White woman who assaulted her. We see it also in Shug, who is castigated as a "loose" woman when she refuses to submit to her father's control over marriage and instead exercises free agency. In the hegemonic domain, racism and sexism have significantly shaped how Celie thinks about God, the world, and herself. Celie envisions God as a "big and old and tall and graybearded" White man with bluish-gray eyes and white eyelashes, a figure who, essentially, could not be less concerned with the life of a poor Black woman (194). In turn, she views herself as someone whose best hope is to survive suffering. This view is further reinforced in the interpersonal domain, which rigidly structures relationships along race and gender hierarchies that position Black women at the bottom of the ladder.

Together, the matrix of power conspires both to abuse Celie and to render her mute about her experience. The same is true for racism and all forms of oppression everywhere. It is especially true of modern-day color-blind racism. Recall chapter 1, where I reviewed Eduardo Bonilla-Silva's conceptualization of the four frames of color-blind racism—abstract liberalism, naturalization, cultural racism, and minimization of racism. Regardless of which frame(s) it employs, color-blind racism perpetuates White supremacy by denying, normalizing, rationalizing, or minimizing the truth of racism at individual, social, and systemic levels. Even Whites who claim to be committed to racial reconciliation are not immune from engaging in this sort of silencing. This is why "Get over it!" and "Why can't we just move on?" are common refrains in discussions of racial oppression. Usually uttered by Whites (and, unfortunately, occasionally also by people of color), these statements betray an impulse to minimize, deny, or forget the ugly and painful truths of oppression.

There is an adage that states, "The devil's greatest trick has been to convince the world that he does not exist." The same could be said of systemic oppression, which maintains its power in part by labeling the oppressed as opportunistic liars who are not to be

---

5. bell hooks, *Talking Back: Thinking Feminist, Thinking Black*, 2nd ed. (Boston: South End Press, 1999), 7.

trusted about the telling of their own stories. There is no person of color who has not heard some version of the rebuttal, "That's not really racism," when discussing her or his experiences of racism with a White person. Characterizing women of color as deceitful, untrustworthy, and incapable of innocence has been a particularly recurrent strategy of White patriarchal supremacy, which is partly why the stereotypic tropes of the Jezebel, the spicy Latina, the China doll/geisha, and the squaw have been heavily used to represent African American, Latinx, Asian American, and Native American sexuality, respectively.

Silencing, and self-silencing, is not always about the prevention of speech. Often, it is about censuring what can be voiced. As hooks states, "I was never taught absolute silence, I was taught that it was important to speak but to talk a talk that was in itself a silence."[6] Genuine reconciliation, then, requires a certain type of speech. It requires speech that exposes, rather than conceals, the powers at work within and behind systems of oppression. It requires risky utterances that lay bare the sin of oppression and force us to gaze at its raw, oozing wounds. It requires confrontational truth-telling.[7]

Tell the Truth and Shame the Devil

For Celie, truth-telling begins with God. There is some safety in confessing her truths to God, even with her conflicting God-images: the loving, caring God who might intervene on her behalf, and the White male deity who is indifferent to her. But there is risk as well. Celie's letters are a form of lament, a record of the "cries and prayers [that] . . . erupt from the human heart and voice in the grip of a painful experience."[8] She writes letters to God in order to voice truths that

---

6. hooks, *Talking Back*, 7.

7. Desmond Tutu distinguishes between three types of truth: (1) forensic factual truth, that is, facts that are verifiable and documentable; (2) social truth, which is shaped through interpersonal interaction and communication; and (3) personal truth, or the "truth of wounded memories"(Desmond Tutu, *No Future without Forgiveness* [New York: Doubleday, 1999], 26).

8. Sally A. Brown and Patrick D. Miller, "Introduction," in *Lament: Reclaiming*

are too horrific to be expressed even in prayer. Consistent with the biblical form of lament, her letters are "at one and the same time the voice of pain and the voice of prayer."[9] As Miller states, "To recover the voice of lament is to recover the voice of prayer as it has defined the human reality before God. The lament is utterly human and pro-foundly theological. It arises out of the reality of human existence; it assumes there is something beyond that reality that can transform existence without destroying it. The laments of Scripture make clear what is present in every human cry for help, the assumption that God is there, God can be present, and God can help. As such, the voice of lament, the cry for help we call lament, is always our prayer."[10] Celie's letters are the voice of pain in that her writing forces her to revisit, rehearse, and record painful experiences of physical, sexual, and emo-tional abuse and neglect. It forces her to confront the hard truth that, with the exception of her sister Nettie, no one has ever loved her. At the same time, though, her letters are the voice of prayer. Celie writes to the "God who hears" in expectation that there is a power beyond her reality that sees and cares about her suffering.

While Celie's truth-telling begins in the safe space of her rela-tionship with God, it does not end there. Her journey to liberation is marked by three confrontational moments in which revealing the truth of her experiences is central. The first comes when she begins to share her story with a person whom she trusts, Shug, who is the first person to whom Celie reveals that her own father raped her, sired her two children, and stole them from her. It is Shug to whom Celie confesses that she has never experienced love: "My mama die, I tell Shug. My sister Nettie run away. Mr. _____ come git me to take care his rotten children. He never ast me nothing about myself. He clam on top of me and fuck and fuck, even when my head bandaged. Nobody ever love me, I say" (112). Celie's use of profanity is espe-cially important. This particular letter begins with Celie telling God that Shug says "fuck" instead of "making love" (111). By adopting

---

Practices in Pulpit, Pew, and Public Square, ed. Brown and Miller (Louisville: Westminster John Knox, 2005), xiii.

    9. Patrick D. Miller, "Heaven's Prisoners," in Brown and Miller, *Lament,* 16.

    10. Miller, "Heaven's Prisoners," 17.

the language herself, Celie makes a decisive break from her lifelong attempt to be a "good" Christian woman who honors her parents and husband no matter how they treat her. In an earlier encounter with Sofia, Celie states,

> I can't even remember the last time I felt mad, I say. I used to git mad at my mammy cause she put a lot of work on me. Then I see how sick she is. Couldn't stay mad at her. Couldn't be mad at my daddy cause he my daddy. Bible say, Honor father and mother no matter what. Then after while every time I got mad, or start to feel mad, I got sick. Felt like throwing up. Terrible feeling. Then I start to feel nothing at all. . . . Well, sometime Mr. _____ git on me pretty hard. I have to talk to Old Maker. But he my husband. I shrug my shoulders. This life soon be over, I say. Heaven last all ways. (41–42)

Telling the truth of her experiences to Shug begins to loosen the yoke of repression created by Celie's internalization and interpretation of biblical teachings that encouraged her to submit to oppression. It also frees her to live fully into a part of her identity that she has known but repressed since childhood: her identity as a same-gender-loving woman. Immediately afterward, Celie and Shug make love for the first time. Thus, in telling the truth to Shug about her life, Celie begins to accept the full truth of who she is and to reject the lie of who the oppressive society has told her that she must be.

This, in turn, leads to the second truth-telling confrontation, wherein Celie shifts from voicing the truth *to* God to voicing the truth *about* God. After finding the letter from Nettie revealing the story of their true parentage, Celie writes to God for the last time, this time directly expressing her sense of abandonment. "Dear God, My daddy lynch. My mama crazy. All my little half-brothers and sisters no kin to me. My children not my sister and brother. Pa not pa. You must be sleep" (177). When Shug discovers that Celie is no longer writing to God and asks why, Celie responds, "He give me a lynched daddy, a crazy mama, a lowdown dog of a step pa and a sister I probably won't ever see again. Anyhow, I say, the God I been praying and writing to is a man. And act just like all the other mens

I know. Trifling, forgitful and lowdown" (192). Shug and Celie's conversation about God reveals how deeply Christian theology and tradition are embedded into the internalized oppression of women of color. Because understandings of what it means to be female are linked to our understanding of God, "a reconstruction of womanhood requires a reconstruction of God."[11]

Celie's liberation begins in earnest when she frees herself from worshipping a White supremacist patriarchal God and finds God for herself beyond the constraints of organized Christianity. It is Shug who tells Celie that God is not housed within the walls of the church, but within the people who come to the church, within her very self. "Any God I ever felt in church I brought in with me. And I think all the other folks did too. They come to church to share God, not find God" (193). Whereas telling the truth to Shug may have been only slightly risky, telling the truth of one's feelings and beliefs *about* God *to* God is considerably riskier, as it could possibly jeopardize one's eternal salvation. Fortunately, for Celie, in addition to her image of God as distant White male authority figure, she has also internalized an image of God as carer and lover of her soul. When Celie relinquishes her negative God-images, she discovers within herself and within all of creation the God who desires more for her than survival, the God whose desire is for her to experience the joy of the color purple.[12]

It is her newly discovered and strengthened relationship with the Divine that enables Celie's third truth-telling confrontation: telling the truth to her oppressor. First, Celie confronts her stepfather, Alphonso. Then, she confronts her husband. "I curse you," Celie says to Albert as he attempts to prevent her from leaving him. The mute, invisible, mousy captive has found her voice. In front of all the people whose opinions Albert cares about, she confronts him with the truth of who he is: "a lowdown dog." She stops making him comfortable

11. Karen Baker-Fletcher and Garth Kasimu Baker-Fletcher, *My Sister, My Brother: Womanist and Xodus God-Talk* (Maryknoll, NY: Orbis Books, 1997), 148.

12. The book's title comes from a conversation between Celie and Shug about the nature of God, when Shug states, "I think it pisses God off if you walk by the color purple in a field somewhere and don't notice it" (196).

and instead holds him accountable. She demands justice: "Until you do right by me, everything you touch will crumble. . . . Until you do right by me . . . everything you even dream about will fail." But this is not just a moment of confrontation; it is a moment of Spirit-filled truth-telling. As noted in this chapter's epigraph, Celie identifies her words as stemming from a source beyond herself. The words come *to* her as much as they come *from* her. They come from the trees, from the air, and from the dust—from the very creation in which she has found God.

> Every lick you hit me you will suffer twice, I say. Then I say, You better stop talking because all I'm telling you ain't coming just from me. Look like when I open my mouth the air rush in and shape words. . . . A dust devil flew up on the porch between us, fill my mouth with dirt. The dirt say, Anything you do to me, already done to you. (206–7)

Celie's truth-telling is not driven by a desire to hurt Albert; nor is her curse driven by a desire for vengeance. Inspired and enabled by the Spirit, her curse is a prophetic utterance, an "act of resistance, a political gesture that challenges politics of domination that would render [her] nameless and voiceless. As such, it is a courageous act—as such, it represents a threat. To those who wield oppressive power, that which is threatening must necessarily be wiped out, annihilated, silenced."[13]

Celie's growth from silent, passive victim to curse-issuing truth-teller parallels the process that womanists and feminists often term *coming to voice*, or as bell hooks puts it, *talking back*: "Moving from silence into speech is for the oppressed, the colonized, the exploited, and those who stand and struggle side by side a gesture of defiance that heals, that makes new life and new growth possible. It is that act of speech, of 'talking back,' that is no mere gesture of empty words, that is the expression of our movement from object to subject—the liberated voice."[14]

---

13. hooks, *Talking Back*, 8.
14. hooks, *Talking Back*, 9.

The truth-telling that we witness in *The Color Purple* is quite distinct from the approach that is dominant in today's racial reconciliation movement. With its focus on symmetrical treatment and bridge building, it encourages White people and people of color to tell the truth about their lives so that they might equally repent of the ways in which they have contributed to racial separatism and then find common ground upon which to build "reconciled" relationships. It calls for both oppressor and oppressed to remember the truth in ways that facilitate the building and maintenance of relationships, what Miroslav Volf calls "remembering rightly."[15] The symmetrical treatment approach to truth-telling is a therapeutic approach that focuses on being neutral, avoiding taking sides, and minimizing feelings of guilt and shame. It may work well in conditions of equal power between dialogue partners. But when power is unequal, this strategy is ill advised, perhaps even dangerous. This is why, for example, many therapists view conjoint sessions between domestic violence perpetrators and victims as contraindicated.[16] When power is unequal, the victim will usually modify her narrative in order to keep the abuser comfortable. Consequently, the counseling will never get to the heart of the matter, and the power dynamics will remain unchanged. The other alternative, encouraging open discussion of the abuse, is dangerous and professionally irresponsible in that it risks violent retaliation from the abuser.

In racial reconciliation, this strategy is clearly geared toward the comfort of Whites, because it implies that they are only half of the problem and that some of the responsibility for racism lies

---

15. Volf explores this notion at length in his book *The End of Memory*. While Volf gives some credence to the importance of justice and accountability, he ultimately argues that forgiving "rightly" requires forgetting the memory of wrongdoing. For him, reconciliation reaches completion when "a wrongdoing is both condemned and forgiven; the wrongdoer's guilt is canceled; through the gift of nonremembrance, the wrongdoer is transposed to a state untainted by the wrongdoing; and bound in a communion of love, both the wronged and the wrongdoer rejoice in their renewed relationship" (Volf, *The End of Memory: Remembering Rightly in a Violent World* [Grand Rapids: Eerdmans, 2006], 149).

16. Nandini Maharaj, "Perspectives on Treating Couples Impacted by Intimated Partner Violence," *Journal of Family Violence* 32 (May 2017): 431–37.

with people of color. But racism is not neutral; it chooses sides, the side of White supremacy, the side of evil. The primary goal of truth-telling in racial reconciliation is not to build bridges; it is to reveal the powers and principalities so that we can tear them down. To diminish this in any way is not truth-telling; it is catering to the very White supremacist system that we claim to be trying to eradicate. It is being complicit with evil. The truth that must be told—and retold over and over again—is this: Racism is alive and well. It did not happen by accident or as an act of omission, but it is an intentional way of structuring society so that White people have material, economic, social, and political power and advantages over nonwhite peoples. Racism is constructed in such a way that White people benefit from it even when they do not actively or consciously participate in it. Racism negatively impacts the historical and contemporary realities of people of color in complex, layered ways that have been shaped over centuries. We cannot root it out unless we reveal how deeply it is embedded into our systems, relationships, and lives. This, however, demands conditions of safety and solidarity in which the oppressed can grow to acknowledge and voice their truths. To force them to attempt to mitigate the impact of this truth upon the oppressor is in itself an act of violence and oppression. The oppressed are well skilled in taking care of the needs of the oppressor. The very nature of oppression demands that they learn to placate the privileged in order to avoid the wrath of their power. Black feminist historian Darlene Clark Hine coined the term "dissemblance" to describe this process among African American women.

> Because of the interplay of racial animosity, class tensions, gender role differentiation, and regional economic variations, Black women, as a rule, developed and adhered to a cult of secrecy, a culture of dissemblance, to protect the sanctity of inner aspects of their lives. The dynamics of dissemblance involved creating the appearance of disclosure, or openness about themselves and their feelings, while actually remaining an enigma. Only with secrecy, thus achieving a self-imposed invisibility, could ordinary Black women accrue the psychic

space and harness the resources needed to hold their own in the often one-sided and mismatched resistance struggle.[17]

Coming to voice, then, requires unlearning the arts of dissemblance, the time-tested and often deeply entrenched strategy that Black women have developed to hide their true selves in oppressive conditions under which revealing one's truth is dangerous.

Telling the truth about racism requires us to examine and confess how even our understandings of God are shaped by White supremacy. Racial oppression and gender oppression are rooted in theological understandings about who God is and who God intends for us to be. Essentially, they are based in the idea that God expects and sanctions the suffering and self-sacrifice of women and people of color relative to men and White people. Redefining our identities, then, requires challenging our individual and collective imaginings of God as One who condones unjust suffering. It necessitates confessing, confronting, and resisting White supremacist patriarchal God-images.

Genuine racial reconciliation, then, does not begin with soothsaying. More often than not, it begins with a curse. Like Celie, victims of racial oppression must boldly proclaim the truth of their experiences and demand justice and accountability. And, as I will demonstrate shortly, oppressors must use that proclamation as a mirror in which to see the truth about themselves and as an opportunity for repentance. Indeed, many understandings of racial reconciliation emphasize repentance from White supremacy as the critical response to truth-telling. After all, it makes sense that repentance follows confession. However, placing our primary emphasis upon the transformative work that must happen for White Christians in racial reconciliation actually reinforces White supremacy. When we prioritize the narratives of women of color, we realize that the victims of racial oppression have considerable work of their own to do, work that is both independent of and connected to that of White repentance. This is the work of liberation and healing.

17. Darlene Clark Hine, "Rape and the Inner Lives of Black Women in the Middle West: Preliminary Thoughts on the Culture of Dissemblance," *Signs* 14, no. 4 (Summer 1989): 915.

Liberation and Healing

The image of the cross is often used to illuminate the vertical and horizontal dimensions of reconciliation. Reconciliation is vertical in that it restores us to right relationship with God. It is horizontal in that it returns us to right relationship with one another. There is, however, another dimension of reconciliation that is also evident in the cross metaphor, namely, the starting locus at the intersection of the horizontal and vertical, the point that represents ourselves. Reconciliation is about restoring us to right relationship with God, with humanity and creation, and with ourselves. For the victims of racism, the restoration of selfhood involves healing the damage that has been wrought by oppression and marginalization. In chapter 2, I identified several gendered forms of racism that are evident in the narratives and experiences of women of color, including colorism, sexual trauma and shaming, and mammification. I also discussed the impact that oppression has on the self-perception of the oppressed. The call to racial reconciliation has overwhelmingly emphasized between-group processes, that is, the relationships between Whites and people of color, or between different racial/ethnic minority groups. By and large, it has ignored the depth and severity of internalized oppression among people of color and the enormous need for healing these wounds. Repeated and systemic experiences of dehumanization not only inflict direct harm; they diminish the capacity of the oppressed to recognize themselves as human and, moreover, as beloved by God. As Archbishop Desmond Tutu states, "One of the most blasphemous consequences of injustice, especially racist injustice, is that it can make a child of God doubt that he or she is a child of God."[18] An important element of the work of reconciliation, then, is restoring the oppressed's image of themselves as being knit in the image and likeness of God, the *imago Dei*.

18. Tutu, *No Future*, 197.

Claiming the Right to Wholeness

An important critique levied by womanist and Black liberationist theologians about the racial reconciliation movement has been its tendency to prioritize conciliation between Whites and people of color over—and often at the expense of—freedom from oppression. This was the crux of the historic debate between James Cone and J. Deotis Roberts.[19] In his 1986 foreword to Cone's *A Black Theology of Liberation*, Paulo Freire wrote: "Any reconciliation between oppressors and oppressed, as social classes, presupposes the liberation of the oppressed, a liberation forged by themselves through their own revolutionary praxis."[20] In *The Color Purple*, we find an understanding of liberation and reconciliation that aligns more closely with Cone's assertion of the primacy of the need for freedom from oppression. There is no one point at which Celie's healing and liberation occur. It is a continuous process of discovery that begins with her very first letter to God. Memory and narrative are healing in and of themselves. In *Sisters of the Yam*, bell hooks notes that "Healing takes place within us as we speak the truth of our lives. . . . Commitment to truth-telling is thus the first step in any process of self-recovery."[21] Members of South Africa's Truth and Reconciliation Commission often note this in their observations about the process. Tutu, for example, noted that "many who came to the commission attested afterward to the fact that they had found relief, and experienced healing, just through the process of telling their story."[22] But telling the truth alone does not transform Celie's circumstances, including the inherently abusive state of her marriage. What it does, however, is transform Celie's beliefs and expectations of what ought to be. Naming her oppression enables Celie to envision and desire a life that is free from it. In a context that has demanded her brokenness, Celie desires to be made whole.

---

19. Cf. James H. Cone, *God of the Oppressed*, rev. ed. (Maryknoll, NY: Orbis Books, 1997); J. Deotis Roberts, *Liberation and Reconciliation: A Black Theology*, 2nd ed. (Maryknoll, NY: Orbis Books, 2005).

20. James H. Cone, *A Black Theology of Liberation* (Maryknoll, NY: Orbis Books, 2010), ix.

21. bell hooks, *Sisters of the Yam: Black Women and Self-Recovery* (Boston: South End Press, 1993), 19.

22. Tutu, *No Future*, 165.

She recognizes, however, that her wholeness—that is, her healing—hinges upon one crucial factor: the oppression must end. This assumption is central to womanist and Black liberation theologies. Healing necessitates liberation. And in this case, liberation necessitates leaving. As Cone states, "Reconciliation means that God enters into black history and breaks down the hostility and racism of white people. . . . God's reconciliation means destroying all forms of slavery and oppression in white America so that the people of color can affirm the authenticity of their political freedom."[23] Sometimes the only way for oppression to end is for the oppressed to claim their agency in leaving the context in which it occurs. This again stands at odds with typical models of racial reconciliation, which, having reduced racism to an issue of separatism, focus on maintaining relationship between the oppressed and the oppressor. These approaches would almost undoubtedly require that Celie and Albert engage in ongoing dialogue about their mutual feelings of hurt and harm and their expressions of forgiveness toward one another. But that is not what happens in *The Color Purple*. Celie breaks contact with the source of her oppression because it is the only way that the abuse will end. It is important to note that Celie leaves with no expectation of returning, that is, with no hope or expectation of reconciliation with Albert. Leaving is an end in itself. It is an act of salvation and transformation that subverts the authority and dominance of the powers—the structural, disciplinary, hegemonic, and interpersonal systems that maintain her subordination. Her leaving is a holy act, a reclamation of her agency as one who is created in the image of God and who is imbued with the capacity for co-creation. It is only when the harm has come to an end and she is ensconced in safety that Celie is able to embark upon the quest for wholeness in earnest.

Breaking the Chains of Bondage

While liberation begins with removing the forces that perpetuate harm, it is not complete until the legacies of that harm are also re-

23. Cone, *God of the Oppressed*, 216.

moved. This is the work of healing. In a womanist ethic of reconciliation, the primary focus of healing is not the relationship between
the oppressed and the oppressor; it is the restoration to wholeness
of the victim herself. Racism is a holistic system of oppression that
constrains, controls, and commodifies the bodies, minds, and relationships of the oppressed. As Howard Thurman states, "When the
need to be cared for is dishonored, threatened, or undermined, then
the individual cannot experience his [or her] own self as a unity and
his [or her] life may become deeply fragmented and splintered. In its
extreme form the disturbance upsets the balance of the mind and a
[person] gradually loses his [or her] sense of humanity."[24] White supremacy dishonors, threatens, and undermines the needs and opportunities of nonwhite peoples by waging an all-out ideological assault
upon every aspect of their humanity. It employs every level of the
matrix of domination to convince not just Whites but also people of
color themselves that they are inferior. Consequently, many people
of color suffer from what Cornel West describes as an "existential
angst [derived] from the lived experience of ontological wounds and
emotional scars inflicted by white supremacist beliefs and images
permeating US society and culture."[25] These beliefs and images, in
turn, attack the intelligence, ability, beauty, and character of people
of color on a daily basis.[26] Moreover, when oppression becomes embedded into the psyches of the oppressed, its mechanics no longer
have to operate as overtly because the oppressed learn to "carry the
oppressive system in their psyches."[27]

Racial reconciliation, then, must be invested in healing the
bodily, mental, socioemotional, spiritual, and financial wounds
inflicted by White supremacy. Pastoral theology defines healing as
"the process of being restored to bodily wholeness, emotional well-
being, mental functioning, and spiritual aliveness."[28] Healing in the

24. Howard Thurman, *Disciplines of the Spirit* (Richmond, IN: Friends United, 2003), 107.
25. Cornel West, *Race Matters* (New York: Vintage, 1994), 27.
26. West, *Race Matters*, 27.
27. Homer U. Ashby Jr., "Is It Time for a Black Pastoral Theology?" *Journal of Pastoral Theology* 6, no. 1 (1996): 2.
28. Larry Kent Graham, "Healing," in *Dictionary of Pastoral Care and Counseling*,

aftermath of systemic injustice must also be concerned with financial restoration, or reparations. All of this is evident in *The Color Purple*, which bell hooks identifies as one of several books by African American women writers that provides a constructive map for healing from the "deep, often unnamed psychic wounding that takes place in the daily lives of black folks in this society."[29]

Celie's healing begins with the task of individuation. She has to construct her identity for herself, an identity that is not defined by others. This requires unlearning the negative self-images that she has internalized from her abusers and from the larger society. It is, in essence, a process of decolonization. "Here decolonization refers to breaking with the ways our reality is defined and shaped by the dominant culture and asserting our understanding of that reality, of our own experience."[30] Celie has to unlearn who society says that she is: a poor, ugly, worthless Black woman whose only skill is serving others; who is powerless over her body, her sexuality, and her livelihood; who is unloved and abused by others; and whose best chances for survival lie in a life of submission to and dependency upon men. She reconnects with her sister, develops genuine friendships based upon mutuality and reciprocity, discovers work that she loves, and becomes economically self-sufficient. She freely transgresses social norms about who she should be, whom she should love, and how she should dress. She releases her shame and redefines her relationships on her own terms. She becomes whole, writing in one of her letters to her sister, "I am so happy. I got love, I got work, I got money, friends and time" (215). By the time Celie returns to Georgia, her healing has transformed her to the degree that Albert does not even recognize her when he first sees her.

Celie's process of healing embodies what bell hooks terms self-recovery, which is an inherently liberatory act for targets of systemic oppression. "Black female self-recovery, like all black self-recovery, is an expression of a liberatory political practice. . . . Before many of us can effectively sustain engagement in organized resistance strug-

---

expanded ed., ed. Rodney J. Hunter et al. (Nashville: Abingdon, 2005), 497.

29. hooks, *Sisters of the Yam*, 11.

30. hooks, *Sisters of the Yam*, 2.

gle, in black liberation movement, we need to undergo a process of self-recovery that can heal individual wounds that may prevent us from functioning fully."[31] This healing, in turn, makes reconciliation possible.[32]

The Healing Power of Relationship

While Celie's healing includes individuation, it does not occur in isolation. Healing for Celie is made possible through the solidarity that she experiences with other Black women, especially Nettie, Shug, Sofia, and Mary Agnes. Notably, these women have competing interests: Nettie received the education that Celie desired; Shug is having an affair with Celie's husband; Mary Agnes is partnered with Sofia's ex. Despite these conflicts, however, they repeatedly and consistently stand together against racial-gender domination. Celie nurses Shug to health after a potentially fatal illness. Mary Agnes risks sexual assault to intervene on behalf of Sofia when she is incarcerated. When Mary Agnes decides to pursue her dream of becoming a singer, Shug assists her and Sofia raises her children.

Together, these women form a network of mutual support and empowerment that enables Celie's healing and liberation. In the midst of familial and societal environments that enact emotional, physical, and spiritual violence against them daily, they love, affirm, and challenge Celie toward healing. Before she is capable of doing so, they speak the truth about her condition and encourage her to resist. Even Mr. _____'s sisters speak up for Celie, demanding that he take better care of her and telling her that she deserves better than the treatment that she is receiving (19–21). Both Nettie and Sofia encourage her to fight back and to prevent Mr. _____ and his children from taking advantage of her. "Don't let them run over you. . . . You got to fight," Nettie tells her (17). Sofia and Shug provide living models of what it means to fight against White supremacist patriarchy within and beyond their own families. Ultimately,

31. hooks, *Sisters of the Yam*, 14–15.
32. hooks, *Sisters of the Yam*, 163.

it is Celie's experiences of love, affirmation, support, and respect within this network of solidarity that enable her to imagine an existence free from abuse and that infect her with the courage to leave the certainty of Albert's house (and later Shug's) and to build a new life for herself.

Healing the Legacy of Harm

Feminist ethicist Margaret Urban Walker uses the term "moral repair" to describe the process of healing in the aftermath of wrongdoing and harm.

> Moral repair is the process of moving from the situation of loss and damage to a situation where some degree of stability in moral relations is regained. This process of restoration or recreation is not always possible; in cases of serious wrong, if repair is possible in some degree, it will usually be at some cost—for the victim, the cost of absorbing some irreparable loss, pain, and anger; the wrongdoer, the cost of some shame, vulnerability, and compensating action; for communities, the costs of providing acknowledgment and vindication for victims, placing responsibility and its demands on wrongdoers, and showing that standards are affirmed and enforced.[33]

For the victim of "serious, violent, traumatic, and shattering harm," moral repair includes not only coming to voice and being validated by others (both part of the truth-telling process), but also efforts to address their needs.[34]

> Another's faulty, disrespectful or violent action inflicts costs on the victim. The costs are often material, almost always emotional and moral, and sometimes they are difficult or impossible to bear. It is justice for the victim to have these costs reduced

---

33. Urban Walker, *Moral Repair*, 6.
34. Urban Walker, *Moral Repair*, 7, 19.

or relieved, ideally by the responsible party; to the extent and in the ways that this is achieved, victims are vindicated. What victims seek and deserve, then, has to do not only with what the victim or society can do to the offender, such as demanding accountability, voluntary or otherwise, but also with what the victim needs the offender or the community to do for her or him. Victims also need and deserve support in seeking to do things for themselves that are integral to restoring what they have lost: to regain self-respect, to avoid self-blaming, to re-establish moral equilibrium, to trust again, to hope, to live without terror, to feel safe from those who have harmed them, to forgive if they choose.[35]

The victims of racism within the United States have lacked any meaningful opportunity or resources for voice, validation, or vindication. Even within the racial reconciliation movement, there have been no large-scale attempts to provide people of color with space to tell their truths without worrying about the impact that such truth-telling will have upon the feelings of White people. And when people of color have tried to create this space for themselves, it is often met with resistance and accusations of being separatist and counter to reconciliation—a far cry from the validation necessary for moral repair. There is even less attention to the work of healing that needs to be done for people of color.

Any reconciliation that does not liberate and heal the oppressed from the consequences of oppression is not reconciliation at all. At best, it is cheap grace, an easy balm that offers forgiveness for the sin of White supremacy without seeking to correct the harm that it has inflicted.[36] At worst, it is an affirmation of White supremacy in

35. Urban Walker, *Moral Repair*, 19.

36. Bonhoeffer used the term "cheap grace" as the antithesis of "costly grace," explaining that cheap grace asks for forgiveness without repentance. "Cheap grace is the preaching of forgiveness without requiring repentance, baptism without church discipline, Communion without confession, absolution without personal confession. Cheap grace is grace without discipleship, grace without the cross, grace without Jesus Christ, living and incarnate" (Dietrich Bonhoeffer, *The Cost of Discipleship* [New York: Touchstone, 1959], 44–45).

that it prioritizes the needs of White people to feel better about their relationships with people of color over the needs of people of color to recover from the psychological and material impact of oppression. This work is much more complex than that of establishing relationships. Toi Derricotte writes in *The Black Notebooks*, "So often white people, when a deep pain with regard to racism is uncovered, want it to be immediately addressed, healed, released. Black people have had to live with the wounds of racism for generations. Even goodwill and hard work won't make the person's hurts cease."[37] The hurt must end and the wounds must be healed. This means that racial reconciliation must attend to correcting overt inequities in the areas of health, economics, education, labor, and housing—inequities that are centuries in the making and that will not be undone without reparations and massive systemic overhaul.

Moreover, racial reconciliation must take up the even more difficult work of restoring the capacity of racial/ethnic minorities to view themselves as being made in the image and likeness of the God who wants us to delight in the color purple. People of color must learn to love themselves—their physicality, sexuality, and ways of being in the world—without mediating their love through the gaze of White supremacist cultural ideals. As Miroslav Volf notes:

> The dominant values and practices can be transformed only if their hold on the hearts of those who suffer under them is broken. This is where repentance comes in. To repent means to resist the seductiveness of the sinful values and practices and to let the new order of God's reign be established in one's heart. For a victim to repent means not to allow the oppressors to determine the terms under which social conflict is carried out, the values around which the conflict is raging, and the means by which it is fought. Repentance thus empowers victims and disempowers the oppressors. It "humanizes" the victims precisely by protecting them from either mimicking or dehumanizing the oppressors.[38]

37. Toi Derricotte, *The Black Notebooks* (New York: Norton, 1997), 189.
38. Miroslav Volf, *Exclusion and Embrace: A Theological Exploration of Identity,*

While I agree with Volf's sentiment, I disagree with his use of "repentance" language to describe this process for people of color in that it runs the dangerous risk of symmetrical treatment, namely, identifying the work of people of color as identical to that which is necessary for Whites. It is certainly the case that people of color may have to repent for sinful acts committed as a response to oppression (such as Celie's attempt to kill Albert). But Jesus's acts of healing for the marginalized are distinct from his calls for their repentance. The damaged self-identities of people of color in a White supremacist context are a form of psychospiritual sickness that requires healing, not an act of sin calling for repentance and atonement. Without such healing, equity in cross-racial relationships, whether interpersonal or systemic, is impossible.

"We Are Not Reconciled"

Furthermore, it is vital to recognize that, as is the case with Celie, healing and liberation from oppression often begin with the act of leaving. Leaving is a theme that arises frequently in the writings and conversations of women of color who are engaged in work for justice, whether in religious or secular settings. One of the earliest examples of intersectional feminist writings, *This Bridge Called My Back*, began after the editors (Cherríe Moraga and Gloría Anzaldúa) left a national feminist writers organization when, after two years, the group continued to refuse to address issues of elitism and racism. In formal and informal gatherings of women of color who are engaged in Christian social justice ministry in predominantly White and/or male circles, a recurrent question is: "How do we know when it's time to leave?" Whereas leaving organizations and relationships out of concern for one's well-being is not unique to women of color, it may represent a particularly pronounced struggle for them for multiple reasons. A significant component of gender socialization involves

---

Otherness, and Reconciliation (Nashville: Abingdon, 1996), 114. Volf further notes that "Jesus called to repentance not simply those who falsely pronounced sinful what was innocent and sinned against their victims, but *the victims of oppression themselves*" (114).

conditioning girls and women to place the needs of others above our own. Despite the advances made by the women's movement, the legacy of the cult of true womanhood remains strong.[39] A significant component of this legacy is women's tendency to be faithful and submissive to male authority, whether it is in the home, church, or work. Racism further compounds the issue. Because the femininities of women of color in the United States are consistently under cultural assault, we often react by not only "doubling down" on our performance of hegemonic femininity, but also by casting ourselves as sacrificial offerings for "the race."[40] At the same time, however, our intersectional identities mean that we are more likely to experience micro- and macroaggressions in predominantly White or predominantly male organizational environments where we are often in the minority both numerically and in terms of power.

The irony, then, is that women of color may be more likely to stay in unhealthy environments longer than are White women and men of color. Conversely, we may have to consider leaving more frequently than do White women or men of color, which means that we more frequently experience the feelings of loss, grief, anxiety, and shame that come with transition. It is important, then, that *The Color Purple* grants us permission to release the guilt and shame that we may experience. It affirms Anzaldúa's statement that "We are not reconciled to the oppressors who whet their howl on our grief. We are not reconciled."[41] Moreover, it points to the potentially transformative power of breaking relationship, which may not only facilitate the liberation and healing of the oppressed but also the repentance and repair of the oppressor.

---

39. Barbara Welter has identified the cult of true womanhood as the hegemonic ideal of White femininity throughout much of the nineteenth century. Its four cardinal virtues of piety, purity, submissiveness, and domesticity were widely disseminated through women's literature of the era (Barbara Welter, "The Cult of True Womanhood: 1820–1860," *American Quarterly* 18, no. 2 [1966]: 151–74).

40. In *Too Heavy a Yoke*, I explain how the myth of the StrongBlackWoman represents such an attempt at atonement among women of the African diaspora.

41. Gloría Anzaldúa, "Speaking in Tongues," in *This Bridge Called My Back: Writings by Radical Women of Color*, ed. Cherríe Moraga and Gloría Anzaldúa, 4th ed. (Albany: State University of New York Press, 2015), 171.

Repentance and Conversion

While the paramount tasks of self-recovery for victims of oppression are liberation and healing, a distinct process is necessary for the oppressors, that of repentance and conversion. "I curse you," Celie says when she finally confronts Albert. Celie's cursing and leaving provoke the critical tension necessary for Albert's transformation. Her assertion of agency and refusal to submit to continued oppression immediately transpose their relationship. Celie becomes the subject—the narrator and architect of her own story—while Albert becomes the object. As the proverb says, "When the lion tells the story, the hunter will not always win." Celie's truth-telling has an enormous cost for Albert. While it brings liberation for her, it brings condemnation for him. It provides a mirror in which Albert finally sees the truth of who he has become: Mr. _____, a hateful man who has exploited and abused a young, innocent girl. It is a hard truth to recognize, one that drives Albert into a deep depression after Celie leaves. He does not eat or bathe for a prolonged period of time. He refuses to leave the house and will not let anyone else in. Eventually, his own thoughts betray him. He begins to imagine the house closing in upon him and the furniture moving to attack him. "But the worse part was having to listen to his own heart. It did pretty well as long as there was daylight, but soon as night come, it went crazy. Beating so loud it shook the room. Sound like drums" (190–91). The weight of a guilt-laden heart is unbearable. One must either relieve the weight or go insane. Albert has three options available to relieve the weight: he can deny the truth of Celie's claim; he can seek her forgiveness; or he can change his heart. The first option is the path of repression and minimization. The second option is the route of absolution, which in this case is not possible because Celie refuses to have contact with him. The third option, and the route that Albert chooses, is repentance and repair, in other words, doing right by Celie.

Doing the Right Thing

Repentance is a central theme in both the Hebrew Bible and the New Testament, where it is also translated as conversion, indicating that the two concepts are linked. Biblically and theologically, repentance has a double meaning. It signifies a turn away from sin (and a commitment to refrain from, or forsake, further sinning) and a turn toward God. The Hebrew words translated as conversion— *shuh, strephein, epistrephein*—"connote the alterations in people's thoughts, feelings, and actions as they turn from idols to the true God or when they repent, that is, return to the covenant relationship with God."[42] The Greek counterpart, *metanoia*, connotes a change in direction. In *America's Original Sin*, Jim Wallis states, "In Scripture, repentance means literally to stop, make a radical turnaround, and take an entirely new path. It means a change of mind and heart and is demonstrated by nothing less than transformed behavior. Repentance means we now have to think, act, and live differently than we did before, when we were still under sin."[43] In the case of systemic oppression, repentance requires an end to and a transformation of oppression and its enactors.

We see this embodied in Albert's transformation. For Albert, repentance begins with atonement. Notably, he cannot undo the harm that he has done to Celie. He cannot escape what Hannah Arendt termed "the predicament of irreversibility—of being unable to undo what one has done."[44] He cannot erase the history or memories of physical or emotional abuse. As a poor Black man in the Jim Crow South, he does not have the capacity to repay Celie for the years that she spent working his fields, caring for his children, and tending his house as he lazily watched. He cannot erase her experience of trying to be a good wife even as her husband openly chased another woman. And he cannot give back the years that she

42. Shelly Rambo, "Conversion," in Hunter et al., *Dictionary of Pastoral Care and Counseling*, 228.

43. Jim Wallis, *America's Original Sin: Racism, White Privilege, and the Bridge to a New America* (Grand Rapids: Brazos Press), 58.

44. Hannah Arendt, *The Human Condition* (Chicago: University of Chicago Press, 1958), 237.

spent trying to conform to heteronormative ideals and repressing her sexuality. The debt that Albert owes Celie is greater than he could ever repay. Nevertheless, repentance requires recognition and accountability. Albert thus responds to Celie's demand for justice with a simple act: sending Celie the letters from her sister that he has hid for years. The act is both an admission of wrongdoing and recognition of the harm that he has caused. Albert's act fits Margaret Urban Walker's definition of reparations: "reparations are made when those who are responsible for repair of a wrong intentionally give appropriate goods to victims of wrong in a specific act (or process) that expresses acknowledgment of the wrong, responsibility for the wrong or its repair, and the intent of rendering just treatment to victims in virtue of that wrongful treatment."[45]

But Albert does not stop there. He goes above and beyond what Celie asks for. He does not only do right by her; he does right by everyone. He commits to living justly, completely transforming his relationships and ways of being in the world. Sofia later tells Celie, "I know you won't believe this . . . but Mr. _____ act like he trying to git religion. . . . He don't go to church or nothing, but he not so quick to judge. He work real hard too. . . . He out there in the field from sunup to sundown. And clean that house just like a woman" (222). Like Celie's liberation, Albert's conversion includes freedom from obligation to heteropatriarchal norms, in other words, freedom from his socialization into an unjust cultural system. He starts to cook and to sew. He stops mistreating and taking advantage of others; for the first time, he learns to care for people rather than simply using them for his own financial and sexual benefit. His relationships with his children and grandchildren become marked by love, nurture, and genuine interest. When Celie moves back to Georgia, where she repeatedly encounters Albert during visits to Sofia and Harpo, she notices the change:

> Look like he trying to make something out of himself. I don't mean just that he work and he clean up after himself and he

---

45. Margaret Urban Walker, *What Is Reparative Justice?* (Milwaukee: Marquette University Press, 2010), 19.

appreciate some of the things God was playful enough to make. I mean when you talk to him now he really listen, and one time, out of know where in the conversation us was having, he said Celie, I'm satisfied this the first time I ever lived on Earth as a natural man. It feel like a new experience. (260)

Repentance, for Albert, is not a onetime event involving expressions of apology and forgiveness. It is the gateway to moral repair and to new life, that is, the gateway to conversion. Albert experiences what William James describes as a shift at the "habitual center" of his being. "It occurs as something deep and fundamental, reshaping [his] entire life from that moment forward."[46]

Repairing the Oppressor's Soul

As I argued in the prior chapter's explanation of moral injury, systemic oppression does not only shatter the psyche of the oppressed; it also wounds the soul of the oppressor. It inflicts moral injury, which in turn requires moral repair, albeit of a different sort than that which is necessary for the victims of oppression. In their ethnographic analysis of military veterans, Brock and Lettini refer to this as "soul repair."[47] Central to moral repair for perpetrators of oppression is making amends. "Accepting responsibility for one's actions and their consequences, and acknowledging that those actions or their consequences are wrong or harmful, is the minimal condition

46. Daniel L. Pals, *Nine Theories of Religion*, 3rd ed. (Oxford: Oxford University Press, 2010), 203. James likewise points out the similarities and distinctions between psychological and religious use of "conversion." He states: "To be converted, to be regenerated, to receive grace, to experience religion, to gain an assurance, are so many phrases which denote the process, gradual or sudden, by which a self hitherto divided, and consciously wrong inferior and unhappy, becomes unified and consciously right superior and happy, in consequence of its firmer hold upon religious realities. This at least is what conversion signifies in general terms, whether or not we believe that a direct divine operation is needed to bring such a moral change about" (William L. James, *The Varieties of Religious Experience* [New York: Philosophical Library, 2015], 270).
47. Rita Nakashima Brock and Gabriella Lettini, *Soul Repair: Recovering from Moral Injury after War* (Boston: Beacon Press, 2012).

for those who have harmed or offended against others to 'set things right' with them."[48] It is this type of moral repair—or conversion—that we witness in Albert in *The Color Purple,* which is consistent with a restorative justice framework. Restorative justice has gained considerable attention since it became the foundational process of South Africa's Truth and Reconciliation Commission, which began in 1995. "Restorative justice embodies a view of crime or violence as a violation of people and relationships that entails an obligation to set things right, repairing victims and communities, and ideally humanizing and reintegrating offenders. The emphasis for restorative justice is on repairing relations through acknowledging the needs of victims and requiring accountability of those responsible for harm, through truth-telling, apology, and restitution or compensation."[49]

Repentance from America's Original Sin

America's "original sin" is White supremacy and its concomitants—imperialism, colonialism, slavery, genocide, Jim Crow, mass incarceration, capital punishment, and the everyday forms of racism experienced by African Americans, Asian Americans/Pacific Islanders, Native Americans, and Latinx peoples. "There is only one remedy for such a sin, and that is repentance. If genuine, it will always bear fruit in concrete forms of conversion and changed behavior, with both rejections and reversals of racism," observes Wallis.[50] Repentance for racism must not be reduced to simply issuing apologies and receiving forgiveness. Forgiveness is a largely interpersonal process between specific parties related to specific transgressions. White supremacy is not an interpersonal, or even a specific, transgression. Imagine, for example, the sheer magnitude of the sins committed to maintain chattel slavery for just one day in the United States. There is no single individual or entity that owns the right of forgiveness or apology. Even today, while White individuals may offer apology

48. Urban Walker, *Moral Repair*, 191.
49. Urban Walker, *Moral Repair*, 15.
50. Wallis, *America's Original Sin*, 55.

for specific acts of racial discrimination, those apologies—and any forgiveness granted—do not extend to the system of racism.

In chapter 1, I argued that racism forms the very powers and principalities that Paul wrote about in Ephesians. I have maintained an emphasis on racism as a matrix of power for this very reason. As Walter Wink notes in his *Powers* trilogy, "the language and reality of power pervade the New Testament because power is one of the primary ways the world is organized and run. No human activity can be described without recourse to this language."[51] The powers are spiritual and material, divine and human, internal and external, invisible and structural forces.[52] In the New Testament, the powers are alternately represented as human authorities and institutions, spiritual beings (both positive and negative), earthly or heavenly kingdoms, and abstract forces of death, life, dominion, and majesty. As part of God's created order, Wink argues, power is neither inherently good nor inherently evil, but it can be fallen. Apology and forgiveness are irrelevant concepts when we are talking about the powers. Instead, Wink notes, "The church's task, then, in making known the manifold wisdom of God now to the principalities and powers in the heavenly places, does not involve the arduous and hopeless effort of bringing the Powers to a place they have never been, or to a recognition they have never shared. It involves simply reminding the Powers Whose they are, a knowledge already encoded in their charter, titles, traditions, insignia, and money."[53]

If White supremacy is a manifestation of the powers and principalities, then not only have White Americans neglected to do battle, but they have also been complicit in and benefited from them. They have been agents of the evil one. Repentance from racism thus requires White Americans to face the horrific reality of racial oppression in all its forms. It requires them to confess the ways that they have participated in and benefited from it and to commit to the ongoing work of systemic and structural reform that is necessary to

51. Walter Wink, *Naming the Powers: The Language of Power in the New Testament* (Minneapolis: Fortress, 1984), 99.

52. Wink, *Naming the Powers*, 7–12.

53. Wink, *Naming the Powers*, 116.

eliminate racism. It requires a willingness to admit that the poison of White supremacy is embedded deep within every aspect of US society and will not be eliminated without massive structural overhaul.

Moral repair from the sin of racism requires communal and societal acceptance of responsibility for sins in which individuals may not have directly participated. As Margaret Urban Walker points out, moral repair is not only the responsibility of those who directly participate in wrongdoing; it is the responsibility of communities.[54] "Communities" in this case may include families, churches, neighborhoods, cities, or societies.[55] In particular, "communities are responsible for seeing that injustice to the victim does not go unaddressed, or, more precisely, that the *victim* does not go unaddressed, but receives acknowledgment that the treatment by the wrongdoer was unacceptable to the community, and assurance that this is a matter of record and due importance to the community. . . . [The importance of this] is magnified where those who are responsible for wrongful harm are unidentifiable, unavailable, or unwilling to acknowledge their responsibility and their obligations of repair."[56]

Repentance from White supremacy means that whiteness itself must be transformed. No one is innocent here. Even a refusal to engage the powers is an abdication of responsibility. For Christians, it is an explicit betrayal of our baptismal covenant, which regardless of denomination includes a statement of our commitment to repent from and resist evil in all its forms. Resisting White supremacy means that White Christians must become more Christian than White. It means that White people broadly must undergo a process of rehumanization. That is, they must recover the fullness of their humanity—the *imago Dei*—that was lost through cooperating with the powers. Gobodo-Madikizela asserts that humanization for the oppressor comes through dialogue, self-examination, confession, and repentance:

> Sustained, engaged, ordered dialogue thus forces the offender to unearth what moral sensibilities he has buried under a fa-

54. Urban Walker, *Moral Repair*, 29–34.
55. Urban Walker, *Moral Repair*, 30.
56. Urban Walker, *Moral Repair*, 31.

cade of "obedience to orders" or righteous "duty to my country" and to face what he has done, not in the heady climate
of the period of mayhem but in the sobering atmosphere of
reflection on ordinary human lives now shattered. But it also
thereby invites him, if he can, if he dare to negotiate the chasm
between his monstrousness and the world of the forgiven. It
thus encourages him to stop denying the suspected truth: that
all along, he knew that he was human and knew right from
wrong. The act of humanizing is therefore at once punishment
and rehabilitation.[57]

Notably, Gobodo-Madikizela's reflections were shaped by the forty-
six hours of individual interviews that she conducted with Eugene
de Kock over a six-month period. De Kock was the South African
police colonel who headed the apartheid regime's counterinsurgency
unit. Known throughout the country as "Prime Evil," de Kock was a
notorious assassin, responsible for the regime's most horrific acts of
violence. Yet throughout the six months of interviews he insisted to
Gobodo-Madikizela that he was not a racist and that he was simply
abiding by the law and following orders.[58] His rationalization is not
different from that of many White Christians in the United States
who defend their (or their ancestors') participation in racial segregation on the basis that they were following the law or from that of
those who lambast the civil disobedience tactics of movements such
as Black Lives Matter.

De Kock was one of only three white South Africans who were
sentenced to prison for their participation in the apartheid regime
after 1994. His conviction came because the Truth and Reconciliation Commission concluded that he had not been fully forthcoming about his crimes, which was a condition for amnesty. He served
20 years of a 212-year sentence before being paroled in 2015. During
his time in prison, he began engaging the families of victims, helping
them to find the remains of loved ones whom he had killed. Some,

---

57. Pumla Gobodo-Madikizela, *A Human Being Died That Night: A South African
Woman Confronts the Legacy of Apartheid* (New York: Houghton Mifflin, 2003), 119–20.
58. Gobodo-Madikizela, *A Human Being Died That Night*, 17.

therefore, have touted him as an exemplar of restorative justice.[59] It is important to note, however, that de Kock's supposed shift actually marks a considerable degree of consistency in his behavior. Just as he followed the law under the apartheid regime, he is following the law under the post-apartheid government. His process of ethical decision making has not necessarily changed. The critical issue for White Christians is not how they embody their humanity when the legal system supports justice, but how they do so when it does not.

Rehumanization for White Christians, then, involves far more than learning to abide by a new set of socially sanctioned rules for interacting with people of different racial backgrounds. It requires a wholistic conversion, a re-orienting toward God and away from White supremacy. The question remains as to whether and how whiteness—a cultural identity created and maintained via the subjugation, suppression, and extermination of nonwhite peoples across the globe—can be redeemed. Further, the question remains whether the church can and will take an active role in encouraging, supporting, and leading the moral repair of a White supremacist society. Reconciliation, after all, can never be separated from religious experience. "The experience of God reconciles all the warring parts that are ultimately involved in the life of every [person] as against whatever keeps alive the conflict, and its working is healing and ever redemptive."[60]

Building Beloved Community

Although commonly attributed to Martin Luther King Jr., the term "beloved community" was coined by Josiah Royce, a White philosopher who had been a teacher of W. E. B. DuBois.[61] For Royce, the beloved community denoted a community united in love by persons

---

59. Antjie Krog, "Can an Evil Man Change?" *New York Times*, March 13, 2015, https://www.nytimes.com/2015/03/14/opinion/sunday/the-repentance-of-eugene-de-kock-apartheid-assassin.html.

60. Thurman, *Disciplines of the Spirit*, 121.

61. Rufus Burrow Jr., "The Beloved Community: Martin Luther King, Jr. and Josiah Royce," *Encounter* 73, no. 1 (Fall 2012): 48.

who have been transformed by the power of love. It was an antidote to individualism, egocentrism, moral independence, and separation.[62] It is unclear whether Royce's view of beloved community explicitly included racial equality. However, his concept was influential upon thinkers such as Howard Thurman, who frequently wrote and preached about community. For example, Thurman wrote:

> That which makes any community become the beloved community is the quality of the human relations experienced by the people who live within it. The term itself is an abstraction. It becomes concrete in a given time and place in the midst of living human beings. It cannot be brought into being by fiat or by order; it is an achievement of the human spirit as men seek to fulfill their high destiny as children of God. As a dream of the race, it has moved in and out on the horizon of human strivings like some fleeting ghost. And yet, it remains to haunt and inspire men in all ages and all conditions. In some sense, it is always vague, and the blueprint for it is often outmoded before it can be translated into living texture. The beloved community in the context of our discussion involves the social climate with all that is meant by the dimensions of freedom brought into focus by the cataclysms of the civil rights revolution in which we are engulfed. It sees the revolutionary activity as means, not as ends. Steadfastly, it refuses to separate the means open to revolution from the ends to be achieved by revolution.[63]

Since King had been a student of Thurman, it is not surprising, then, that beloved community became "the chief regulating principle of King's theological social ethics."[64] King believed that the beloved community was at least a partially achievable reality that could be accomplished "with relentless cooperative endeavor between persons

62. Kipton Jensen, "The Growing Edges of Beloved Community," *Transactions of the Charles S. Peirce Society* 52, no. 2 (Spring 2016): 241–43.

63. Howard Thurman, "Desegregation, Integration and Beloved Community," 17–18, http://www.bu.edu/htpp/files/2017/06/1965-Desegregation-Integration-Beloved-Community.pdf.

64. Burrow, "The Beloved Community," 44.

and God."[65] For him, "the beloved community is one in which persons as such have inherent dignity and worth and must—every one of them—be respected and treated accordingly."[66] King's primary focus, of course, was racial equality, which would be evidenced by "integration with power," an inclusive community governed by the principles of love, fairness, and justice.[67]

Lewis V. Baldwin notes that King's concept of beloved community included four basic principles:

> (1) the impartiality of God in creating and dealing with human beings; (2) a sacramentalistic idea of the cosmos as echoed by the psalmist, "the earth is the Lord's, and the fullness thereof—the world, and they that dwell therein"; (3) a belief in the dignity and worth of all human personality; and (4) a solidaristic view of society and the world, which holds that each person is a distinct ontological entity who finds growth, fulfillment, and purpose through personal and social relationships based on the agape love ethic. This final principle is best characterized in King's use of the metaphor of the "great world house" or the "world-wide neighborhood," which suggests a totally integrated human family, unconcerned with human differences and devoted to the ethical norms of love, justice, and community.[68]

For King, then, the beloved community was a wholistic vision that included humanity's relationship with God, the created order, and one another. It was a collectivist vision that emphasized individual well-being and self-actualization as well as harmonious and just social relationships.

Womanist and feminist scholars have critiqued King's concept of beloved community for its lack of explicit attention to gender jus-

---

65. Burrow, "The Beloved Community," 45.
66. Burrow, "The Beloved Community," 49.
67. Burrow, "The Beloved Community," 52.
68. Lewis Baldwin, *Toward the Beloved Community: Martin Luther King Jr. and South Africa* (Boston: Pilgrim Press, 1995), 2.

tice. While King spoke frequently about the "triple evils" of racism, classism, and militarism, he did not attend to the import of sexism, including the ways in which it amplified the effect of other systemic oppressions.[69] Together with his failure to treat women as equals and his affirmation of redemptive suffering, the lack of intersectionality in King's philosophy and activism has been a cause for considerable ambivalence toward engaging his work for womanist and feminist scholars, according to Karen Guth.[70] Still, however, womanist and Black feminist scholars have engaged the concept of beloved community, using the lived experiences and constructed narratives of African American women as authoritative sources from which to expand King's concept. One example of this is Joy James's *Seeking the Beloved Community*.[71] Further, Paul Tewkesbury argues effectively that Alice Walker's 1976 novel, *Meridian*, interrogates King's notion of beloved community.[72] Even Walker's definition of the term "womanist" embodies the concept. A womanist loves herself, loves creation, and loves her people. She works for the survival and wholeness of all people, male and female (and today Walker would most likely add gender-nonconforming, transgender, and queer).

"These My Peoples"

The Color Purple, then, continues Walker's exploration of what building beloved community might look like in the aftermath of oppression. The end of the novel finds Celie and Albert (as well as Shug, Harpo, Sofia, and Mary Alice) building a new world for themselves, one in which Celie no longer sees Albert as enemy or oppressor, but

69. Karen V. Guth, "Reconstructing Nonviolence: The Political Theology of Martin Luther King Jr. after Feminism and Womanism," *Journal of the Society of Christian Ethics* 32, no. 1 (2012): 75.

70. Guth, "Reconstructing Nonviolence," 76.

71. Joy James, *Seeking the Beloved Community: A Feminist Race Reader* (Albany: State University of New York Press, 2013).

72. Paul Tewkesbury, "Keeping the Dream Alive: *Meridian* as Alice Walker's Homage to Martin Luther King and the Beloved Community," *Religion and the Arts* 15, no. 5 (2011): 603–27.

rather as her "peoples" (287). This is more than a simple reconfiguring of relationship. Having separately undergone significant transformation, when Celie and Albert reencounter one another, they do so as new people, two people who are liberated and healed, repentant and converted. Like the risen Christ who appears in the upper room to the disciples, though, they both bear the wounds of their pasts. Celie does not readily trust Albert, nor is she initially interested in relationship with him. Albert still feels the sting of Celie's leaving and longs for reconciliation, but he also accepts her right to autonomy. It is only their mutual love for and relationships with Sofia, Harpo, Mary Alice, and their families that bring them within proximity of one another. It is their mutual experience of heartbreak caused by Shug Avery that forms the initial strand of their connection. Slowly and cautiously, they establish a new relationship.

This new relationship has several critical aspects. First, the relationship happens on Celie's terms. Albert would love nothing more than for him and Celie to live again as husband and wife; he even proposes to her again, "this time in the spirit as well as in the flesh" (283). Celie, however, says no, affirming her identity as a same-gender-loving woman and offering instead that they be friends. Second, the relationship does not forget, deny, or minimize the past. Celie and Albert come together as new people with an old history. They do not pretend that the history does not exist. They address it openly and repeatedly. And when they do, Albert makes no demands for Celie to "move on" or "get over it." He owns who he was—and the evil for which he was responsible—just as much as he owns who he has become.

Finally, and most importantly, the relationship itself is a new form. Celie's rejection of Albert's marriage proposal opens the space for them to create an entirely new relational structure, one that has no precedent in a world gripped by the powers and principalities. They defy social and religious norms about how women and men are to exist in the world and in relation to others. Their liberated and converted identities are authentic expressions of their personhood, rather than attempts to conform to or survive the racial-gender status quo. Within their corner of the world, they create a microcosm of beloved community in which identities, relationships, and opportunities are not governed by racial-gender hierarchies, but rather by social, political, and economic equality. They create a world that is not ruled by the powers of domination, but rather by an ethic of justice, liberation, love for self and others, authenticity, reciprocity, interdependence, and agency. In this new world, when Celie is reunited with her sister and children, she introduces Albert to them as "my peoples." Liberated people in transformed relationships creating a new world together—that is the work of building beloved community.

Building without a Blueprint

This same work is required in racial reconciliation, but at a systemic level. The *telos*, or divine "endgame," for racial reconciliation is not restored relationship between Whites and people of color. It is not, as one ministry colleague, activist Onleilove Alston, once sarcastically described it, the image of "a big Black dude and a White dude on a stage, hugging it out with a single tear rolling down their cheeks."[73] It is the establishment of a just world, one in which racial inequities have been abolished. This means that the current practices, policies, and societal norms that disadvantage people of color or advantage White people must be abolished and corrected. Further, there must be intentional, sustained, and large-scale effort to remediate the economic, educational, political, social, physical, and psychological harm inflicted upon people of color by racism. Particular, although not exclusive, attention must be given to restoring the economic, physical, and socioemotional well-being of Native Americans and the descendants of enslaved Africans that has been eroded over centuries of displacement, brutality, and subjugation.

All sectors of society, including the church, must undertake the task of building beloved community. Inasmuch as the Christian church articulated and disseminated the theology that justified European imperialism, the genocide of Indigenous peoples, the enslavement of Africans, and the segregation and oppression of all people

73. Onleilove Alston, personal communication, September 20, 2016.

of color, so too it must lead the way in forming a culture in which repentance, conversion, and reparations are expected responses to US racial history. The church must enable the public to imagine a new society in which a person's wholeness is unaffected by her or his racial identity. A challenge, of course, is that this type of society has never existed. The quest to build beloved community in the aftermath of racial oppression requires us to build something that has never been seen, something for which we have no blueprint. In the history of the world, there has been no time in which racial categories (as opposed to ethnic and national categories) have existed but racism did not. Race and racism (i.e., White supremacy) go hand in hand. We have no model for a world that recognizes race without subscribing to racial hierarchy.

Does it follow, then, that the very idea of race must be eliminated in order to build beloved community? Many people involved in racial reconciliation would say so. At the minimum, they would argue that whiteness must be eliminated. This argument is faulty. It is akin to saying that the way to eradicate sexism is to abolish gender. While racial identities can be fallen, to believe in the power of the risen Christ means that we must also believe that they can be redeemed. Brian Bantum explores this notion in more depth in *The Death of Race*:

> Race is the incarnation of a desire to live untethered from one another, from the ground. And if one cannot imagine living with others or as a creature with other creatures, how can they say they want to live or to know God? . . . The truth of our bodied lives, of the story of our beginnings in the Garden of Eden, is that we cannot choose who is with us. We cannot choose the differences that will give us life or the differences that we need. The difference inherent in our bodily lives, in race, gender, sexuality, is the constant reminder that God does not create us to be alone. But the community of God is only possible in the embrace of the one who is not like us.[74]

74. Brian Bantum, *The Death of Race: Building a New Christianity in a Racial World* (Minneapolis: Fortress, 2016), 152.

Bantum thus affirms the value of racial identities while also calling for the death of the notion that racial identities are mutually exclusive and independent of one another.

Building beloved community does not require the abolition of race, but it does require the abolition of White supremacy, as well as the establishment of racial justice. And while there is no historical model for a racially diverse and just society, our theological imagination might be guided by the prophet Isaiah as he proclaims the "jubilee year of release from slavery."[75]

> The LORD God's spirit is upon me, because the LORD has anointed me. [The LORD] has sent me to bring good news to the poor, to bind up the brokenhearted, to proclaim release for captives, and liberation for prisoners, to proclaim the year of the LORD's favor and a day of vindication for our God, to comfort all who mourn, to provide for Zion's mourners, to give them a crown in place of ashes, oil of joy in place of mourning, a mantle of praise in place of discouragement. They will be called Oaks of Righteousness, planted by the LORD to glorify [Godself]. They will rebuild the ancient ruins; they will restore formerly deserted places; they will renew ruined cities, places deserted in generations past. (Isa. 61:1–4)

Building beloved community, then, requires that we be actively involved in the work of dismantling White supremacy and establishing the period of jubilee for peoples whose historical legacies include racially based displacement, detention, enslavement, and genocide at the hands of White Christians. Jubilee does not happen without sacrifice or effort. It requires the privileged to give up what they have acquired, even when that acquisition has happened through legal and socially sanctioned means. And the deserted places do not rebuild themselves; rebuilding requires time, money, and labor. As Bantum puts it, "To say that race must die is to actualize your gifts, your vocation, your voice, and your body for the freedom of those in your job, your community, and your school, and to work fervently

---

75. Text note on Isa. 61:1, *New Oxford Annotated Bible*.

to ensure that their lives might be imbued with hope."[76] It is to employ our words, our actions, and our economic, social, and political resources to build the beloved community.

Conclusion

"Everybody talkin' 'bout heaven ain't going there," and neither is everybody talking about racial reconciliation. The prevailing models of racial reconciliation within largely White evangelical and mainline Christian communities fall far short of what is needed to adequately address racism and repair its legacy. Having been disproportionately articulated and advocated by White Christians, racial reconciliation has heavily emphasized the importance of proximity, dialogue, bridge building, forgiveness, and friendship, while largely excluding issues of liberation, justice, and transformation. Much of what passes for racial reconciliation feels like an interracial playdate. Whites leave the playground feeling good about their new friend of color, but the material realities of people of color are unchanged.

Even after four decades and significant outpourings of money on conferences, workshops, and projects, racial reconciliation has failed to progress beyond the important critique that James Cone levied in his 1975 text, *God of the Oppressed*:

> I cannot accept a view of reconciliation based on white values. The Christian view of reconciliation has nothing to do with black people being nice to white people as if the gospel demands that we ignore their insults and their humiliating presence. It does not mean discussing with whites what it means to be black or going to white gatherings and displaying what whites call an understanding attitude—remaining cool and calm amid racists and bigots. . . . We black theologians must refuse to accept a view of reconciliation that pretends that slavery never existed, that we were not lynched and shot, and that

76. Bantum, *The Death of Race*, 153.

we are not *presently* being cut to the core of our physical and mental endurance.[77]

My attempt throughout this book has been to put forward an understanding of race, racism, and reconciliation that pushes the movement beyond its playing ground of White comfort. In this chapter, I have offered a model of racial reconciliation consistent with what Thurman calls "the discipline of reconciliation . . . [which] applies not only to ruptured human relations but also to disharmony within oneself created by inner conflict. The quality of reconciliation is that of wholeness; it seems to effect and further harmonious relations in a totally comprehensive climate."[78] Alice Walker's *The Color Purple* exemplifies the wholistic nature of reconciliation that Thurman describes. It demonstrates how the lives and the narratives of women of color contain tremendous power to reveal the intersectional nature of oppression, the complicated legacy that it leaves, and the incredibly complex work that is required for liberation, healing, and transformation. It reveals that, more often than not, genuine racial reconciliation does not begin with an invitation to bridge building; neither does it require forgiveness of behaviors, attitudes, and social systems whose evil is of such a magnitude that they could be forgiven only by God. Instead, true racial reconciliation often begins with a curse. "Until you do right by me" is the cry that must be uttered by the oppressed, and it is the challenge that must be met by the oppressor.

To revisit and expand the definition that I offered in the introduction to this volume, racial reconciliation is part of God's ongoing and eschatological mission to restore wholeness and peace to a world broken by systemic injustice. Racial reconciliation is a social justice movement that focuses upon dismantling White supremacy, the systemic evil that denies and distorts the image of God inherent in all humans based upon the heretical belief that White aesthetics, values, and cultural norms bear the fullest representation of the *imago Dei*. White supremacy thus maintains that White people are superior to

77. Cone, *God of the Oppressed*, 207–8.
78. Thurman, *Disciplines of the Spirit*, 105.

all other peoples, and it orders creation, identities, relationships, and social structures in ways that support this distortion and denial. Racial reconciliation is a wholistic process that requires confrontational truth-telling, the liberation and healing of the oppressed, the repentance and conversion of the oppressor, and an ongoing commitment to building beloved community. Reconciliation is an iterative process. The tasks are neither linear nor mutually exclusive, and they are often cyclical in nature as our journey into reconciliation draws us ever deeper into confrontation with the ugliness of racism and the hidden ways in which it has infected our psyches, our relationships, and our world. Genuine efforts toward racial reconciliation are at once spiritual, political, social, and psychological. They are rarely comfortable; more often than not, they are painful. And the seeming intractability of racism within our world makes reconciliation feel more like "mission impossible" than the mission of God.

Chapter Five

Our Spiritual Strivings

They seemed to be staring at the dark,
but their eyes were watching God.

　　　　Zora Neal Hurston, *Their Eyes Were Watching God*

The framework that I have used throughout this text reveals that race and racism are far more complex than typically acknowledged in Christian efforts toward racial reconciliation. Nowhere is this complexity revealed more than in the experiences of women of color. Race is intertwined with gender and other categories of identity, just as racism is intertwined with sexism and other forms of systemic oppression. Racism is about a matrix of power and domination that is designed to support and maintain white supremacy. It is not merely about relationship. Indeed, racism structures relationships in such a way that even when separatism is overcome, power imbalances remain. This understanding of racism obliterates the conventional Christian notion that reconciliation can be achieved simply through a focus on interpersonal friendships between people of different races. At the same time, however, reconciliation cannot be reduced to simple economic reparations. Racial justice must certainly include financial reparations to mitigate the multigenerational impact of displacement, stolen labor and land, inadequate education, and discrimination in employment, housing, environmental policy, healthcare, and the criminal justice system. This, however, is the entry point into reconciliation, not its *telos*. As focusing on the narratives of women of color demonstrates, the wounds of race extend far beyond external disparities. Thus, reconciliation must also include explicit efforts to redress the psychological, physical, spiritual, and relational impact of white supremacy upon all peoples.

When the complexity of the task of remediating racism is laid bare, it begs the question as to whether racial reconciliation is even possible, or perhaps more appropriately, whether it is a social movement worth engaging. Confronting the realities of racism—whether through dialogue or social action—is unrelentingly difficult. It is emotionally and psychologically arduous, even traumatic, labor that can take a tremendous toll on our well-being and our relationships. Yet it is precisely this complexity and this difficulty that point to the necessity of God's redemptive work in racial reconciliation. That is, racial reconciliation is ultimately part of the mission of God to restore a broken world. It is both an Edenic and an eschatological mission, one that began in the Genesis creation story and that will ultimately be completed by God. Yet it requires our participation, as God has called us to be ambassadors of reconciliation.

> So then, from this point on we won't recognize people by human standards. Even though we used to know Christ by human standards, that isn't how we know him now. So then, if anyone is in Christ, that person is part of the new creation. The old things have gone away, and look, new things have arrived! All of these new things are from God, who reconciled us to himself through Christ and who gave us the ministry of reconciliation. In other words, God was reconciling the world to himself through Christ, by not counting people's sins against them. He has trusted us with this message of reconciliation. So we are ambassadors who represent Christ. God is negotiating with you through us. We beg you as Christ's representatives, "Be reconciled to God!" (2 Cor. 5:16–20)

To be a Christian, then, is to be committed to God's mission of reconciliation. This means that racial reconciliation is neither a solely interpersonal nor a solely economic interaction. It is our responsiveness to God's offer of new life in Christ. We cannot opt out of it. We are either working toward justice and reconciliation, or we are not Christian—period.

The question for Christians is not whether racial reconciliation is possible. Our faith calls us to believe in the impossible every day. The story of our faith is that the Three-in-One so loved the world that they sent the Son to earth, where he was gestated in and birthed from the womb of a teenaged virgin Jewish girl; he grew up alongside humans; he engaged in the mundane activities of feeding, foot washing, and healing the sick; he flouted the religious authorities and was sentenced to death like a common criminal; he rose from the dead after lying in a dark, airless tomb for several days; he rose into heaven; and he will someday return to earth. In merely human terms, racial reconciliation is most certainly impossible. But as followers of Christ, possibility is not a criterion for our faithful obedience.

The more pressing question, then, is how we sustain our quest toward the impossible. Racial reconciliation is a social and spiritual movement in which our identities, our relationships, our social structures, and indeed our world are to be transformed. It is not about feel-good moments or having friendships with people of other races. It is, rather, part of God's ongoing action in the world to create a people who will act as though they have been created in the image of God. It is a painful, costly, and often lonely struggle that requires a particular skill set to engage and maintain over the long haul. As Katongole and Rice state, "In a world where loyalty to Christ is constantly contested, the ministry of reconciliation calls forth a specific kind of everyday leader who is able to unite a deep vision with the concrete skills, virtues and habits necessary for the long and often lonesome journey of reconciliation."[1] Thus, I conclude this book by offering tools for the journey; that is, six spiritual commitments that enable and sustain our participation in God's mission: being held captive, confessing and lamenting, standing in solidarity, keeping Sabbath, cultivating grace, and watching God.

---

1. Emmanuel Katongole and Chris Rice, *Reconciling All Things: A Christian Vision for Justice, Peace, and Healing* (Downers Grove, IL: InterVarsity Press, 2008), 124.

Being Held Captive

I am writing this chapter in the wake of Donald Trump's election to the US presidency by a largely White Christian supporter base, after a campaign filled with overtly racist, misogynist, and ableist rhetoric and behavior.[2] To say that I feel like abandoning my work for racial reconciliation among Christians in this context would be an understatement. Indeed, many notable leaders have dropped their use of the term "reconciliation," swapping it out for what they consider to be clearer and more realistically attainable goals: racial conciliation, racial justice, cultural credibility, intercultural integrity, and so on.[3]

For me and many others, only one thing keeps us on a journey in which we are destined to encounter people who devalue our personhood: captivity. That is, we are held captive by the understanding that reconciliation is core to the gospel, that it reflects God's intention for humanity, and that it is central to our identity as Christians. As Lederach articulates:

> God is working to bring all things together. The purpose is to heal and to reconcile people with each other and with God. God's mission is also ours. We have been given the same ministry of reconciliation (2 Corinthians 5:18–20). This ministry, as articulated by Paul, is not just about individual salvation. It is about facing divisions and restoring people in their relationships with others and with God. It is about joining God in the mission of reconciliation by building bridges and bringing down the dividing walls of hostility between individuals and groups. True atonement and holiness place us on the journey

2. Daniel Cox, Rachel Lienesch, Robert P. Jones, "Beyond Economics: Fears of Cultural Displacement Pushed the White Working Class to Trump," *PRRI/The Atlantic Report,* May 9, 2017, https://www.prri.org/research/white-working-class-attitudes-economy-trade-immigration-election-donald-trump/; Emma Green, "It Was Cultural Anxiety That Drove White, Working-Class Voters to Trump," *The Atlantic,* May 9, 2017, https://www.theatlantic.com/politics/archive/2017/05/white-working-class-trump-cultural-anxiety/525771/.

3. Brenda Salter McNeil, *Roadmap to Reconciliation: Moving Communities into Unity, Wholeness, and Justice* (Downers Grove, IL: InterVarsity Press, 2015)., 21.

to make real the reconciling love of God in our lives and to heal our broken communities across the globe. Our mission is to walk the path by which all things come together.[4]

When we are held captive by the belief that reconciliation is our central mission as Christians, reconciliation becomes the primary theme through which we read and interpret Scripture and through which we do ministry. Salter McNeil demonstrates captivity to this understanding of Scripture when she interprets the call to reconciliation as rooted in Genesis 1:28, which she refers to as " 'the cultural mandate,' or the command to fill the earth."[5] I try to fulfill that mandate each time that I teach my introductory pastoral care class, when I begin the semester by taking students through a scriptural journey that traces the themes of rupture and reconciliation from Genesis through the epistles.

This sense of captivity is a reversal of the way that the term is used in the Hebrew canon, where the people of Israel are exiled into captivity as divine punishment for their failure to honor YHWH and to live faithfully, justly, and with integrity. In the Hebrew canon, in essence, the people of Israel are made captive because they have refused to pursue peace, justice, and reconciliation. In contrast, when we are held captive to God's mission of reconciliation, we are bound in such a way that we cannot help but pursue peace, justice, and reconciliation. We become like Paul, prisoners of Christ Jesus and of the gospel who are compelled to enter into the breaches—the lives, relationships, institutions, and systems that are ruptured by racial oppression, sexual-gender injustice, classism, and ableism—and to live there in solidarity with others as we together proclaim God's word of liberation, justice, and reconciliation. We are captive in the sense that we could not do otherwise; we could not even will to do otherwise. Having tasted from the spring of living water, we are unable to thirst for anything else, even when we, like Paul, are imprisoned, beaten, or shipwrecked because of our obedience (cf. John 4:1–14).

4. John Paul Lederach, *Reconcile: Conflict Transformation for Ordinary Christians* (Harrisonburg, PA: Herald Press, 2014), 130–31.
5. Salter-McNeil, *Roadmap to Reconciliation*, 23.

The commitment to captivity is not, however, a commitment to color-blind reconciliation. We are bound to the mission of reconciliation because we know and are aware of the deeply painful realities of racism. To be held in captivity to God's mission of racial reconciliation does not mean that we deny that racism exists. Rather it means, as James Cone puts it, that we must possess the theological imagination to believe that the cross can, and indeed must, redeem the lynching tree. In his masterful text *The Cross and the Lynching Tree*, Cone effectively argues that while a "powerful religious imagination" is necessary to see redemption and salvation in the cross, a different type of imagination is required for those who can connect the message of this symbol of state-sanctioned violence to our current social and political reality.[6] This imagination can be formed only by standing in solidarity with those who have known the terror of the lynching tree and, because of the active role of the church in sanctioning white supremacy, of the cross. It is "God's loving solidarity [that] can transform ugliness—whether Jesus on the cross or a lynched black victim—into beauty, into God's liberating presence."[7]

Captivity shapes not only why we engage in the movement for reconciliation, but also how we do it. As captives, we recognize that we are not in control, neither of our own journey nor of that of others. While we may choose our path on any given day, we do not control its direction or its destination. We must release our need to control the direction of dialogue and action, instead taking a position of submission and service. This requires us to relinquish ego, competition, pride, and fear, replacing them with humility, cooperation, and trust. Captivity also demands that we open ourselves to the possibility of personal and institutional change that does not take the shape that we expect or the form with which we are comfortable. Entering the breach requires us to see and touch the places of brokenness in ourselves, in others, and in our world. In these broken spaces, we glimpse God in new ways and we risk being made new.

6. James H. Cone, *The Cross and the Lynching Tree* (Maryknoll, NY: Orbis Books, 2013), 157–58.

7. Cone, *The Cross and the Lynching Tree*, 161.

In essence, the commitment of captivity means that we surrender to being swept along a journey that is not about us but that requires our active participation. It is an eschatological movement whose outcome we can neither predict nor control. Indeed, the deeply entrenched and intersectional nature of racial oppression in the United States and globally means that those of us living today will likely never glimpse the world that we are struggling to cocreate with God. We will be fortunate indeed if, following in the footsteps of Moses and Martin Luther King Jr., we are blessed to glimpse a vision of the promised land (cf. Deut. 34:1–4). For the vast majority of us, though, captivity to God's mission of reconciliation means that we must repeatedly confront the painful realities of division, oppression, and subjugation in the world that we inhabit. This brings us to the next commitment: confessing and lamenting.

Confessing and Lamenting

In chapter 4, I argued that racial reconciliation begins with confrontational truth-telling. It makes sense, then, that confession is an important spiritual practice for the journey of reconciliation. Confession, though, is a particular type of truth-telling, one that names our complicity with and repentance from sin in light of our understanding of God's grace and forgiveness. When we confess, we name our specific sins, not just our general patterns of sinning. This means, of course, that we must know what our sins are. While that seems as if it should be an easy task, it is difficult for most people in the United States. Modern US culture has a strong aversion to claiming responsibility for one's behavior. While people tend to point to millennials as exemplars of this, it is a trait that crosses generations, socioeconomic classes, races, and genders. This becomes obvious when we examine how we talk about our mistakes. Popular language in the United States has evolved in such a way that we overwhelmingly use passive language and omit subjectivity when we talk about our errors. For example, we say, "the vase broke" rather than "I broke the vase" (as if the vase just suddenly became animate and jumped off the table).

If we have difficulty confessing *mistakes*, then we are even more resistant to confessing *sins*, especially those that involve the complicity with systemic racism that we have been conditioned to not notice. But racial reconciliation requires precisely that: confession, that is, the capacity and willingness to notice, name, and accept specific responsibility for one's active participation in and passive complicity with white supremacy. It means that rather than fighting or defending against the accusation of racism when it is levied against us (for people of color this is often internalized racism), we examine ourselves to determine how we have been racist in this instance. Since color-blind racism operates largely through normalizing and rationalizing itself, this is usually a corporate effort. Perpetrators of racism often cannot see the harm that they do to others unless the oppressed name it for them. Moreover, because of the extent to which racism shapes our thoughts, behaviors, relationships, and social structures, a single act of confession neither absolves us from nor protects us against further complicity. Thus, confession needs to be continual, a repetitive practice in which we engage as we work toward liberation. "The practice of public confession is a way of unlearning innocence. As we learn to go out of our way to draw near and tarry with the pain of the world in concrete places, the challenge is to keep naming the truth, keep being disturbed, keep remembering the awful depth of brokenness."[8]

It is confession's tendency to bring us face to face with the "awful depth of brokenness" that gives rise to the need for lament. Several scholar-practitioners have written in depth about the importance of lament in reconciliation. Katongole and Rice, for example, describe lament as "a cry directed to God. It is the cry of those who see the truth of the world's deep wounds and the cost of seeking peace. It is the prayer of those who are deeply disturbed by the way things are."[9] In his commentary on Lamentations, Rah notes that "Laments are prayers of petition arising out of need. But lament is not simply the presentation of a list of complaints, nor merely the expression of sadness over difficult circumstances. Lament in the Bible is a litur-

8. Katongole and Rice, *Reconciling All Things*, 92.
9. Katongole and Rice, *Reconciling All Things*, 78.

gical response to the reality of suffering [that] engages God in the context of pain and trouble. The hope of lament is that God would respond to human suffering that is wholeheartedly communicated through lament."[10]

Like confession, lament is a practice largely absent from the liturgies of US churches. While lament constitutes 40 percent of all psalms, it is remarkably underrepresented in the hymnals of mainline denominations.[11] Instead, US church services are dominated by triumphalist praise and worship. While victory and triumph are important themes in the Christian tradition, they are incomplete without also giving expression to the grief, pain, and anger that arise from protracted suffering, such as that which is experienced by the victims of systemic oppression. Moreover, an exclusive focus on triumphalism tends to comfort the privileged, allowing them to continue to ignore injustice.[12]

Lament, like confession, is intrinsically linked to truth-telling. It makes no attempt to minimize, excuse, or deny the reality of suffering. Rah demonstrates this with his analysis of Lamentations 1, which he says "uncompromisingly describes the true status of the situation."[13] Lament does not pull punches or engage in clever wordplay in order to soothe the consciences or protect the feelings of the perpetrator. It demands honesty, both before God and before other people.[14] It is not an intellectual exercise but rather a deeply felt practice that engenders feelings of shame, guilt, anger, resentment, and even depression.[15] Lament presents the full realities and complexities of suffering as it pleads for God's intervention in the midst of suffering.

10. Soong-Chan Rah, *Prophetic Lament: A Call for Justice in Troubled Times* (Downers Grove, IL: InterVarsity Press, 2015), 21

11. Rah, *Prophetic Lament*, 21–22. Rah further states, "The American church avoids lament. The power of lament is minimized and the underlying narrative of suffering that requires lament is lost. But absence doesn't make the heart grow fonder. Absence makes the heart forget. The absence of lament in the liturgy of the American church results in the loss of memory. We forget the necessity of lamenting over suffering and pain. We forget the reality of suffering and pain" (22).

12. Rah, *Prophetic Lament*, 19–20.

13. Rah, *Prophetic Lament*, 46.

14. Rah, *Prophetic Lament*, 47.

15. Rah, *Prophetic Lament*, 56.

Racial reconciliation requires confession and lament because both practices counter the ahistorical tendencies that privilege white supremacy. "True reconciliation, justice and *shalom* require a remembering of suffering, an unearthing of a shameful history and a willingness to enter into lament. Lament calls for an authentic encounter with the truth and challenges privilege, because privilege would hide the truth that creates discomfort."[16] Moreover, confession and lament are critical to racial reconciliation because they point us to the God who sees, who hears, and who acts. They remind us that while we must diligently work for liberation and justice as the hands and feet of God in the world, the magnitude of suffering ultimately requires divine intervention. Confession and lament are our acknowledgment that reconciliation is God's journey, and thus we expect God to act.

Standing in Solidarity

Conversations about racial reconciliation often invoke the language of love and friendship. Far too often, though, this language is used to manipulate victims of oppression into silent complicity with their quotidian experiences of racism, including those that occur in relationship with White Christians who claim to be pursuing reconciliation. Consider, for example, the case of a friend in ministry, a Latinx woman on the ministerial staff at a large, wealthy, predominantly White congregation. After several years of being the target of racially inappropriate behavior by a White male minister on the staff, she made a formal complaint. The White male senior pastor, forced to intervene after years of ignoring the behavior (much of which had been in group settings), consulted with several widely recognized evangelical leaders about how to handle the situation. After one such meeting, he shared with my friend the advice that he had received from an older African American male: "Tell all your younger pastors that in our world of greater brokenness in spite of

---

16. Rah, *Prophetic Lament*, 58.

all the studies being done about race and gender, always run toward friendship."[17]

This advice, which the senior pastor perceived as "a word from the Lord," was highly problematic. It sought to put a relational bandage on a systemic broken arm. Friendship, at a minimum, presumes equal power, mutual respect, and safety from harm. None of those were present in this case. Again, we must return to Patricia Hill Collins's understanding of power here. Racism, at both the individual and systemic levels, is predicated upon unequal power distribution that always favors whiteness. Racism is not an interpersonal situation in which both partners are equally culpable. There is a victim and there is an oppressor. The problem in this case was a White man's gendered racism against a Latinx woman. Expecting her to pursue a relationship with a person who clearly devalued her was emotionally manipulative and spiritually abusive. It was the equivalent of expecting a deer to run toward a lion.

The posture needed here, and in racial reconciliation broadly, is not that of friendship, but that of solidarity. In friendship, people run toward one another. In solidarity, people run together toward a greater objective. In racial reconciliation, that objective is threefold: the destruction of white supremacy, the healing and repair of the historical wounds of racism, and the establishment of a racially just society. With solidarity, it is not only important that we come together; it also matters how we come together. We have to do the work internally and externally. That is, we must align with one another in ways that embody the society that we are attempting to build. For Christians engaged in racial reconciliation, in particular, solidarity is based upon our shared identity as followers of Christ who are bound together through our baptismal covenant. Thus, our solidarity must be evinced by what Duane Bidwell identifies as the characteristics of "helpful and healthful covenant partnerships": (1) relational justice (the sharing of power, opportunity, and rewards); (2) equal regard (an ethic of interdependent mutuality in which partners empathize with and seek the flourishing of one another); (3) mutual empowerment (the capacity to influence and be influenced by others without

17. Personal communication, May 17, 2017.

domination or losing one's identity); (4) respect for embodiment (honoring the body of the other, including their lived realities, as a reliable and trustworthy informant about them, the world, and the Divine); (5) and resistance to colonization (working to prevent and dismantle the internalization of harmful cultural beliefs).[18] Moreover, for men of color, White women, and White men to stand in solidarity with women of color (and for us to stand in solidarity with one another) requires them to adopt an ethic of caring, a position of receptivity, trust, and empathy toward the truths that women of color tell as well as the emotional expressiveness with which we tell it.[19]

Solidarity does not require the perfect attainment of these characteristics. Rather, it requires active striving toward them and accountability for them in our relationships and actions.[20] Without solidarity, the search for beloved community is impossible. It is solidarity that, as Brita Gill-Austern asserts, enables us to become, shape, and form persons and communities

> first, who have the emotional and intellectual maturity and skills to live constructively with difference and who are enriched rather than threatened by otherness; second, who are able to open the doors of their hearts and minds to those who have been excluded; and third, who can understand that justice, as Martin Luther King Jr. once said, "is love enfleshed in history," and who make a commitment to justice-making in a concrete and particular arena, while at the same time seeing its connections to other arenas. . . . Practical solidarity means

18. Duane Bidwell, *Empowering Couples: A Narrative Approach to Spiritual Care,* Creative Pastoral Care and Counseling (Minneapolis: Fortress, 2013), 21–25.

19. Collins describes the ethic of caring as one of four elements of a Black feminist epistemology, which also includes (1) reliance upon lived experience as a criterion of meaning; (2) the use of dialogue to assess knowledge claims; and (3) an emphasis upon personal accountability. The ethic of caring itself has three components: (1) regard for individual expressiveness; (2) respect for emotionality as an aide for, rather than hindrance to, dialogue; and (3) the capacity for empathy (Patricia Hill Collins, *Black Feminist Thought: Knowledge, Consciousness, and the Politics of Empowerment,* 2nd ed. [New York: Routledge, 2000], 262–64).

20. Bidwell, *Empowering Couples,* 24.

that we do not simply feel compassion and empathy for others, but commit ourselves to be in the struggle for justice with them. We do not simply suffer with people; we also struggle alongside of them.[21]

Lederach refers to this idea of alongsideness as "accompaniment," which he identifies as one of three core reconciliation arts that Jesus embodied in his life and ministry.[22] He states, "Accompaniment requires us to walk together with those who are estranged."[23] In reconciliation, our love of God is specifically embodied in how the privileged accompany those who are suffering.

> God chose alongsideness, shared suffering, and the fullness of the vulnerability in the human condition. . . . To reconcile requires a commitment to see the face of God in the other, to feel the world from their perspective, and to place ourselves not in control of but *alongside* the human experience and condition. . . . If we consider this the root art of reconciliation, then loving God, the first of the three, requires a willingness to dwell alongside human suffering, to be with others in the way God has chosen to be with us.[24]

Lederach's description of accompaniment clearly evokes the kenotic (that is, self-emptying) love of Christ described in Philippians 2.

> Adopt the attitude that was in Christ Jesus: Though he was in the form of God, he did not consider being equal with God

21. Brita L. Gill-Austern, "Engaging Diversity and Difference: From Practice of Exclusion to Practices of Practical Solidarity," in *Injustice and the Care of Souls: Taking Oppression Seriously in Pastoral Care,* ed. Sheryl Kujawa-Holbrook and Karen B. Montagno (Minneapolis: Fortress, 2009), 35.

22. Drawing on the Great Commandment, Lederach argues that the three reconciliation arts—noticing the humanity of others, self-reflection and self-care, and accompaniment—correspond to the love of neighbor, love of self, and love of God, respectively (Lederach, *Reconcile*, 47–54).

23. Lederach, *Reconcile*, 57.

24. Lederach, *Reconcile*, 55–56.

something to exploit. But he emptied himself by taking the form of a slave and by becoming like human beings. When he found himself in the form of a human, he humbled himself by becoming obedient to the point of death, even death on a cross. Therefore, God highly honored him and gave him a name above all names, so that at the name of Jesus everyone in heaven, on earth, and under the earth might bow and every tongue confess that Jesus Christ is Lord, to the glory of God the Father. (Phil. 2:5–11).

While the Philippians passage has several important lessons in demonstrating the type of solidarity necessary for racial reconciliation, there are also a few critical limitations in the use of this as a model of human solidarity. First, there is an important difference in the directionality of movement in Christ's incarnation and in human solidarity. In the incarnation, God the Son moved downward toward humanity in order to elevate us toward the Divine. Jesus's power was and is ontologically located in his being. Thus, his incarnation did not alter his divinity and his relation to power was unchanged. In essence, Christ became human in order to center himself in human lives so that we might become better humans.

With solidarity, however, the privileged make an outward movement. In racial reconciliation, this means that White people must move from the center to the margins because they finally realize that the white supremacy that lies at the center of the human imagination is not actually divine; it is an idol. They recognize that their view of themselves, the world, and the Three-in-One has been so thoroughly shaped by the idolatry of white supremacy that they are unable to imagine what authentic human existence ought to look like. Thus, they move toward the margins because it is the only way to decenter and thus de-idolize themselves. It is only by being on the margins that the oppressor and the oppressed can work together to deconstruct the center.

This leads to the second lesson from the Philippians passage, namely, that solidarity does not require abnegation of identity or choice. There is an inherent paradox in the Philippians text. Even in human form, Christ maintained his full divinity. And though he "took the form of a slave," it was by choice, a choice that he reaffirmed each day that he awoke in human form. In other words, the incarnation was meaningful precisely because Christ freely chose it (he was not banished to earth by God the Father) and because he remained who he was while also becoming something else. Likewise, when human solidarity calls us to shift our positionality or our perspective—so that we can learn to see the world through another's lens—we do so freely and out of a firm sense of our starting (and returning) place. Thus, Gill-Austern states that the first movement of practical solidarity is to "know home." This means that our gaze is not always directed toward the other. We must be "ruthlessly self-aware": knowledgeable of the ways in which our intersectional identities shape our experiences of and complicity in privilege and oppression; cognizant of the familial and cultural ways of being and doing that shape how we think, feel, and act; and capable of identifying and reflecting on our core assumptions about identity, faith, and justice.[25] "We need to know and own the cultural milieu in which we have been formed and rooted. We need to see the network of commitments that bind us to a place and a people and the social arrangements in which we are inextricably linked that disconnect us from the lived realities of others."[26] Our identities and lives matter. This is especially important for the oppressed. Far too often, in the interest of racial reconciliation, people of color are made to feel that we must sacrifice the centrality of our racial identities. Thus, we often negate our needs for belonging, safety, and care in an effort to be absorbed in a melting pot of whiteness. Solidarity makes no such demand. Indeed, it requires us to know and affirm our own beauty and value. Solidarity does not ask the deer to run toward the lion whose mouth is still stained with our blood from its last attack. It invites the oppressor onto our turf, but it also sets ground rules in order to preserve our safety. Solidarity is always a choice, never an imposition. It is sustained through disciplines of presence, accountability, mutual submission, and commitment.[27] It is also sustained by knowing when, and how, to withdraw.

25. Gill-Austern, "Engaging Diversity and Difference," 36–37.
26. Gill-Austern, "Engaging Diversity and Difference," 37.
27. Lederach, *Reconcile*, 102.

Keeping Sabbath

Sabbath is a difficult practice to maintain for most US Christians. It contradicts both our Protestant work ethic and capitalist rhythms, which teach us that our value, success, and salvation are dependent on how much we work and produce. We live in a society where one of the first questions people ask us is, "What do you do?" It is countercultural, then, to sustain a practice of ceasing our doings. This practice is even more difficult for individuals with an activist personality, who are deeply aware of systemic injustice and motivated to dismantle it. Many activists have an understanding of call that echoes that of the prophet Jeremiah.

> Every time I open my mouth, I cry out and say, "Violence and destruction!"
> The LORD's word has brought me nothing but insult and injury, constantly.
> I thought, I'll forget him;
> I'll no longer speak in his name.
> But there's an intense fire in my heart, trapped in my bones.
> I'm drained trying to contain it;
> I'm unable to do it. (Jer. 20:8–9)

Likewise, for many of us, the propulsion toward justice is the fire shut up in our bones. It consumes us and will not let up. We remain hypervigilant for the signs and costs of racial oppression. When we work from an intersectional framework, our alertness is multiply magnified. Our social media feeds are filled with news and commentary about the latest high-profile incident of systemic oppression. Indeed, our close connections with other racial justice workers often mean that we learn about these incidents before they gain national media attention. We are always ready to engage and to act when these incidents arise.

Sabbath is the antidote to our hypervigilance and state of constant activity. Sabbath quite literally means to stop, or to cease. Judeo-Christian traditions have historically understood and practiced this as a full day of rest from labor. Sabbath-keeping, after all, is one of the earliest principles in Scripture, first appearing in Genesis when God rests on the seventh day and blesses it: "On the sixth day God completed all the work that he had done, and on the seventh day God rested from all the work that he had done. God blessed the seventh day and made it holy, because on it God rested from all the work of creation" (Gen. 2:2–3). In Exodus, God raises the stakes, commanding Israel to observe a complete day of rest on the Sabbath as an act of obedience.

> Remember the Sabbath day and treat it as holy. Six days you may work and do all your tasks, but the seventh day is a Sabbath to the LORD your God. Do not do any work on it—not you, your sons or daughters, your male or female servants, your animals, or the immigrant who is living with you. Because the LORD made the heavens and the earth, the sea, and everything that is in them in six days, but rested on the seventh day. That is why the LORD blessed the Sabbath day and made it holy. (Exod. 20:8–11)

Notably, whereas the other commandments of the Decalogue (with the exception of the injunction against idolatry) are phrased in one or two sentences, the command to keep the Sabbath receives a full paragraph, perhaps because God foresaw that it would be the most difficult for us to keep. Importantly, the issuance of the Decalogue comes just a few chapters after some of the people of Israel violate the Sabbath by gathering manna, despite having been provided enough food for two days on the sixth day.

Sabbath rest is not just physical; it is also meant to be a respite from spiritual, emotional, intellectual, and social striving. This includes our work for the kingdom. Far too often, though, Christian leaders—whether they are clergy, activists, or academics (Lord have mercy on those of us who are all three!)—use the plentiful harvest as justification to overtly ignore the needs that we have as laborers. We routinely and unreflectively violate the Sabbath in ways that we would never think of breaking the other commandments. In doing so, we not only do a grave injustice to ourselves, but we also dishonor God.

Regular practices of ceasing and resting revitalize, renew, and restore our spiritual, emotional, physical, and relational well-being. In *Soul Feast*, Marjorie Thompson reminds us that ceasing our labor every seven days helps to restore us to the natural rhythms that God has established in the world.[28] This, in turn, reduces our risk for burnout and sustains our capacity for ministry over the long haul. In racial reconciliation, the discipline of Sabbath often means that, in addition to daily and weekly practices of rest and renewal, we need extended periods of leave from our regular places of engagement. Thus, Lederach describes the journey of reconciliation as paradoxical, including movements toward and away from conflict. While entering into dialogue, relationships, and activism are critical points in the journey, "moving away, seeking space apart, has a place in the choreography of reconciliation. . . . Forcing someone into engagements and relationships, which we often do under the rubric of spiritual obligation, without fully attending to the preparation and authenticity of that choice, is equally damaging."[29] This is particularly the case for people of color who are located in predominantly White contexts, since being culturally isolated usually demands inordinately high levels of emotional, spiritual, physical, intellectual, and social labor over a prolonged period. In these cases, Sabbath also requires periods when we withdraw to cultural enclaves, spaces where we are surrounded by people who look, talk, eat, dance, sing, and worship like us.

But Sabbath is not just about rest *from* labor; it is also about rest *with* God. Otherwise, as Thompson states, it is merely vacation. "The essence of Sabbath is rest and renewal for the soul. In good Jewish fashion, this naturally includes our bodies and minds. Yet if rest does not reach the depth of soul it is merely vacation, not Sabbath. We need time out with God, not just time off from work"[30] Indeed, Sabbath is distinguished from mere—albeit important—rest in that the former requires a profound trust in God and a sense of God's

---

28. Marjorie J. Thompson, *Soul Feast: An Invitation to the Christian Spiritual Life* (Louisville: Westminster John Knox, 2014), 70.

29. Lederach, *Reconcile*, 36.

30. Thompson, *Soul Feast*, 70.

time. Because racial reconciliation, like all justice ministry, is "love in action," we tend to measure our faithfulness to the mission by what we do and what we have produced. Our belief that "injustice anywhere is a threat to justice everywhere" means that we feel the need to respond to every injustice with a sense of urgency. An unavoidable occupational hazard of this ever-pressing need for urgent action is egocentrism. Too easily and too often, we can come to believe that progress toward beloved community can be made only if *we* are in *that* meeting, *that* conference, or *that* project at *that* particular time. The practice of Sabbath—stopping work at predetermined times regardless of the work that remains to be done—reorients us toward God and God's time. By not engaging in our usual activity and realizing that the world goes on anyway, we discover that "all the work committed to us by God can be done in God's timing, for the grace that entrusts the work to us also empowers it."[31] More importantly, we remember that we are not God and that the mission of racial reconciliation is not ours but God's.

Further, it is vital that we hold our role as ambassadors of God's mission of reconciliation together with our obedience to God's commandment to rest. "God wants to teach us how to rest even as we work for peace and harmony in the world, secure in the knowledge that God loves us and is able to give us the rest we need."[32] In racial reconciliation, we embody this best when we establish rhythms of journeying and rest, activity and reflection, serving and being served, engagement and retreat, and doing and becoming.

Cultivating Grace

If there were only one "fruit of the Spirit" critical to interracial dialogue and racial justice work, it would be grace. "Grace" is a multivalent term that includes dimensions of compassion, accountability, and humility. It shapes how we view the racial/ethnic other, how we

31. Marva J. Dawn, *The Sense of the Call: A Sabbath Way of Life for Those Who Serve God, the Church, and the World* (Grand Rapids: Eerdmans, 2006), 37.

32. Katongole and Rice, *Reconciling All Things*, 60.

understand and demand accountability for racism, and how we view ourselves. South African pastor Trevor Hudson says that each of us stands beside a pool of tears, the summation of our historical and current experiences of pain, hardship, and oppression.[33] Those who venture near us too insensitively run the risk of stepping, perhaps stomping, on our pain and thus wounding us even more deeply. The commitment to grace, then, is about honoring the pools of tears of the individuals (and groups of people) we encounter on the journey toward racial reconciliation, many with whom we will find ourselves in deep conflict. Grace enables us to see beyond the superficialities of a person's being and to imagine that there is always more beneath the surface of any person (or group of people) than can easily be seen. It prompts us to resist the tendency to reduce others to one-dimensional stereotypes and to instead remember that all individuals, racial/ethnic groups, and organizations have complex histories and multilayered identities. It reminds us to imagine the systemic forces that have shaped the racial/ethnic other and to recognize that given a similar set of circumstances, we would be very much like them. In other words, grace empowers our intersectional systemic frameworks!

Grace is largely about compassion, which as Lederach notes, "starts with a quality of attentiveness that requires the simple act of noticing the other as a person," that is, a recognition of shared humanity. [34] This type of compassion is not a feeling as much as it is a discipline, a commitment to see the other, including the collective racial other, as made in the image of God. Like empathy, grace imbues us with a deeply compassionate cultural curiosity that prompts us to continually ask ourselves the questions, "Who is missing from my journey? Whose stories do I not understand? Whose truth differs from mine? Which marginalized peoples do I need to learn from in order to enhance my intersectional understanding of oppression and liberation?" Grace fills us with such deep love for all of God's creation that we are determined to keep learning until we under-

33. Trevor Hudson, *A Mile in My Shoes: Cultivating Compassion* (Nashville: Abingdon, 2005), 91.

34. Lederach, *Reconcile*, 48.

stand the perspectives of our sisters and brothers, even if we do not agree with them. We do this without expecting a reciprocal gesture. Indeed, more often than not, grace expects not to receive anything. In intercultural dialogue, this means that we open ourselves up to a person with whom we radically disagree without any expectation that the person will become more conforming to our sensibilities.

This stance of compassionate cultural curiosity requires humility, which is a practice in itself. Lederach describes two essences of humility that are especially relevant for the journey of reconciliation: (1) acknowledging that we are small yet significant parts of a bigger whole and (2) knowing "that learning and truth seeking are lifelong adventures."[35] Humility guards against jealousy, arrogance, territoriality, and rigidity. It requires that we approach contexts with care and respect; that we watch and listen to those on the margins; and that we assume that they always have something to teach us (even those of us who also live on the margins!).[36] Listening is a critical foundational skill for maintaining the humility and grace necessary for reconciliation. "When we understand listening as a spiritual discipline, as prayer, and as seeking God, then we recognize that God speaks to us through others. Our capacity to listen to God is only as great as our capacity to listen to each other when we are in conflict. . . . We test our real capability to listen, not when it is easy, but when it is most difficult. Listening is much more than a technique devised to improve communication. Listening is about the process of relationship, engaging Truth, and finding God."[37]

While experiences of privilege may make these practices more difficult for some racial-gender groups, they are relevant and necessary for all of us engaged in the struggle for racial justice. For example, for me as a cisgender, heterosexual, African American Christian woman, this has meant intentionally listening to and learning from the experiences of Asian American, Latinx, Indigenous, and multiracial peoples; from transgender, queer, and gender-nonconforming persons; from lesbian, gay, bisexual, and pansexual persons; and from

35. Lederach, *Reconcile*, 107.
36. Lederach, *Reconcile*, 107.
37. Lederach, *Reconcile*, 122.

non-Christian people (including adherents to other religions, agnostics, and atheists) who are deeply committed to racial justice. Just as the intersectional existence of women of color yields critically important information about the nature of racism and racial justice, so too do the experiences of those located at the intersections of gender, race, sexuality, and religion.

While our practices of grace, humility, and listening orient us to the other, they are not done for the sake of helping the other. They are done for the sake of our own liberation. African American Buddhist sensei Angel Kyodo Williams states this well in her book addressing racism within Dharma communities: "One abiding theory that emerges from the practice of a radical dharma that presents itself is that you should know this, attend to that, be aware of these things, but you must do them for your liberation, not mine."[38] Likewise, compassionate presence is not something that we practice only toward others; we must learn to practice it toward ourselves. "Our inner self requires patience, accompaniment, care, and reflection on the fullness of who we are—light and shadow included. . . . The capacity for self-acceptance and care, coupled with practices of self-reflection, nurture the elements necessary for compassionate practice."[39] Part of the grace that we have to learn to extend to ourselves is the forgiveness for our failures to be all things to all people. Many of us drawn to the journey of reconciliation have a deeply held sense of responsibility for others. This is especially the case for women of color, who often endure the pain of reconciliation out of a sense of duty to make the world better for others. Grace means that we must learn to see ourselves with compassion, to embrace our full imperfect humanity, and to listen to the truths that emerge from our own lives.

Cultivating a spirituality of grace also has significant implications for our understanding of justice and accountability for the sins of racism. It requires us to go beyond our notions of fairness. Grace is decidedly unfair. Rather than the "eye for an eye" logic of retributive justice, it aims for restorative justice, recognizing that "acts of injus-

---

38. Angel Kyodo Williams, Lama Rod Owens, and Jasmine Syedullah, *Radical Dharma: Talking Race, Love, and Liberation* (Berkeley, CA: North Atlantic, 2016), 2.

39. Lederach, *Reconcile*, 51.

tice can be punished, repented of, publicly named and denounced, or even repaid, but they can never be undone."[40] Indeed, the magnitude of white supremacy in the United States and globally is so great that full compensation is impossible. This does not mean, however, that we relinquish our demands for accountability and reparations. Rather, it means that we make these demands knowing that what is owed will not match what is repaid. This paradox is precisely why racial reconciliation is a mission in which Christians have a particular stake. We know what it means to be recipients of such grace. Christ's incarnation and death are the exemplars of paying a debt that one does not owe while also not receiving the honor that one is owed. This, too, is the paradox of grace in racial reconciliation. For White Christians, grace means that the debt they pay may not be one that they personally incurred. And for people of color, it means that the payment we receive is far less than what we are owed. It is a paradox that creates profound tension, which can be soothed only by focusing our attention on the Three-in-One who makes even the hope of reconciliation possible.

Watching God

The epigraph for this chapter comes from a climactic scene in *Their Eyes Were Watching God*, when a hurricane bears down upon the Everglades. Most people have already fled the area, but Janie, Tea Cake, and several of their friends have decided to ride out the storm. As others pack and leave, they revel, spurred on by the elation of thinking that they are stronger, smarter, and braver than those who flee. They spend the day dancing, shooting dice, and showing off. But when night comes, so do the wind, the darkness, and the water. As the storm pounds, they sit huddled together in the dark, watching for God.

When we embark on the journey toward racial reconciliation, we often experience a similar feeling of elation. Perhaps we are people of color who have long understood racism as an inescapable part

40. Katongole and Rice, *Reconciling All Things*, 32.

of our lives, and we feel empowered by acting to create structural change. Or perhaps we are White Christians whose awareness has finally been opened to the realities of racism, and we are inspired that our faith gestures toward a different reality. We become excited as we undertake new projects, engage in activism, find community with fellow travelers who think like us, and glimpse signs of progress. Over time, though, our excitement gives way to pessimism, apathy, or despair. We learn that everything we have tried has been tried before, with little avail, and that what looked like progress has turned into stagnation or even regression. Those people are not really our people, and many of them have walked away, searching for cheap grace instead of meaningful, sustained social change. The winds of hatred have picked up steam, ushering in a new political shitstorm. What should we do when this happens? We sit in the dark, watching for God.

It is easy, and all too common, to confuse watching for God as a passive acceptance of reality. But watching for God is an act of holy observation and subversive hope. In the midst of turmoil, chaos, and despair, it asks, "What is God doing, and what would God have us to do?" Lederach refers to this as the moral imagination, "the capacity to imagine something rooted in the challenges of the real world yet capable of giving birth to that which does not yet exist."[41] Although not exclusively the domain of Christianity or religion broadly, this capacity is at the heart of the Christian story.[42] We often talk of it as the "now and not yet," the liminal space between our present reality and the Christian ideal. In racial reconciliation, the moral imagination exists in the tension between (1) a deep understanding of and rootedness in the realities, legacies, and challenges of systemic racism and (2) a creative imagination that refuses to be contained by the boundaries of race and racism and that envisions a new possibility.[43]

41. Lederach, *Reconcile*, 29.
42. For Lederach, the moral imagination is not the domain of religion. He cautions against moral dogmatism and against reducing the moral imagination to an ethical or religious inquiry. In part, however, his caution seems to be based on his assumption that religion is not concerned with the political (Lederach, *Reconcile*, 28).
43. John Paul Lederach, *The Moral Imagination: The Art and Soul of Building Peace* (Oxford: Oxford University Press, 2005), 5.

Lederach identifies four disciplines for sustaining a moral imagination: relationship, paradoxical curiosity, creativity, and risk.[44] For racial reconciliation, I translate these as follows: (1) taking seriously the notion that our baptism enters us into a new identity characterized by diving in community in the body of Christ, by the commandment to love our neighbors as ourselves; (2) resisting dualisms (simplistic notions that divide the world into either/or categories) and embracing complexity; (3) maintaining hope that there is another way beyond what we can see; and (4) being willing to endure pain and insecurity, faithfully believing that death is followed by resurrection. It is the Easter story, after all, that makes—or ought to make—Christians particularly equipped to enter sites of pain and risk. As Katongole and Rice put it: "This is the very nature and essence of the church: to exist as the sign of a reality beyond itself. It is not that the church is the new reality. The church's mission is to gesture to this reality beyond us. The promise of new life is what gives the church its uniqueness as well as its challenge namely, to be an imperfect yet compelling demonstration plot of the new creation we announce."[45]

To watch for God means that we dream with God. We are aware of reality, yet we do not allow what is to constrain our vision of what ought to be.

When we look realistically at our world, peace seems a utopian fantasy held by people who must be a little out of touch with reality. We must be careful, however, with our embrace of objective knowledge and realism, for both involve a subtle premise. Realism assumes that what is now and what must be in the future are the same. Tomorrow is seen as the slave of today. Too often we find ourselves succumbing and adapting to the way things are. . . . We adapt and give up our dreams to

44. Lederach describes the four disciplines as (1) the capacity to imagine ourselves in a web of relationships that includes our enemies; (2) the ability to sustain a paradoxical curiosity that embraces complexity without reliance on dualistic polarity; (3) the fundamental belief in and pursuit of the creative act; and (4) the acceptance of the inherent risk of stepping into mystery of the unknown that lies beyond the far too familiar landscape of violence (Lederach, *The Moral Imagination*, 173).

45. Katongole and Rice, *Reconciling All Things*, 113.

fit the way things are. . . . But we must not permit ourselves to be defined by the realities those challenges represent.[46]

Lederach argues that there are two approaches to dreaming of reconciliation: realism, whereby we observe what is and make predictions based upon it, and using our prophetic eyes and voice, whereby we live according to unseen realities.[47] I suspect that much of the debate about racial reconciliation is really a tension between two types of personalities: dreamers (or idealists) and realists (or pragmatists). Racial reconciliation requires both. We must dream of beloved community while also remaining grounded in the realities of a society that is stratified by intersectional racism. The dreamers are those whose hope for reconciliation spurs them to keep working for it even when all signs point to failure. The realists, in turn, keep the dreamers grounded in the reality of what is. Without the realists, the dreamers' efforts would be like a balloon filled with air: pretty to look at but containing no substance. The realists provide the heavy weight against which the balloon must struggle. It is all well and good to float toward heaven without carrying a load. But it is another thing entirely to try to lift the inordinately heavy pain of this world up so that it might be healed and transformed. Racial reconciliation requires the latter.

When we watch for God and dream with God, we join our imaginations with the ancestors of our African American, Asian American, Latinx, and Native American foremothers, for whom God has always made a way out of no way. We watch the God who has always lifted the load that is too heavy for us to bear. We watch the God of enslaved Black women, the Jesus "who provides empowerment for resistance, survival, healing, and liberation in times of trouble."[48] We watch the God of Latina women, the Jesucristo who, "having already set the captive free through his suffering and death and resurrection, still walks with us in our very real everyday suffering and death to-

46. Lederach, *Reconcile*, 25.

47. Lederach, *Reconcile*, 22–26.

48. Karen Baker-Fletcher and Garth Kasimu Baker-Fletcher, *My Sister, My Brother: Womanist and Xodus God-Talk* (Maryknoll, NY: Orbis Books, 1997), 74.

ward our daily resurrection and abundant life."[49] We watch the God of Filipino women, the Jesus who lived as a fully liberated human being who befriended the marginalized and challenged the religious and political authorities.[50] We watch the God of Korean women, Jesus, the priest of *han*, "a shaman who consoles the broken-hearted, heals the afflicted and restores wholeness through communication with the spirits."[51] We watch knowing that God, the Three-in-One, also watches. Just as God did with Hagar and Ishmael in the wilderness, God sees, God hears, and God provides.[52]

Conclusion

In *The Moral Imagination*, Lederach poses the question, "How do we transcend the cycles of violence that bewitch our human community while still living in them?"[53] In this book, I have applied this question to racial reconciliation, asking more specifically, "What can we learn from the experiences of women of color about how we can transcend the oppressive matrix of intersectional racism while still living within it?" When we center the experiences and perspectives of women of color, we realize that racism and reconciliation are far more complicated than we would be led to believe by the dominant narratives, which have been shaped largely by White and Black men. We come to realize that racial reconciliation in the United States is impossible precisely because it demands that we attempt to transcend white supremacy while still ensconced in the bodies that have been racialized by white supremacy. It demands that we find ways to redeem the

49. Alicia Vargas, "The Construction of Latina Christology: An Invitation to Dialogue," *Currents in Theology and Missions* 34, no. 4 (2007): 274.

50. Kwok Pui-lan. *Introducing Asian Feminist Theology* (Sheffield: Sheffield Academic, 2000), 84.

51. Pui-lan, *Introducing Asian Feminist Theology*, 88.

52. I am indebted to Rev. Alexia Salvatierra for this image from her sermon at the Women of Color Post-Conference Retreat, held in conjunction with the annual conference of the Christian Community Development Association, Memphis, TN, November 15, 2015.

53. Lederach, *The Moral Imagination*, 5.

constructs of race while eradicating racism. It demands that we learn how to become a new people even as White racism continues its assault on people of color. It demands that our struggle against racism also engage sexism, heterosexism, classism, ableism, xenophobia, and all forms of oppression. And it demands that we do this from the margins, being led by those who bear the brunt of oppression, those who live at the intersections. It is impossible. Fortunately, nothing is impossible for God (Matt. 19:26). And as followers of the risen Christ, we are called to believe in the impossible every day. Perhaps what is needed is for us, like Alice in *Through the Looking Glass*, to practice believing in reconciliation.

> Alice laughed. "There's no use trying," she said "one can't believe impossible things."
> "I daresay you haven't had much practice," said the Queen. "When I was your age, I always did it for half-an-hour a day. Why, sometimes I've believed as many as six impossible things before breakfast."[54]

Lord, we believe. Help our unbelief (Mark 9:24).

---

54. Lewis Carroll, *Through the Looking Glass* (Luton, UK: Andrews UK, 2012/ EBSCOhost eBook Collection).

Bibliography

Accapadi, Mamta Motwani. "When White Women Cry: How White Women's Tears Oppress Women of Color." *The College Student Affairs Journal* 26, no. 2 (Spring 2007): 208–15.

Alexander, Michelle. *The New Jim Crow: Mass Incarceration in the Age of Colorblindness.* Rev. ed. New York: New Press, 2012.

Arendt, Hannah. *The Human Condition.* Chicago: University of Chicago Press, 1958.

Ashby, Homer U., Jr. "Is It Time for a Black Pastoral Theology?" *Journal of Pastoral Theology* 6, no. 1 (1996): 1–15.

Baker-Fletcher, Karen, and Garth Kasimu Baker-Fletcher. *My Sister, My Brother: Womanist and Xodus God-Talk.* Maryknoll, NY: Orbis Books, 1997.

Baldwin, Lewis. *Toward the Beloved Community: Martin Luther King Jr. and South Africa.* Boston: Pilgrim Press, 1995.

Ball, Molly. "The Resentment Powering Trump." *The Atlantic*, March 15, 2016. http://www.theatlantic.com/politics/archive/2016/03/the-resentment-powering-trump/473775/.

Banks, Taunya Lovell. "A Darker Shade of Pale Revisited: Disaggregated Blackness and Colorism in the 'Post-Racial' Obama Era." In *Color Matters: Skin Tone Bias and the Myth of a Postracial America*, edited by Kimberly Jade Norwood, 209–35. New Directions in American History. London: Taylor and Francis, 2014.

Bantum, Brian. *The Death of Race: Building a New Christianity in a Racial World.* Minneapolis: Fortress, 2016.

Berry, Wendell. *The Hidden Wound.* New York: North Point Press, 1989.

Bidwell, Duane. *Empowering Couples: A Narrative Approach to Spiritual Care.* Creative Pastoral Care and Counseling. Minneapolis: Fortress, 2013.

Blake, Jamilia J., Verna M. Keith, Wen Luo, Huong Le, and Phia Salter. "The Role of Colorism in Explaining African American Females' Suspension Risk." *School Psychology Quarterly* 31, no. 3 (September 2016): 1–13.

Bonhoeffer, Dietrich. *The Cost of Discipleship.* New York: Touchstone, 1959.

Bonilla-Silva, Eduardo. *Racism without Racists: Color-Blind Racism and the Persistence of Racial Inequality in America.* 4th ed. Lanham, MD: Rowman & Littlefield, 2014.

Brock, Rita Nakashima, and Gabriella Lettini. *Soul Repair: Recovering from Moral Injury after War.* Boston: Beacon Press, 2012.

Brown, Austin Channing. *I'm Still Here: Black Dignity in a World Made for Whiteness.* New York: Convergent Books, 2018.

Brown, Sally A., and Patrick D. Miller, eds. *Lament: Reclaiming Practices in Pulpit, Pew, and Public Square.* Louisville: Westminster John Knox, 2005.

Brownmiller, Susan. *Against Our Will: Men, Women, and Rape.* New York: Ballantine, 1993.

Bryant, Taylor. "How the Beauty Industry Has Failed Black Women." *REFINERY29,* February 27, 2016. http://www.refinery29.com/2016/02/103964/black-hair-care-makeup-business.

Burch, Traci. "Skin Color and the Criminal Justice System: Beyond Black-White Disparities in Sentencing." *Journal of Empirical Legal Studies* 12, no. 3 (Sept. 2015): 395–420.

Burrow, Rufus, Jr. "The Beloved Community: Martin Luther King, Jr. and Josiah Royce." *Encounter* 73, no. 1 (Fall 2012): 37–64.

Burton, Linda M., Eduardo Bonilla-Silva, Victor Ray, Rose Buckelew, and Elizabeth Hordge Freeman. "Critical Race Theories, Colorism, and the Decade's Research on Families of Color." *Journal of Marriage and Family* 72 (June 2010): 440–59.

Byrd, Ayana, and Lori Tharps. *Hair Story: Untangling the Roots of Black Hair in America.* New York: St. Martin's Press, 2014.

Cadet, Danielle. "The 'Straight Outta Compton' Casting Call Is So Offensive It Will Make Your Jaw Drop." *Huffington Post,* July 17,

2014. https://www.huffingtonpost.com/2014/07/17/straight-out-of
-compton-casting-call_n_5597010.html.

Carmon, Irin. "For Eugenic Sterilization Victims, Belated Justice."
MSNBC, June 27, 2014. http://www.msnbc.com/all/eugenic-ster
ilization-victims-belated-justice.

Carnes, Tony. "Lost Common Cause." *Christianity Today*, July 9, 2001,
15–16.

Carter, Jacoby Adeshei. "Does 'Race' Have a Future or Should the Future
Have 'Races'? Reconstruction or Eliminativism in a Pragmatist Philosophy of Race." *Transactions of the Charles S. Peirce Society* 50, no. 1
(2014): 29–47.

Clammer, John. "Performing Ethnicity: Performance, Gender, Body and
Belief in the Construction and Signalling of Identity." *Ethnic & Racial
Studies* 38, no. 13 (2015): 2159–66.

Cleveland, Christena. *Disunity in Christ: Uncovering the Hidden Forces That
Keep Us Apart.* Downers Grove, IL: InterVarsity Press, 2013.

Collins, Patricia Hill. *Black Feminist Thought: Knowledge, Consciousness,
and the Politics of Empowerment.* 2nd ed. New York: Routledge, 2000.

———. *Black Sexual Politics: African Americans, Gender, and the New Racism.* New York: Routledge, 2004.

Collins, Patricia Hill, and Sirma Bilge. *Intersectionality: Key Concepts.*
Cambridge: Polity Press, 2016.

Cone, James H. *A Black Theology of Liberation.* Maryknoll, NY: Orbis
Books, 2010.

———. *The Cross and the Lynching Tree.* Maryknoll, NY: Orbis Books,
2013.

———. *God of the Oppressed.* Rev. ed. Maryknoll, NY: Orbis Books, 1997.

Cooper, Anna Julia. *A Voice from the South.* New York: Oxford University
Press, 1988.

Cooper-White, Pamela. *Braided Selves: Collected Essays on God, Multiplicity,
and Persons.* Eugene, OR: Cascade, 2011.

Craig-Henderson, Kellina M. "Colorism and Interracial Intimacy: How
Skin Color Matters." In *Color Matters: Skin Tone Bias and the Myth of a
Postracial America*, edited by Kimberly Jade Norwood, 260–303. New
Directions in American History. London: Taylor and Francis, 2014.

Crenshaw, Kimberlé. "Mapping the Margins: Intersectionality, Identity

Politics, and Violence against Women of Color." *Stanford Law Review* 43, no. 6 (July 1991): 1241–99.

Dawn, Marva J. *The Sense of the Call: A Sabbath Way of Life for Those Who Serve God, the Church, and the World.* Grand Rapids: Eerdmans, 2006.

Deis, Chris. "The Tea Parties: Built on Fear, Violence and Race Resentment." *Alternet,* April 7, 2010. https://www.alternet.org/story /146190/the_tea_parties%3A_built_on_fear%2C_violence_and _race_resentment.

DelReal, Jose A. "'Get 'em out!' Racial Tensions Explode at Donald Trump's Rallies." *The Washington Post,* March 12, 2016. https://www. washingtonpost.com/politics/get-him-out-racial-tensions-explode -at-donald-trumps-rallies/2016/03/11/b9764884-e6ee-11e5-bc08-3e0 3a5b41910_story.html.

Demby, Gene. "The Ugly, Fascinating History." *Code Switch,* January 6, 2014. http://www.npr.org/sections/codeswitch/2014/01/05 /260006815/the-ugly-fascinating-history-of-the-word-racism.

Derricotte, Toi. *The Black Notebooks.* New York: Norton, 1997.

DiAngelo, Robin. *White Fragility: Why It's So Hard for White People to Talk about Racism.* Boston: Beacon Press, 2018.

Dill, Bonnie Thornton, and Ruth Enid Zambrana. *Emerging Intersections: Race, Class, and Gender in Theory, Policy, and Practice.* New Brunswick, NJ: Rutgers University Press, 2009.

Douglass, Frederick. "Slaveholding Religion and the Christianity of Christ." In *African American Religious History.* 2nd ed., edited by Milton C. Sernett, 102–11. Durham, NC: Duke University Press, 1999.

Emerson, Michael O., and Christian Smith. *Divided by Faith: Evangelical Religion and the Problem of Race in America.* Oxford: Oxford University Press, 2000.

Enck-Wanzer, Darrel. "Barack Obama, the Tea Party, and the Threat of Race: On Racial Neoliberalism and Born Again Racism." *Communication, Culture & Critique* 4, no. 1 (2011): 23–30.

Gill-Austern, Brita L. "Engaging Diversity and Difference: From Practice of Exclusion to Practices of Practical Solidarity." In *Injustice and the Care of Souls: Taking Oppression Seriously in Pastoral Care,* edited by Sheryl Kujawa-Holbrook and Karen B. Montagno, 29–44. Minneapolis: Fortress, 2009.

Gobodo-Madikizela, Pumla. *A Human Being Died That Night: A South African Woman Confronts the Legacy of Apartheid*. New York: Houghton Mifflin, 2003.

Golash-Boza, Tanya. *Race and Racisms: A Critical Approach*. New York: Oxford University Press, 2015.

González, Eduardo, Jr. "Migrant Farm Workers: Our Nation's Invisible Population." http://articles.extension.org/pages/9960/migrant-farm-workers:-our-nations-invisible-population.

Gould, Stephen Jay. "Curveball: A Review of Herrnstein and Murray's The Bell Curve." *New Yorker* 70, no. 39 (November 28, 1994): 139–50.

Goyette, Jared, and Naaman Zhou. "Minneapolis Protests as Police Chief Quits over Justine Damond Shooting." *The Guardian*, July 22, 2017. https://www.theguardian.com/us-news/2017/jul/22/justine-damond-shooting-minneapolis-police-chief-resigns-at-mayors-request.

Graham, Larry Kent. *Moral Injury: Restoring Wounded Souls*. Nashville: Abingdon, 2017.

Guth, Karen V. "Reconstructing Nonviolence: The Political Theology of Martin Luther King Jr. after Feminism and Womanism." *Journal of the Society of Christian Ethics* 32, no. 1 (2012): 75–92.

Harper, Lisa Sharon. *Evangelical Does Not Equal Republican . . . or Democrat*. New York: New Press, 2008.

Harris, Paula, and Doug Schaupp. *Being White: Finding Our Place in a Multiethnic World*. Downers Grove, IL: InterVarsity Press, 2004.

Harvey, Jennifer. *Dear White Christians: For Those Still Longing for Racial Reconciliation*. Grand Rapids: Eerdmans, 2014.

Heller de Leon, Christie. "Sticks, Stones, and Stereotypes." In *More Than Serving Tea: Asian American Women on Expectations, Relationships, Leadership, and Faith*, edited by Nikki A. Toyama and Tracey Gee, 19–35. Downers Grove, IL: InterVarsity Press, 2006.

Hill, Daniel. *White Awake: An Honest Look at What It Means to Be White*. Downers Grove, IL: InterVarsity Press, 2017.

Hine, Darlene Clark. "Rape and the Inner Lives of Black Women in the Middle West: Preliminary Thoughts on the Culture of Dissemblance." *Signs* 14, no. 4 (Summer 1989): 912–20.

hooks, bell. *Sisters of the Yam: Black Women and Self-Recovery*. Boston: South End Press, 1993.

————. *Talking Back: Thinking Feminist, Thinking Black*. 2nd ed. Boston: South End Press, 1999.

Hudson, Trevor. *A Mile in My Shoes: Cultivating Compassion*. Nashville: Abingdon, 2005.

Hunter, Margaret L. "Buying Racial Capital: Skin-Bleaching and Cosmetic Surgery in a Globalized World." *Journal of Pan African Studies* 4, no. 4 (June 2011): 142–64.

————. "Colorism in the Classroom: How Skin Tone Stratifies African American and Latina/o Students." *Theory into Practice* 55, no. 1 (Winter 2016): 54–61.

Hunter, Rodney J., Nancy J. Ramsay, H. Newton Malony, Liston O. Mills, and John Patton, eds. *Dictionary of Pastoral Care and Counseling*. Expanded ed. Nashville: Abingdon, 2005.

Hussenius, Anita, Kathryn Scantlebury, Kristina Andersson, and Annica Gullberg. "Interstitial Spaces: A Model for Transgressive Processes." In *Illdisciplined Gender: Engaging Questions of Nature/Culture and Transgressive Encounters*, edited by Jacob Bull and Margaretha Fahlgren, 11–30. Cham, CH: Springer International Publishing, 2015.

Irving, Debby. *Waking Up White, and Finding Myself in the Story of Race*. Cambridge, MA: Elephant Room Press, 2014.

Jacob, Michelle M. "Native Women Maintaining Their Culture in the White Academy." In *Presumed Incompetent: The Intersections of Race and Class for Women in Academia*, edited by Gabriella Gutiérrez y Muhs, Yolanda Flores Niemann, Carman G. González, and Angela P. Harris, 242–49. Boulder: University Press of Colorado, 2012.

James, Joy. *Seeking the Beloved Community: A Feminist Race Reader*. Albany: State University of New York Press, 2013.

James, William L. *The Varieties of Religious Experience*. New York: Philosophical Library, 2015.

Jennings, Willie James. *The Christian Imagination: Theology and the Origins of Race*. New Haven: Yale University Press, 2010.

Jensen, Kipton. "The Growing Edges of Beloved Community." *Transactions of the Charles S. Peirce Society* 52, no. 2 (Spring 2016): 239–58.

Jinkerson, Jeremy D. "Defining and Assessing Moral Injury: A Syndrome Perspective." *Traumatology* 22, no. 2 (2016): 122–30.

Katongole, Emmanuel, and Chris Rice. *Reconciling All Things: A Christian*

Vision for Justice, Peace, and Healing. Downers Grove, IL: InterVarsity Press, 2009.

Keith, Verna M. "A Colorstruck World: Skin Tone, Achievement, and Self-Esteem among African American Women." In *Shades of Difference: Why Skin Color Matters,* edited by Evelyn Nakato Glenn, 25–39. Stanford: Stanford University Press, 2009.

Khang, Kathy. "Freedom in Sexuality." In *More Than Serving Tea: Asian American Women on Expectations, Relationships, Leadership, and Faith,* edited by Nikki A. Toyama and Tracey Gee, 88–100. Downers Grove, IL: InterVarsity Press, 2006.

Kim-Kort, Mihee. *Making Paper Cranes: Toward an Asian American Feminist Theology.* St. Louis: Chalice Press, 2012.

Kimmel, Michael S. *Manhood in America: A Cultural History.* 2nd ed. New York: Oxford University Press, 2006.

Krog, Antjie. "Can an Evil Man Change?" *New York Times,* March 13, 2015. https://www.nytimes.com/2015/03/14/opinion/sunday/the-repentance-of-eugene-de-kock-apartheid-assassin.html.

"Ku Klux Klan Supports Donald Trump for President." *Fortune,* November 2, 2016. http://fortune.com/2016/11/02/donald-trump-ku-klux-klan-newspaper/.

Kupenda, Angela Mae. "Facing Down the Spooks." In *Presumed Incompetent: The Intersections of Race and Class for Women in Academia,* edited by Gabriella Gutiérrez y Muhs, Yolanda Flores Niemann, Carman G. González, and Angela P. Harris, 20–28. Boulder: University Press of Colorado, 2012.

Lajimodiere, Denise K. "American Indian Females and Stereotypes: Warriors, Leaders, Healers, Feminists; Not Drudges, Princesses, Prostitutes." *Multicultural Perspectives* 15, no. 2 (May 2013): 104–9.

Lederach, John Paul. *The Moral Imagination: The Art and Soul of Building Peace.* Oxford: Oxford University Press, 2005.

———. *Reconcile: Conflict Transformation for Ordinary Christians.* Harrisonburg, PA: Herald Press, 2005.

Lopez, Johana P. "Speaking with Them or Speaking for Them: A Conversation about the Effect of Stereotypes in the Latina/Hispanic Women's Experiences in the United States." *New Horizons in Adult Education & Human Resource Development* 25, no. 2 (Spring 2013): 99–106.

Lorde, Audre. *The Black Unicorn: Poems.* New York: Norton, 1978/1995.

Lucas, Lauren Sudeall. "Functionally Suspect: Reconceptualizing 'Race' as a Suspect Classification." *Michigan Journal of Race & Law* 20, no. 2 (Spring 2015): 255–85.

Lynn, Richard. *Race Differences in Intelligence: An Evolutionary Analysis.* 2nd ed. Arlington, VA: Washington Summit Publishers, 2015.

Maharaj, Nandini. "Perspectives on Treating Couples Impacted by Intimated Partner Violence." *Journal of Family Violence* 32 (May 2017): 431–37.

Markus, Hazel Rose, and Shinobu Kitayama. "Culture and the Self: Implications for Cognition, Emotion, and Motivation." *Psychological Review* 98, no. 2 (1991): 224–53.

May, Vivian M. *Pursuing Intersectionality, Unsettling Dominant Imaginaries.* New York: Routledge, 2015.

McCormick, John. "Bloomberg Politics Poll: Nearly Two-Thirds of Likely GOP Primary Voters Back Trump's Muslim Ban." *Bloomberg*, December 9, 2015. http://www.bloomberg.com/politics/articles/2015-12-09/bloomberg-politics-poll-trump-muslim-ban-proposal.

McFann, Kristen, Steve Osunsami, and Emily Shapiro. "Prosecutor: Accused Charleston Church Shooter Dylann Roof Stood Over Victims, Shooting Repeatedly." ABCNews.com, Dec. 7, 2016. http://abcnews.go.com/US/prosecutor-accused-charleston-church-shooter-dylann-roof-stood/story?id=44031417.

McNeil, Brenda Salter. *Roadmap to Reconciliation: Moving Communities into Unity, Wholeness, and Justice.* Downers Grove, IL: InterVarsity Press, 2015.

Miller, Kevin A. "McCartney Preaches Reconciliation." *Christianity Today*, June 19, 1995.

Mills, Charles W. *The Racial Contract.* Ithaca, NY: Cornell University Press, 2014.

Mitchem, Stephanie Y. *Introducing Womanist Theology.* Maryknoll, NY: Orbis Books, 2002.

Monk, Ellis P., Jr. "Skin Tone Stratification among Black Americans." *Social Forces* 92, no. 4 (June 2014): 1313–38.

Moraga, Cherríe, and Gloría Anzaldúa, eds. *This Bridge Called My Back: Writings by Radical Women of Color.* 4th ed. Albany: State University of New York Press, 2015.

Bibliography

Moynihan, Daniel. *The Negro Family: The Case for National Action.* Washington, DC: US Government Printing Office, 1965. https://www.dol.gov/general/aboutdol/history/webid-moynihan.

Nadeem, Shehzad. "Fair and Anxious: On Mimicry and Skin-Lightening in India." *Social Identities* 20 (Mar/May 2014): 224–38.

Nelson, Jill. *Straight, No Chaser: How I Became a Grown-Up Black Woman.* New York: Penguin, 1997..

Niemann, Yolanda Flores. "Lessons from the Experiences of Women of Color Working in Academia." In *Presumed Incompetent: The Intersections of Race and Class for Women in Academia*, edited by Gabriella Gutiérrez y Muhs, Yolanda Flores Niemann, Carman G. González, and Angela P. Harris, 446–500. Boulder: University Press of Colorado, 2012.

Nisen, Max. "Legacies Still Get a Staggeringly Unfair College Admissions Advantage." *Business Insider*, June 5, 2013. https://www.businessinsider.com/legacy-kids-have-an-admissions-advantage-2013-6.

Norwood, Kimberly Jade, and Violeta Solonova Foreman. "The Ubiquitousness of Colorism: Then and Now." In *Color Matters: Skin Tone Bias and the Myth of a Postracial America*, edited by Kimberly Jade Norwood, 28–72. New Directions in American History. London: Taylor and Francis, 2014.

Novak, Nicole L., Natalie Lira, Kate E. O'Connor, Siobán D. Harlow, Sharon L. R. Kardia, and Alexandra Minna Stern. "Disproportionate Sterilization of Latinos under California's Eugenic Sterilization Program, 1920–1945." *American Journal of Public Health* 108, no. 5 (May 2018): 611–13.

Olsen, Ted. "Racial Reconciliation Emphasis Intensified." *Christianity Today*, January 6, 1997, 67.

Omi, Michael, and Howard Winant. *Racial Formation in the United States.* 3rd ed. New York: Routledge, 2015.

"Overcoming Apartheid: Building Democracy." African Online Digital Library, African Studies Center, Michigan State University. http://overcomingapartheid.msu.edu/video.php?id=65-24F-A3.

Oyserman, Daphna, Heather M. Coon, and Markus Kemmelmeier. "Rethinking Individualism and Collectivism: Evaluation of Theoretical Assumptions and Meta-Analyses." *Psychological Bulletin* 128, no. 1 (2002): 3–72.

Painter, Nell Irvin. *The History of White People*. New York: Norton, 2010.

Pals, Daniel L. *Nine Theories of Religion*. 3rd ed. Oxford: Oxford University Press, 2010.

Park, Ashley, and Steve Eder. "Inside the Six Weeks Donald Trump Was a Nonstop 'Birther.'" *New York Times*, July 2, 2016. http://www.nytimes.com/2016/07/03/us/politics/donald-trump-birther-obama.html?_r=0.

Pratt, Richard H. "The Advantages of Mingling Indians with Whites." http://historymatters.gmu.edu/d/4929/.

Promise Keepers. "7 Promises." https://promisekeepers.org/promises.

"Promise Keepers and Race." *The Christian Century,* March 6, 1996.

Pui-lan, Kwok. *Introducing Asian Feminist Theology*. Sheffield: Sheffield Academic, 2000.

Quiros, Laura, and Beverly Araujo Dawson. "The Color Paradigm: The Impact of Colorism on the Racial Identity and Identification of Latinas." *Journal of Human Behavior in the Social Environment* 23 (April 2013): 287–97.

Rah, Soong-Chan. *Many Colors: Cultural Intelligence for a Changing Church*. Chicago: Moody Publishers, 2010.

————. *Prophetic Lament: A Call for Justice in Troubled Times*. Downers Grove, IL: InterVarsity Press, 2015.

Randolph, Peter. "Plantation Churches: Visible and Invisible." In *African American Religious History*. 2nd ed., edited by Milton C. Sernett, 64–68. Durham, NC: Duke University Press, 1999.

Richardson, Bradford. "Republican: Obama Most 'Racially Divisive' President Since Civil War." *The Hill*, January 15, 2016. http://thehill.com/blogs/blog-briefing-room/news/266075-republican-obama-most-racially-divisive-president-since-civil.

Roberts, Dorothy. *Killing the Black Body: Race, Reproduction, and the Meaning of Liberty*. New York: Pantheon Books, 1997.

Roberts, J. Deotis. *Liberation and Reconciliation: A Black Theology*. 2nd ed. Maryknoll, NY: Orbis Books, 2005.

Roth, Wendy D., and Biorn Ivemark. "Genetic Options: The Impact of Genetic Ancestry Testing on Consumers' Racial and Ethnic Identities." *American Journal of Sociology* 124, no. 1 (July 1028): 150–84.

Ryabov, Igor. "Colorism and Educational Outcomes of Asian Americans: Evidence from the National Longitudinal Study of Adolescent Health." *Social Psychology of Education* 19 (2016): 303–24.

The Sentencing Project. *Fact Sheet: Trends in US Corrections*. Washington, DC: The Sentencing Project, 2015. http://www.sentencingproject.org /publications/trends-in-u-s-corrections/.

Shay, Jonathan. "Moral Injury." *Intertexts* 16, no. 1 (2012): 57–66.

Smith, Andrea. *Conquest: Sexual Violence and American Indian Genocide*. Durham, NC: Duke University Press, 2015.

———. "Heteropatriarchy and the Three Pillars of White Supremacy: Rethinking Women of Color Organizing." In *Color of Violence: The INCITE! Anthology*, edited by INCITE! Women of Color against Violence, 66–73. Durham, NC: Duke University Press, 2016.

Snyder, Howard A. "Will Promise Keepers Keep Their Promises?" *Christianity Today*, November 14, 1994.

Southern Poverty Law Center. *Ku Klux Klan: A History of Racism and Violence*. 6th ed. Montgomery, AL: Southern Poverty Law Center, 2011. https://www.splcenter.org/sites/default/files/Ku-Klux-Klan -A-History-of-Racism.pdf.

Starbuck, Margot. *Unsqueezed: Springing Free from Skinny Jeans, Nose Jobs, Highlights, and Stilettos*. Downers Grove, IL: InterVarsity Press, 2010.

Sullivan, Shannon. *Good White People: The Problem with Middle-Class White Anti-Racism*. Albany, NY: SUNY Press, 2014.

Swanson, Ana. "The Myth and the Reality of Donald Trump's Business Empire." *The Washington Post*, February 29, 2016. https://www .washingtonpost.com/news/wonk/wp/2016/02/29/the-myth-and -the-reality-of-donald-trumps-business-empire/?noredirect=on &utm_term=.f0bc914e50aa.

Takei, Carl, Michael Tan, and Joanne Lin. *Shutting Down the Profiteers: Why and How the Department of Homeland Security Should Stop Using Private Prisons*. New York: ACLU Foundation, 2016.

Tapia, Andrés T. "After the Hugs, What? The Next Step for Racial Reconciliation Will Be Harder." *Christianity Today*, February 3, 1997, 54–55.

Tewkesbury, Paul. "Keeping the Dream Alive: *Meridian* as Alice Walker's Homage to Martin Luther King and the Beloved Community." *Religion and the Arts* 15, no. 5 (2011): 603–27.

Thompson, Marjorie J. *Soul Feast: An Invitation to the Christian Spiritual Life*. Louisville: Westminster John Knox, 2014.

Thurman, Howard. "Desegregation, Integration and Beloved Community." http://www.bu.edu/htpp/files/2017/06/1965-Desegregation-Integration-Beloved-Community.pdf.

———. *Disciplines of the Spirit*. Richmond, IN: Friends United, 2003.

Tutu, Desmond. *No Future without Forgiveness*. New York: Doubleday, 1999.

"Unique Monument for Commemorating Virtues of 'Mammy' Is Projected." *The Sunday Oregonian*, March 11, 1923.

United States Holocaust Memorial Museum. "The Biological State: Nazi Racial Hygiene, 1933–1939." Washington, DC: United States Holocaust Memorial Museum, July 2, 2016. https://www.ushmm.org/wlc/en/article.php?ModuleId=10007057.

Vargas, Alicia. "The Construction of Latina Christology: An Invitation to Dialogue." *Currents in Theology and Missions* 34, no. 4 (2007): 271–77.

Volf, Miroslav. *The End of Memory: Remembering Rightly in a Violent World*. Grand Rapids: Eerdmans, 2006.

———. *Exclusion and Embrace: A Theological Exploration of Identity, Otherness, and Reconciliation*. Nashville: Abingdon, 1996.

Walker, Alice. *The Color Purple*. Boston: Mariner Books, 1982.

———. *In Search of Our Mothers' Gardens: Womanist Prose*. San Diego: Harcourt Brace Jovanovich, 1983.

Walker, Margaret Urban. *Moral Repair: Reconstructing Moral Relations after Wrongdoing*. Cambridge: Cambridge University Press, 2006.

———. *What Is Reparative Justice?* Milwaukee: Marquette University Press, 2010.

Walker-Barnes, Chanequa. *Too Heavy a Yoke: Black Women and the Burden of Strength*. Eugene, OR: Cascade, 2014.

Wallace-Sanders, Kimberly. *Mammy: A Century of Race, Gender, and Southern Memory*. Ann Arbor: University of Michigan Press, 2008.

Wallis, Jim. *America's Original Sin: Racism, White Privilege, and the Bridge to a New America*. Grand Rapids: Brazos Press, 2016.

Washington Post Staff. "Full Text: Donald Trump Announces a Presidential Bid." *The Washington Post*, June 16, 2015. https://www.washingtonpost.com/news/post-politics/wp/2015/06/16/full-text-donald-trump-announces-a-presidential-bid/#annotations:7472690.

Welter, Barbara. "The Cult of True Womanhood: 1820–1860." *American Quarterly* 18, no. 2 (1966): 151–74.

Bibliography

West, Cornel. *Race Matters*. New York: Vintage, 1994.

Whalin, W. Terry. "Promise Keepers Gathers Black Leaders." *Christianity Today*, April 28, 1997.

Williams, Angel Kyodo, Lama Rod Owens, and Jasmine Syedullah. *Radical Dharma: Talking Race, Love, and Liberation*. Berkeley, CA: North Atlantic, 2016.

Wilson, Clint C., Félix Gutiérrez, and Lena M. Chao. *Racism, Sexism, and Media*. 4th ed. Los Angeles: Sage, 2013.

Wilson, Sherrée. "They Forgot Mammy Had a Brain." In *Presumed Incompetent: The Intersections of Race and Class for Women in Academia*, edited by Gabriella Gutiérrez y Muhs, Yolanda Flores Niemann, Carman G. González, and Angela P. Harris, 65–77. Boulder: University Press of Colorado, 2012.

Wink, Walter. *Naming the Powers: The Language of Power in the New Testament*. Minneapolis: Fortress, 1984.

Wolf, Naomi. *The Beauty Myth: How Images of Beauty Are Used against Women*. New York: Anchor Books, 1991.

Wong, Jaclyn S., and Andrew M. Penner. "Gender and the Returns to Attractiveness." *Research in Social Stratification and Mobility* 44 (June 2016): 113–23.

Index of Subjects

Accapadi, Mamta, 153
activism. *See* antiracist activism
affirmative action, 5–6, 27, 135
Africa, 33, 50n56, 80, 86, 118, 133
  Africans, 25–26, 28, 29–30, 34, 52, 86
  South Africa, xvii, 2, 83, 127, 177,
    191, 194–95
  and transatlantic slave trade, 31,
    51–52, 59, 115, 117–18, 121–22
African Americans, 120
  and collective Blacks, 48–49
  and colorism, 79–80
  communities, 20–21, 110, 154
  education of, 60–61
  identity, 65–70, 131–32
  as legacy Blacks, 50, 51–52, 200
  middle-class, xiv, 46, 66
  popular culture representations of,
    90–91
  and racial capital, 88–91
  and racial identity, 131–32
African American men, 2, 5, 12–13,
  75–76
  incarceration of, 53–54
  lynchings of, 74–75, 110–11
  and rape allegations, 109–11
African American women, 11, 51, 53,
  198
  and colorism, 80–81
  and discrimination experiences, 64,
    75–76
  dissemblance by, 174–75
  girls, 89–90

hypersexuality of, 107–9
identity, self-esteem, 65–70, 94–95
  as jezebels, 107, 108–9, 111–12, 168
  killings of, second nadir, 19–21
  lynchings of, 74–75
  and mammification, 98–101, 107,
    111–12
  and misogynoir, 77–78, 96
  and rape, 108–11
  strength of, xvii, 38, 105
  and womanist theology, 11–15
  See also Black women; women of
    color
Africans, 25–26, 28, 29–30, 34, 52, 86
Alabama, 23
Alexander, Michelle, 54
Alston, Onleilove, 200
America's original sin, 23, 62, 191–95
antiracist activism, 59, 67–68, 111, 114,
  145–46
  and dialogue, 139–40, 146, 150,
    152–55
  organizing, 50, 59, 66–69
  and Sabbath rest, 221–24
Anzaldúa, Gloría, 77, 185, 186
Arendt, Hannah, 188
Armenians, 32, 137
Asian Americans, 5, 33, 48–49, 50, 91
Asian American women, 49, 51, 84, 92
  China doll, geisha girl stereotype,
    101–2, 168
Asians, 28, 83–84, 119
  Chinese, 83–84

Index of Subjects

East, 27–28
  Japanese, 32, 83–84
  orientalism, 56–57
Atlanta, xiii–xvi, 5, 19, 45–47
  Child Murders, xv

Baldwin, Lewis V., 197
Banks, Taunya Lovell, 81
Bantum, Brian, xvii, 201–2, 202–3
beauty, 83–84, 92, 97
  whiteness and, 79–81, 91–96, 151
  women of color and, 91–94
beloved community, 163, 195–98,
  200–203, 224
Benjamin, André, xiv
Berry, Wendell, 122, 128–29, 146–47
Beyoncé, 78
Bible, Scripture, 107, 170, 188, 210
  lament in, 169, 213–14
  on Sabbath, 221–22
  story books, 72–73
Bidwell, Duane, 216
Bilge, Sirma, 44, 68–69
Birmingham, 144–45
Birth of a Nation, The, 19
Black liberation theology, 12, 177–78
Black Lives Matter, 21, 144, 194
Blacks, 5, 53, 115, 153–54
  Caribbean-born, 50n56, 52, 54–55,
    131–32
  collective, 48–49
  criminalization of, 53–54
  enslaveability, 31, 52–54, 80, 118–20
  families, 37–38
  patriarchy, 161–63
  police brutality, antiblack, 19–21, 36,
    62, 145
  racial identity, 131–32
  stereotypes, 98–101, 153–54
  sterilization of, 26–27
  See also African Americans
Black-White binary, 42, 48–49, 52, 132
Black women, 161–63, 166–67, 181. See
    also African American women;
    women of color
Bland, Sandra, 20, 21
Bonhoeffer, Dietrich, 183n36
Bonilla-Silva, Eduardo, 34–35, 36–37,
  48–50, 82

breakfast metaphor, 39–40
bridge building, 173–74, 204, 209
Brock, Rita Nakashima, 130, 190
Brown, Austin Channing, 150n74
Browne, Katrina, 121–22, 143–44
Brownmiller, Susan, 110
Brown v. Board of Education, 41
Buddhism, 162, 227
Burch, Traci, 89
Bush, George W., 57
Byrd, Ayana, 59

Cameron, Barbara, 73–74
capitalism, 221
  genocide and, 55–56
  prison industrial complex (PIC),
    52–54
  slavery and, 51–55, 118, 121–25, 148
capital, racial, 88–91, 154
captivity, 209–11
Caribbean Islanders, 48, 50, 52, 54–55
  Black, 50n56, 52, 54–55, 131–32
Carnes, Tony, 145
Carter, Jacoby Adeshei, 28
Castile, Philando, 21
Catholic Church, Doctrine of Discov-
    ery, 122–23
cheap grace, 183–84, 229
children, xv, 72–73, 89–90
China, 83–84
Chinese Americans, 48, 101–2, 168
Christian Community Development
    Association (CCDA), xvii, 7
Christian racial reconciliation, 1–6,
    33–34, 69–70, 206–8
  and civil disobedience, 144–45, 194
  confession and lament in, 212–15
  mission of God and, 209–12, 215,
    228, 229
  paradigm, 7–10, 23, 62
  patriarchy in, 64–65, 70, 74, 112
  Sabbath keeping, 221–24
  solidarity, 210–11, 215–20
  symmetrical treatment and, 41–43,
    114
  whiteness and, 114–16, 139
Christian theology, xvii, 169–71
Christians, evangelical, 3–6, 7–10,
    108–9, 203, 215

249

Index of Subjects

power, types of, 44–45, 206
repentance of, 129, 163, 175, 184–85,
    187–90, 191–95, 201
as sickness, 127–29, 185
sin of, 3, 7, 23, 127, 114
social constructionism and, 29–34,
    39–41, 47
structural, 8, 44–45, 47, 69, 80, 106,
    121, 132, 141–45, 160
Rah, Soong-Chan, 213–14
Randolph, Peter, 123–24
rape, 108–11, 164–65
realism, 230–31
rehumanization, 193–95
relationships, interpersonal, 7–9,
    14–15, 62, 112–13, 178, 184, 203,
    206–7, 215–16
    healing through, 181–82
reparations, 179–80, 184, 189, 201,
    206–7, 228
repentance, 129, 163, 175, 184–85,
    187–90, 191–95
Republican party, Republicans, 18–19,
    21
restorative justice, 190–91, 194–95,
    227–28
Rice, Chris, xvii, 2, 208, 213, 230
Rice, Tamar, 21
Roberts, Dorothy, 26–27
Roberts, J. Deotis, 177
Roof, Dylann, 109–10
Royce, Josiah, 195–96
Rushin, Kate, 1

sabbath, 208, 221–24
Said, Edward, 56
Salter McNeil, Brenda, 114, 210
Sanders, Tywanza, 109
Schaupp, Doug, 152
science, racial, 27–28, 30, 148
segregation, xiv, 15, 36, 50, 53–54, 120,
    128, 191
    and housing, 45–47
    of Native Americans, 60
    racism and, 34, 39
    in South, 50, 166–67, 188
self-made man, 141–43
Selma, xvi
separateness, 7–8

sexism, 77, 167, 197–98, 201
    racialized, 68, 113
Shaheen, Jack, 58
Shay, Jonathan, 126
silencing, 112, 164–68, 215–16
sin of racism, 3, 7, 23, 127, 114
    as America's original, 23, 62, 191–95
    confessing, 212–13
    of White supremacy, 3, 23, 62, 11,
        148, 168, 183–85, 188, 191–95,
        212–13
slavery, 15, 23, 25, 36, 50–53, 80
    Black families and, 37–38
    chattel, race-based, 50, 51–52,
        59–60, 108–9, 117–20, 121–22, 127
    cultural annihilation supporting,
        59–60
    and DeWolf family, 121–22, 125, 143
    enslaveability of Blacks, 31, 52–54,
        80, 118–20
    indentured servants, White, 117–18
    and mammy stereotype, 98–99
    and Native Americans, 117–18
    prison industrial complex (PIC) as,
        52–54
    rape, institutionalized, 108–9
    transatlantic slave trade, 31, 51–52,
        59, 115, 117–18, 121–22
    violence of, 121–22
    whiteness, making of, 116–20
    White people, impact on, 120–25,
        127–31
Smith, Andrea, 50–51, 52–53, 55, 56–57,
    60
Smith, Christian, 6
social Darwinism, 27
social media, 21, 221
socioeconomic opportunity, 138, 141,
    199–200
solidarity, 181–81, 215–20
South Africa, xvii, 2
    Apartheid in, 83, 127, 194–95
    Truth and Reconciliation Commis-
        sion, xvii, 127, 177, 191, 194–95
South America, 54
South Carolina, xiv, 20, 23, 39–40, 52
    Emanuel AME Church, 109–10
South, United States, 17, 31, 139n76